Locked Out

Locked Out

A Century of Irish Working-Class Life

Edited By

DAVID CONVERY

IRISH ACADEMIC PRESS
DUBLIN

First published in 2013 by Irish Academic Press

8 Chapel Lane,
Sallins,
Co. Kildare,
Ireland

Individual chapters © 2013 Contributors

www.iap.ie

British Library Cataloguing in Publication Data
An entry can be found on request

ISBN 978 0 7165 3201 9 (cloth)
ISBN 978 0 7165 3202 6 (paper)
ISBN 978 0 7165 3221 7 (ebook)

Library of Congress Cataloging-in-Publication Data
An entry can be found on request

Printed in Ireland by SPRINT-print Ltd.

Contents

Contents

List of Plates

the death of John Byrne in an industrial school in 1935. Reproduced courtesy of the Communist Party of Ireland.

10. Corporation Buildings, 'a blatant attempt to house the very poor'. The scene of police brutality during a raid in 1913 which resulted in the death of John McDonagh, they also gave rise to the 'Animal Gang' in the 1930s. Reproduced courtesy of Terry Fagan and the North Inner City Folklore Project.

11. Female munitions workers in Belfast, 1941. The war resulted in increased opportunities for women, helping to redefine traditional gender roles. HOYFM.BT839 C Belfast Telegraph Collection Ulster Folk & Transport Museum.

12. Munster Bar, the winners of the Waterford Pubs League, 1971. L-R: John Toms (Captain, Munster Bar), Jimmy Searson (Chairman, Waterford Junior Football League), Carl Bowe (Guinness representative, Waterford). Reproduced courtesy of John Toms.

13. Female textile workers in Cork's Sunbeam-Wolsey factory, 1940s. Reproduced courtesy of Cork City Library.

14. Joe Heaney, one of Ireland's most accomplished seán-nos singers. 'The Rocks of Bawn' was one of his many recordings. Reproduced courtesy of the Joe Heaney Archive, National University of Ireland, Galway.

15. Robert Noonan, better known under his pen-name Robert Tressell, author of *The Ragged Trousered Philanthropists*. His work, though widely acclaimed in Britain, has been neglected along with other working-class writers in Ireland. Reproduced courtesy of Hastings Museum and Archive.

List of Contributors

Dr David Convery received a PhD in history from University College Cork in 2012, funded by the Irish Research Council for the Humanities and Social Sciences. His research focuses on working-class politics and culture in twentieth-century Europe, and he has previously published numerous articles and book chapters on the history and memory of Irish involvement in the Spanish Civil War.

Dr Sarah-Anne Buckley lectures in the Department of History at the National University of Ireland, Galway. She has published articles on a number of topics in Irish history, including child neglect, incest, deserted wives and social work. Her book *The Cruelty Man: Child Welfare, the NSPCC and the State in Ireland* will be published in 2013.

Liam Cullinane is an Irish Research Council-funded PhD student in the School of History, University College Cork. His doctoral research consists of a comparative oral history of Irish Steel, Sunbeam-Wolsey and the Ford Marina plant. He has previously been published in *Saothar*, the journal of the Irish Labour History Society.

James Curry is a Digital Humanities Doctoral Scholar at the Moore Institute, National University of Ireland, Galway and author of *Artist of the Revolution: The Cartoons of Ernest Kavanagh (1884–1916)* (Cork: Mercier Press, 2012). He is also the co-editor (with Francis Devine) of *'Merry May Your Xmas Be & 1913 Free From Care': The Irish Worker 1912 Christmas Number* (Dublin: Irish Labour History Society, 2012).

Dr Fiona Devoy McAuliffe is a research assistant/administrator, qualified secondary school teacher and was awarded a PhD in history from University

College Cork in 2010 for a thesis titled '"A sword of Damocles": the threat of conscription and the dynamics of Irish politics, 1914–18'. She has been published in *History Studies* and the *Irish Review* and is editor and researcher of the revised edition of the UCC War Record (1919) listing the staff and students of UCC who fought in the First World War.

Donal Fallon holds a BA from the National University of Ireland Maynooth and in 2012 was awarded an MA from University College Dublin for a thesis on gangs and political violence in 1930s Dublin. He is co-editor of the Dublin history-focused website 'Come Here To Me' (www.comeheretome. com), select articles from which were published as *Come Here To Me: Dublin's Other History* by New Island Books in 2012.

Sara Goek comes from DeKalb, Illinois and is a graduate of Boston College. She is currently pursuing a PhD in History / Digital Arts and Humanities at University College Cork. Her research covers oral histories of migration from Ireland to the United States and Great Britain between 1945 and 1970 and the role of music and culture in migrants' lives and communities.

Dr Christopher J.V. Loughlin has recently completed his PhD in history at Queen's University Belfast. He was awarded a J.C. Beckett Bursary in 2008 and was the recipient of an Arts and Humanities Research Council (UK) scholarship from 2009–12. He is currently researching left-wing politics, international political economy and the industrial history of Northern Ireland from 1900–50.

Dr Conor McCabe is a research fellow with the Equality Studies Centre, University College Dublin School of Social Justice, and author of the 2011 publication *Sins of the Father: Tracing the Decisions That Shaped the Irish Economy*. His research interests include money, finance and Irish labour and working-class history.

List of Contributors

Dr Alan J.M. Noonan recently completed his PhD at University College Cork titled 'Wandering Labourers: The Irish and Mining throughout the United States, 1845–1920'. He was the Glucksman Ireland Fellow to New York University 2009–10, and Research Fellow at the University of Montana, 2005–06.

Dr Michael Pierse is a Research Fellow at the Institute for Collaborative Research in the Humanities at Queen's University Belfast. Michael published his first book, *Writing Ireland's Working Class: Dublin After O'Casey*, with Palgrave Macmillan in 2011, and his work includes research on Seán O'Casey, Brendan Behan, Dermot Bolger, and generally on cultural representations of class in Irish life.

David Toms is a Tutorial Scholar at the School of History, University College Cork where he is currently completing a PhD on the social history of sport in Munster, 1880–1930. He is a writer and co-editor of the football blog *The True Ball*, and has published a collection of poetry titled *Soma | Sema* (Merseyside: Knives, Forks and Spoons Press, 2012).

Introduction

David Convery

One hundred years ago, a titanic battle gripped the city of Dublin that polarised Irish society. The Irish Transport and General Workers' Union (ITGWU), led by Jim Larkin, took on the might of one of the biggest Irish capitalists of the day, William Martin Murphy. What began as a strike of ITGWU members over union recognition in Murphy's Dublin United Tramway Company quickly escalated, as Murphy, backed by the state, declared all-out war on the trade union movement. As head of the Dublin Employers' Federation, Murphy was instrumental in securing the backing of more than 400 employers that saw some 25,000 on strike or locked-out of work in a battle that lasted from August 1913 to March 1914. The 1913 Lockout would see large-scale rioting, brutal baton charges from the police, the imprisonment of hundreds of union activists, the importation of strike-breakers from Britain but also substantial donations and sympathetic strike action from British workers, as well as the establishment of the Irish Citizen Army. The Lockout completely overshadowed the other significant historical event of that year, the establishment of the Irish Volunteers in November 1913, an event which has been magnified out of proportion due to subsequent history. Despite tremendous efforts, the workers went down to a bitter defeat. Historians and other commentators have tended to view the 1913 Lockout as a tragic, but unique case in Irish history, which in many ways it was. However, its uniqueness lies mainly in its scale. The working class continued to exist after 1913. It continued to develop its own organisations, its own cultural and leisure activities, its own forms of self-representation and identity. It also continued to engage in strike action and other forms of protest against the employers and ruling establishment. Yet the study of an independent working class is neglected in favour of an all-embracing focus on nationalism in politics, culture and wider society. As highlighted throughout this book, this neglect has stretched at times to an actual denial of the existence of an Irish working class. That class, rather than ethnicity, religion, or the idea of national identity could have a role to play in politics and cultural production is an alien one to mainstream Irish debate. The working class has been locked out of history.

Why this neglect of working-class history and culture? Numerous reasons have been offered as to why this is the case, among them the primarily rural nature of Irish society for most of its independent existence, which has hindered the development of a large industrial working class. This however, is insufficient by itself to explain the issue. In other countries – Russia being a prime example – the working class has had a political and cultural prominence out of proportion to its numerical strength. One of the most important reasons has been the triumph of nationalism in Ireland. Jim Larkin, James Connolly and the ITGWU were vociferous in their efforts to create an independent working-class identity and politics. After the union's defeat in the Lockout, Larkin left for the United States and would not return until 1923. Connolly, meanwhile, would be executed for his role in the Easter Rising in 1916. Despite the huge role of the labour movement from 1918–1923 – a period of intense radicalisation which witnessed mass strikes, occupations and 'soviets', most famously the Limerick Soviet in April 1919 – the new labour leadership lacked the willingness to use its industrial muscle to go beyond the current political boundaries. Labour would consequently take a backseat in politics, allowing the nationalist movement to take centre stage. The nationalist movement was a pan-class alliance that saw nation, not class, as the key determinant in politics and society. That the two main parties in independent Ireland – Fine Gael and Fianna Fáil – came from this movement, coupled with the weakness of the Labour Party – which was content to ride on the respective coat-tails of the aforementioned parties when it was practicable to do so – ensured nationalist ideology a hegemonic role in Irish society. Ireland would be defined by the commonality of people based on ethnicity and religion, united in the task of building an independent state. A Gaelic, Catholic identity was what mattered; as opposed to an English, Protestant one. Class differences, although patently in existence to those who would look, were submerged. Those who presented an outlook at odds with this often encountered censorship, incarceration and ostracism from society. The only viable option for many was to take the boat.

These conditions produced an insular, conservative society that has been reflected in scholarship. The study of the Irish working class has been mostly limited to those who are or have been active in the labour movement or politics. The Irish Labour History Society (ILHS) was established in 1973, and its journal, *Saothar*, in 1975. These have provided a focus and given an enormous boost to the study of Irish working-class history, even though it remains largely neglected by mainstream historiography. However, although they have investigated certain aspects of Irish working-class life and culture from time to time, both have been characterised by an overly empirical approach focused on biographical studies of labour activists and the history of institutions such as the trade unions and the Labour Party. Furthermore, the study of the Irish working class has yet to benefit from the insights that can be achieved by adopting an inter-disciplinary approach. This is understandable given that the lack of mainstream interest meant much of the groundwork of merely gathering documents and developing an outline of Irish working-class history had yet to be done. However, it has meant that the study of the Irish working class is behind that of other countries. This year also marks the fiftieth anniversary of the publication of E.P. Thompson's *The Making of the English Working Class*. In 1963, Thompson faced a similar situation in Britain to that which we find in Ireland today. That is, an academe largely ignorant of and, moreover, unconcerned with investigating English working-class life. Thompson, as he so eloquently put it, set out to rescue the working class 'from the enormous condescension of posterity'. His work, though not without his faults – not least in its neglect of women's history –

was a pioneering effort that spurred on a new, more holistic approach to the study of the working class in Britain. While not aiming to compare to Thompson's work, all of the writers in this volume have been influenced to some extent by it, and feel it appropriate to mark its anniversary and to point a way forward for Irish working-class history in its spirit.

The pioneering efforts of the ILHS have succeeded in creating a scaffold upon which we can begin to build by an examination of aspects of the culture, mentality and everyday life of the Irish working class, as well as the interactions of the working class with the dominant state discourse. This volume has been written entirely by early career researchers, and thus presents the work of a new generation of scholars impacted by developments in contemporary society and educated in a rigorous and inter-disciplinary approach that draws upon methodologies, sources and ideas from disciplines such as sociology, anthropology, literature, diaspora, cultural, women and gender studies, as well as history, to examine aspects of Irish working-class life that have hitherto been neglected, or if examined previously, to offer a new perspective.

We begin the volume with the 1913 Lockout, aspects of which are explored by Conor McCabe and David Convery in the opening two chapters. The Lockout was about more than just trade union recognition, as important as that was. For the protagonists on both sides, it was an all-out class war, fought over competing visions of how society should be run and in whose interests. Radical political visions advanced by socialists clashed with traditional capitalist free market values epitomised in the character of William Martin Murphy. This radical vision of the ITGWU included the development of an independent cultural existence for the working class, a subject which is dealt with in Chapter 3 by James Curry in his study of the prose, poetry and dramatic works of the neglected writer Andrew Patrick Wilson in the pages of the *Irish Worker*.

It was also part of a worldwide process that saw an increase in the organisation and militancy of unskilled workers. Rather than viewing Ireland in isolation from the rest of the world, we should see it as integrated. Processes which unfold abroad are mirrored in Ireland, and similarly Irish events impact elsewhere. Part of this integration is the flow of people throughout the world. Many studies exist on Irish emigrants, but few attempt to integrate them with the ongoing history of Ireland, or to analyse them from a class perspective. It must be remembered that Irish emigrants were, in the main, working class and small farmers, and their history and identity did not end with their departure from Ireland's shores. Two of the chapters in this volume are thus devoted to the study of Irish working-class emigrants. The first of these is Chapter 4, in which Alan J.M. Noonan discusses the impact of Jim Larkin on the politics of Irish-Americans during his stay in the US from 1914–23. Noonan highlights the alienation and incomprehension that could exist between the official socialist movement and its potential audience among working-class Irish immigrants, who, while Catholic, could also be radical – as Noonan demonstrates with the example of Irish miners in Butte, Montana.

In Chapter 5, Fiona Devoy McAuliffe illustrates that despite the defeat of the unions during the Lockout, the conditions created during wartime from 1914–18 facilitated an unprecedented upsurge in union membership and strength, the power of which was demonstrated most forcibly in the general strike against conscription in April 1918. Labour now seemed to be in the driving seat in a country in foment, yet stood aside in the general elections of 1918, allowing Sinn Féin to take the reins of the national struggle. This would have crucial consequences for the position of the working class in independent Ireland, which would lack a significant political voice and be consequently subject to marginalisation and sometimes worse.

In Chapter 6, Donal Fallon investigates the politics of newsboys in inner-city Dublin in the 1930s. He reveals how their initial scuffles with republicans over costs during a newspaper strike would lead to them being smeared as the 'Animal Gang', a seemingly catch-all term later employed to denote groups of working-class youths involved in violence, especially against communists. The state and charitable organisations played a more sinister role in the marginalisation of working-class youth. Institutionalisation of poor, working-class children for a variety of official reasons was widespread, and often resulted in abuse, and in some cases death, as Sarah-Anne Buckley examines in Chapter 7.

In Northern Ireland, the working class had a more prominent place in society due to its numerical and industrial strength. It too, however, would fail to develop a strong, independent political voice due to the sectarian nature of Northern Irish society. Nevertheless, there were times when its industrial strength combined with extreme political and social circumstances to effectively push its demands forward. In Chapter 8, Christopher J.V. Loughlin highlights one such example in the major engineering strikes that rocked Belfast in October 1942, which, more than simply being about wages and conditions demonstrated competing visions of how and why the Second World War was being fought.

In Chapter 9, David Toms examines a central aspect of working-class cultural life – sport. A vibrant sporting life centred on the workplace existed in Ireland for decades, with teams of workers competing in self-organised local, regional and national leagues in association football, Gaelic football and hurling, as well as other sports. These played a central role in generating working-class identity and workplace solidarity.

One of the main barriers to investigating working-class history is that, for the most part, working-class people did not write about their experiences and thoughts and therefore it can be very difficult to understand their mentality. Methods to deal with this have been developed in other parts of the world, but have been slow in their incorporation into Irish scholarship. Numerous chapters in this volume, however, highlight the insights that can be gained by utilising some of these techniques and sources. In Chapter 4 Noonan uses Irish-language poetry, situated in the context of known historical events, to gain an understanding of the mentality of Irish miners in Butte, Montana. Similarly, in Chapter 10, the second chapter on Irish working-class emigrants, Sara Goek utilises oral history and song to great effect in her examination of gender and class among Irish workers in post-war Britain. In Chapter 11, Liam Cullinane uses oral history to gain insights into the importance

Introduction

of class, gender and status among the mostly female workforce of the now-defunct Sunbeam-Wolsey factory in Cork city. In both chapters, through the voices of the workers themselves, the authors enable us to see that, although class may not be defined using traditional terminology, class distinctions were apparent to workers who distinguished them in multiple ways from geography to accent, to seating arrangements. To conclude the book, Michael Pierse offers a wide-ranging reflection in Chapter 12 on the class divide in Irish cultural production and education over the past century and presents a damning indictment of the continuing censorship and misrepresentation of working-class culture in contemporary Ireland.

In this 'decade of centenaries' much energy will be expended on how we can remember the narrative of national struggle. As such, it will merely continue the focus on the place of nation in politics, culture and society in most scholarly writings on Ireland. Through this volume, we offer a different perspective, using the occasion of the centenary of the 1913 Lockout to highlight the neglected history and culture of the Irish working class. In doing so, we hope to kindle an interest among the general public and academics alike in a subject that is rich, varied and worthy of serious study.

Chapter One

'Your only God is Profit': Irish Class Relations and the 1913 Lockout[1]

Conor McCabe

On Tuesday 26 August 1913 the Irish Transport and General Workers' Union (ITGWU) called a strike of its Dublin United Tramway Company (DUTC) members in a move that had been debated and talked about in public for weeks beforehand. In the case of the company's director, William Martin Murphy, he had been planning to confront the ITGWU directly since at least 1911. He was one of the main forces behind the creation of the Dublin Employers' Federation, established specifically to prevent strikes and protect the interests of employers.[2] This was no ordinary lobby group. It could draw on the support of the courts and police, and wielded the threat of unemployment to keep the workforce in line. Dublin was a city that paid starvation wages, and a single week's pay was often the difference between poverty and penury. At its heart the 1913 Lockout, which developed out of the August strike, was not about union recognition or even wages; it was about class power. The employers knew this, and so did the ITGWU. The nature of the conflict in 1913, the issues at hand, the winners and losers, provide insights into the social forces that would go on to shape independent Ireland.

At the time of Larkin's arrival in 1907 it had been almost a hundred years since Dublin could lay claim to the title of second city of the British Empire.

Its once-opulent Georgian squares were now for the most part tenements – private rented accommodation in the hands of slum landlords – and business consisted mainly of port trade and administration. Dublin was not an industrial centre. 'If you mount the Nelson Column in Sackville Street you may, if you are particularly observant' wrote Arnold Wright in 1914, 'count as many factory shafts as you have fingers on your two hands, but you will have to look for them.'[3] The factories which produced for export were focused on food production and alcohol. It was a city through which goods passed mainly on their way to Britain, in particular live cattle that were shipped to the slaughterhouses of England.

A large part of the city's activity was centred on services within the city itself. Of the 397,957 persons listed with occupations in Dublin in the 1911 census, 167,479, or 42 per cent, were general service class – that is, unskilled, low-paid and casual.[4] The skilled working class – the artisans – made up 25 per cent of the working population, and were concentrated primarily in building, clothing and food supply trades. The number of families listed in the city census stood at 62,365, of which just over 54 per cent 'occupied one or two-room dwellings'.[5] The Rev. P.J. Monaghan, a Roman Catholic clergyman, gave evidence to the government inquiry into Dublin housing conditions in November 1913 and mentioned 'an instance in which 107 human beings occupied one tenement house, stating that there were only two water-closets in the entire building for both sexes.'[6] The intense poverty gave Dublin, at twenty-two deaths per 1,000, the highest mortality rate of the cities of the UK.[7]

Dublin also suffered from tax flight. Throughout the nineteenth century the prim and pious middle classes left for the new suburbs which were being erected on the outer edge of the two canals which encircle the city. This made them exempt from city rates, yet still within tram distance of their business and social interests. Those who extracted their wealth from the economic dynamics of Dublin paid little towards its sustenance and reproduction. Dublin became 'a cribbed, cabined and confined city between the Royal and Grand Canals, with an increasingly impoverished population in ever deteriorating buildings.'[8] In his evidence to the Royal Commission on the Housing of the Working Classes in 1885, the city's superintendent medical officer, Charles Cameron, talked of one builder who moved his premises from Richmond Street to 'immediately over the bridge to premises adjoining the canal outside the city'. 'By that change of position he escapes perhaps a rate of one [shilling] in the pound on his premises,' said Cameron, 'and at the same time he has all the advantages of the city; all his timber and stone are drawn through the city to his works, and all his workmen live in the city, and if they get knocked up they go to our hospitals.'[9] By 1913 the city's tram system was an essential part of this doughnut structure of slum core and leafy low-tax periphery.

The unskilled and casual occupations which dominated Dublin's economic structure were not part of the traditional cache of trade unionism. This slowly began to change in the 1880s with the rise of New Unionism, the focus of which was the establishment of mass membership organisations that would achieve labour gains, not through the monopoly of artisan trades – as with the craft unions – but through sheer strength of numbers. The tactics eventually adopted would reflect this strategy, including violent strike action and the blacking of strike-breakers. New Unionism also recognised the importance of political representation and legislative reform, symbolised most clearly by the demand for an eight-hour day. The movement tended to focus on recruiting workers in transport and essential services, as these were the 'sectors where strikes of unskilled workers were most likely to succeed.'[10] This was the case in Ireland where railwaymen were among the first to embrace the ideology of New Unionism.

The initial wave of New Unionism in the 1880s and 1890s saw a short spike in trade union activity. Its fortunes did not rise again in Ireland until the arrival of Larkin to Belfast in 1907. In 1909 he formed the ITGWU, winning some early victories. In the summer of 1911 there was a spate of strike action involving New Unionism across Great Britain and Ireland. In September of that year the Irish branches of the Amalgamated Society of Railway Servants (ASRS) engaged in a sympathetic strike with the ITGWU that not only failed in its objectives, but saw 10 per cent of the strikers laid off in an overt and unapologetic act of victimisation undertaken by the chief director of the Great Southern and Western Railway, Sir William Goulding. It affected relations between the railwaymen and the ITGWU, and played no small part in the absence of the railwaymen from direct action during the 1913 Lockout. Whereas in Britain successful strike action had led to significant concessions and increased membership, in Ireland trade union development on the railways was frozen, and remained so for the next five years. The September 1911 strike was broken by boardroom militancy, and this had a sizable effect on employer attitudes to the Irish trade union movement, particularly around recognition and legitimacy – core elements of the 1913 Lockout. William Martin Murphy said that the strikers 'were beaten to the ropes' by the militant stance of the employers, and that lesson stayed with him.[11] With the railwaymen seemingly broken, the next collective action by the employers would be against the ITGWU itself.

'WE ARE LIVING IN STIRRING TIMES.'
–*Irish Worker*, 12 August 1911.

The opening act in the 1913 Lockout occurred not on the trams but in the offices of the *Irish Independent,* owned by William Martin Murphy. On Friday 15 August around forty dispatchers were paid off after they refused to leave the ITGWU. 'The city newsboys, learning of this action, refused to sell the *Evening Herald* [also owned by Murphy] in the streets in order to show their sympathy with the *Independent* employees and their demands' and by that evening it was almost impossible to buy the newspaper in the city centre.[12] The newsboys had already been unionised by Larkin. The boycott of Murphy's newspapers spread to the parcels department of the DUTC and to Eason's newsagents, and by 'Sunday 17 August, Murphy had dismissed two hundred tramway workers for refusing to handle his newspapers or to carry out other instructions.'[13] Two days later the ITGWU held a meeting of its tramway members where strike action was discussed but not formally accepted. Either way, the DUTC took it as a declaration of intent and issued a statement saying that it would ask all its workers to sign a loyalty pledge stating that they would remain at their post 'should a strike of any of the employees of the company be called for by Mr. James Larkin of the Irish Transport Workers Union'.[14]

It was clear that Murphy and the Dublin employers wanted to smash Larkinism – that is, militant trade unionism underpinned by sympathetic strike action – yet the phenomenon was in no small part a creature of their own making, as Emmet O'Connor notes, 'The root of Larkinism lay in employer hostility to the unionisation of unskilled workers'.[15] Larkinism was such a militant force because the employers were themselves militant and implacable. In other words, against such a hostile enemy, Larkinism seemingly offered a way of countering their power and improving the lives of the city's unskilled workforce. This was a world where the moderate voice was ignored, where structural poverty was excused as personal failing and where the powerless were simply brushed aside.

At the same time that the DUTC was making plans to expel the ITGWU from its workplace, Murphy was making arrangements with the Dublin Metropolitan Police to counter any possible disruptions by Larkin and the union. These included the mobilisation of contingents of the armed national police force – the Royal Irish Constabulary – into the city. Larkin, for his part, attended a meeting of the Dublin Trades Council on Monday 25 August in order to gain its backing. This was not a straightforward matter, and it was made all the more complicated by Larkin's unpredictable and antagonistic character. No mention was made of the tramway company. Instead the council voiced its support of the strikers in the *Independent*'s offices. Larkin left the meeting and went to Liberty Hall where tramcar men were waiting for him. It was at this meeting that the decision to strike was taken. The next morning, Larkin issued a note from Liberty Hall to the ITGWU tramway members. It simply read: 'Members. Strike declared. Stop at once by order of union'.[16]

Shortly before 10am on Tuesday 26 August 1913 around 200 of DUTC's 650 tram workers followed Larkin's order and left their cars. 'The conductors went to the company's offices and handed over their tickets and cash boxes, while the motormen gave up possession of the driving handles.'[17] Murphy, however, 'had taken time by the forelock' and had 'made arrangements for dealing with this strike, and accordingly he had put a body of men remaining faithful on the cars.'[18] Within half an hour the Dublin Metropolitan Police were out in numbers, supported by armed members of the RIC, and within forty minutes, according to the *Freeman's Journal*, 'the tram service was again running pretty smoothly.'[19] Seven ITGWU tramway men were arrested for breach of contract. The impact of the strike on the tram service had been minimal, although the DUTC cancelled all evening services as a safety precaution. At a meeting of around 7,000 people at Beresford Place the vice-president of the Dublin Trades Council, William O'Brien, said that they were 'in the midst of the greatest labour battle ever fought in Dublin' and that it was 'a battle of organised employers against organised trade unionism.'[20] Murphy, not surprisingly, saw the scale of the events quite differently. 'I am familiar with the history of all the tramway strikes in these countries and abroad' he told the press on the evening of 26 August, 'and Mr. Larkin's so-called strike today was the feeblest and most contemptible attempt that was ever made.'[21] The strike had failed to seriously affect services. The advantage was with Murphy and the DUTC.

On the morning of Thursday 28 August the police arrested Larkin and four other ITWGU activists – P.T. Daly, William Partridge, William O'Brien and Thomas Lawlor – at their homes and brought them to Chancery Lane police station 'where charges of seditious libel, seditious conspiracy, and unlawful assembly were entered against them.'[22] The police said that based on the evidence of detective officer Revelle 'and other credible witnesses' the accused were guilty of conspiring to disturb the public peace and to raise 'discontent and hatred between ... the working classes of Dublin and the police forces [and soldiers] of the Crown.'[23] Somewhat surprisingly, the magistrate granted bail after the defendants gave assurances that they would not hold any illegal meetings or use inflammatory language. The police drew attention to Larkin's promise to speak at a meeting on Sunday that had been proclaimed, but the magistrate said that was a matter for the police. On Friday 29 August Larkin said that he would address the Sunday meeting 'dead or alive'. A warrant was issued for his arrest and he went into hiding. An alternative rally destined for Fairview was organised by William O'Brien. However, on Sunday morning a heavily-disguised Larkin entered the Imperial Hotel on Sackville Street (O'Connell Street), also owned by Murphy, and announced his presence from a first-floor balcony. Almost immediately he was arrested and taken away. A crowd gathered and cheered on Larkin. And then the police attacked.

There had been riots in the city on the night of Saturday 30 August, but the crowd on O'Connell Street on Sunday 'was peaceable and composed mainly of curious onlookers, church-goers and Sunday strollers going about their lawful business'.[24] It is not known who gave the order to draw batons – if indeed any order was given – but within minutes of Larkin's arrest the police were striking at all and sundry outside the Imperial Hotel and down the side-streets. Somewhere between four and six hundred people were injured that day, with one fatality: James Nolan, a labourer who was struck by police as he left a pub. Another labourer, John Byrne died on 4 September as a result of injuries received when he was batoned on Burgh Quay during the Saturday night riots. The events became known as Bloody Sunday and made headlines across the Atlantic, with the *New York Times* quoting one witness who said that all the crowd 'were guilty of was cheering Larkin like a hero'.[25] The class conflict at the heart of the dispute – with capital and the state on one side and organised labour on the other – was laid bare by Bloody Sunday. It also brought the British labour movement directly, if somewhat reluctantly, into the fight.

The response of the British Trades Union Congress (TUC) was to support the strikers with funds and food ships but not with industrial action. This was essentially the same response given by the British-based leadership of the ASRS in 1911 when the Irish railwaymen went on strike. It was the default stance of the British labour leadership when dealing with Ireland – lofty speeches and logistical support, but a line drawn at industrial solidarity. Bloody Sunday may have raised emotions and galvanised support and sympathy, but as with 1911, Ireland's fight would be on Ireland's shores. When it came to industrial action 'Dublin', the Irish historian Francis Devine observed, 'was not Derby or Dundee'.[26]

James Connolly was also in custody. He had been arrested along with William Partridge on Saturday 30 August. At their hearing, Connolly said that he did not recognise the proclamation that banned Sunday's meeting 'because I do not recognise English government in Ireland at all. I do not recognise the King except when I am compelled to do so'.[27] He refused to give bail of £300 in a person recognisance and two sureties of £150 each, and was sentenced to three months' imprisonment.[28] He was released on 13 September after a week on hunger strike. On 1 September Larkin was once again brought before the court, only this time he was refused bail.

James Nolan's funeral took place on 3 September and people showed up in their thousands. The funeral procession turned into 'a show of strength that stretched for over a mile'.[29] It stopped the trams and the police kept their distance. It passed off peacefully. The same day, around 400 Dublin employers agreed at a meeting to join with Murphy in his move against the ITGWU. They pledged themselves 'in future not to employ any persons who continue to be members of the Irish Transport and General Workers' Union and that anyone refusing to obey instructions shall be instantly dismissed'.[30] A similar stance was taken by the heads of the city's shipping firms, the Master Carriers' Association, the Society of Motor Manufacturers and Traders, as well as by members of the Coal Merchants Association. On 1 September Jacob's factory had come out in support of Murphy and locked out ITGWU members of its workforce. It meant that practically every workplace where the ITGWU was organised had agreed to dismiss the union's members – unless, of course, they left the union. 'The battle against Syndicalism', wrote the *Irish Times*, 'or, as it is called in Dublin, Larkinism, may, therefore, be said to have begun.'[31] The strike had become a city-wide lockout, affecting over 25,000 trade unionists who refused to handle tainted goods or repudiate the ITGWU.

'JIM LARKIN'S METHODS ARE NOT THOSE OF THE ROSE LEAF OR THE KID GLOVE.'
–*Keir Hardie*, 3 September 1913.[32]

Larkin was granted bail at a special hearing on the morning of Friday 19 September and almost immediately he left for Britain. He arrived in Glasgow the next day and addressed a crowd at a meeting in St Andrew's Hall which was held under the auspices of the Glasgow Independent Labour Party. On Sunday he spoke at Birkenhead. From this stage onwards until early December Larkin's role in the dispute was primarily, but not exclusively, to campaign for support among the British labour movement for the blacking of goods to and from Dublin while 'Connolly, when not in jail, deputized for him in Liberty Hall.'[33] On 27 September the first food ship arrived in Dublin. This was the physical outlay of the financial support that had been guaranteed by the TUC – £5,000 immediate payment followed by a weekly subvention. At the same time the Dublin Employers' Federation issued a circular to its members calling for the promotion of a fund 'to be devoted to carrying on the present campaign of combating the syndicalistic methods of the Irish Transport and General Workers' Union, and for securing the freedom of trade as vital to the best interests of the country...'[34] The Federation, with one eye on the promised Home Rule state, ended the circular by stating that it was important 'to make some permanent arrangements for the continuance of these elementary rights in the future'.

A public inquiry into the causes of the dispute opened in Dublin on 29 September. Larkin appeared as counsel for the workers and under this role he cross-examined William Martin Murphy, much to the delight of the public. On 21 October Mrs Dora Montefiore's 'Save The Kiddies' scheme, which planned to give the children of locked-out workers a holiday with families in England, was met with vitriol and protests from the city's Catholic hierarchy and laity. Archbishop William Walsh called it 'proselytising'. Mrs Lucille Rand, daughter of an American senator, was arrested at Kingston harbour and charged with abducting two children under fourteen years of age. Mrs Montefiore was also arrested and charged. The scheme was abandoned on 28 October, the same day that Larkin was sentenced to seven months' imprisonment for sedition. His committal to Mountjoy Prison unleashed a torrent of protest and he was released on 13 November having served only seventeen days.

At a rally outside Liberty Hall, Larkin announced a speaking tour of Britain 'to tell the working classes of England, Scotland and Wales what was going on in Dublin.'[35] Larkin called it his fiery cross tour, and it led to a second wave of sympathetic strikes, in Liverpool and South Wales, involving up to 30,000 railwaymen. The first wave occurred on 16 September when railwaymen in Liverpool refused to handle goods for Dublin, leading to suspensions and walk-outs involving over 13,000 men. The earlier wave was eventually settled by J.H. Thomas, leader of the National Union of Railwaymen and a fierce opponent of sympathetic strike action.[36] Larkin was becoming a threat to the leadership of the TUC, who began to question both the man and his tactics for the first time in public since the Lockout began. For his part, Larkin responded with his immense talent for losing friends and alienating people. Speaking at the Free Trade Hall in Manchester on 16 November, Larkin berated the British Empire – to a shout of 'shame' from the audience – and called for Home Rule for Ireland. He talked about assassins stalking him in the lobby of the Imperial Hotel and the personal attacks he suffered while in prison. Then he moved on to the British labour movement itself:

> It is time we woke up. If you disgrace your manhood and the Union by pretending you are friendly, and sending us money help, but at the same time sending us scab labour, I say, damn you and your money; we don't want it. We want to carry out the fundamentals and ethics of trade unionism so don't scab us.

Are you going to allow us in Dublin to be offered as a sacrifice? If not, send a message to our leaders, and tell them that the employing class in Dublin will not get any help from this side of the water.[37]

Larkin had a point. The strike and blackening of goods and workers was being broken in Dublin by non-unionised labour arriving from Britain. And this was no ordinary strike. The employers had made it clear that they saw it as a struggle against Syndicalism and Larkinism. The problem for Larkin was that on this issue, the employers and the British trade union leadership were in agreement. Syndicalism and Larkinism were threats to them both. And the trade union leadership, as with the employers, moved to protect themselves.

On Friday 5 December representatives of the British trade union movement and the Dublin Employers' Federation met in Dublin to discuss a possible settlement to the Lockout. It seemed that while both sides agreed that Larkinism needed to be contained, the problem remained as to how the labour movement could extricate itself from the situation without losing face.[38] The meeting broke up without agreement. On 9 December the TUC met in special congress in London. The attendance was made up of trade union officials, though not rank-and-file. The meeting voted against a general strike in support of the ITGWU in Dublin, but voted to retain financial support for the locked-out members. 'Larkin got his innings,' said J. Havelock Wilson, the moderate trade unionist and former Liberal party MP, and one of the strongest opponents of Syndicalism in Britain.[39] Syndicalism may have been popular among the rank-and-file, but the rank-and-file didn't make policy. The defeat of support for sympathetic industrial action meant that there was no chance of victory for the ITGWU. It was time to settle, with the advantage firmly on the side of the employers.

On 11 December James Connolly said that the ITGWU was willing to co-operate in any move for peace. The employers agreed to 'withdraw the circulars, posters and forms of agreement … presented to their employees' on condition that the workers agreed 'to abstain from any form of sympathetic strike action pending a board of wages and conditions of employment being set up by March 17th 1914.'[40] A further conference was organised, but it broke up over the issue of reinstatement. On 15 January 1914 Connolly wrote to William O'Brien, saying that he had advised Larkin to announce a 'general resumption of work, and the handling of all goods pending a more general acceptance of the doctrine of tainted goods by the trade union world.'[41] The money and food supplies had allowed the ITGWU to hold out for longer than expected, but the strike was not won or lost on funding from Britain. Sympathetic action was key, and this was not forthcoming. Speaking in Glasgow on Friday 30 January 1914 Larkin said 'we will admit we are beaten, we will make no bones about it,' before stating defiantly, 'but we are not too badly beaten still to fight!' The next day the United Building Labourers and General Workers' Union signed an agreement with the Dublin Building Trades' Association which stated that none of its members 'would remain, or become future members of, the Irish Transport Workers' Union.'[42] There were a few more workers who held out but effectively the lockout was over.

It was clear to the *Irish Times*, however, that although the employers had won the battle, this was no outright victory.

> Everybody is thankful, of course, that the strike is at last at an end; but few people, we think, will be satisfied with the manner of its ending. The settlement is the worst kind of settlement – virtually 'settlement by starvation.' Our unemployment problem is grievously aggravated. Many of those who have regained their employment have gone back to work with the resentful feelings of hopelessly beaten men. There can be no element of finality about such a settlement.[43]

A similar sentiment was expressed by Connolly the previous month, when he told O'Brien that 'the cross-channel unions had definitely resolved not to assist us in fighting the battle against the Dublin sweaters in the only way it could be fought, viz: by holding up their goods…'[44] The nature of the support from the British trade union movement – food and supplies but no sympathetic strike action – ensured the strike remained an Irish affair. 'The education of Irish workmen in the advantages of English intervention begun by the railway strike a few years ago', continued the *Irish Times* in its editorial, 'is vastly advanced by these sorry and cynical proceedings.'

The 1913 Lockout was naked class conflict. The economic structure of the city demanded a large body of unskilled and low-paid workers in order to sustain the profit-seeking mechanisms it had in place. The fact that the workers were unskilled meant that they were outside the catchment area of the older and more established craft unions. This is why the ITGWU was seen as such a threat. It organised outside of the craft unions, and brought together as a powerful industrial force the workers who were dismissed as rabble. Its power came from its numbers and from its use of sympathetic strikes. The employers, especially Murphy, saw this and moved against the union, armed with substantial economic power and with the backing of the courts and, indeed, the State itself. But Syndicalism, and its Irish variant, Larkinism, was also a threat to conservative trade unionism. From September to December 1913 the ITWGU was fighting on two fronts, and it lost on both.

Jim Larkin often said that his vision for Ireland was that of a co-operative commonwealth but that this world was far ahead in the future. With Home Rule seemingly on the horizon, the purpose of the Lockout was to make sure it stayed that way. Whatever Ireland would become as an independent nation, Murphy and the employers wanted to make sure that it was one where business had free reign, and where the working class knew their place. And despite some setbacks and mealy-mouthed compromises, from its foundation in 1922 the Irish state held true to that vision.

Chapter Two

Uniting the Working Class: History, Memory and 1913

David Convery

Come on along, come on along
And join Jim Larkin's union.
Come on along, come on along
And join Jim Larkin's union.
You'll get a loaf of bread and a pound of tea
And a belt of a baton from the DMP.[1]

This year marks the centenary of the 1913 Lockout, an event likely to be passed over for the most part by the mainstream media and political establishment concerned almost solely with the nationalist pantheon in the 'decade of centenaries'. But for working-class people, the Lockout has far greater resonance. In public meetings, demonstrations, debates and commentary, the words Larkin, Connolly and 1913 are often invoked when pointing to the type of leadership that is needed to combat the effects of austerity today.[2] That events of 100 years ago are used as symbols to inspire today's struggles shows a level of dissatisfaction with what came after, but also demonstrates the towering, almost mythical nature of these two figures and the project they headed in the Irish Transport and General Workers'

Union (ITGWU). All of these points are indeed, related. It has often been claimed that Ireland is a 'classless' society. The negative effect of this sort of proposition is clear. Rather than facilitate a level playing field, it has reinforced the privileged status of those who already had wealth and access to power and through this, has advanced their cultural hegemony. Historiography and cultural criticism is thus marked by a conservative and insular orientation with a distinct focus on constitutionalism, institutions and high politics and culture, rather than on the lives, history and expression of the great mass of people. As outlined in the introduction and demonstrated repeatedly in the other chapters of this book, the working class, for the most part, has been written out of history. The emphasis on the national question and the process of state building has, furthermore, facilitated ignorance, intentional or otherwise, of Ireland's place internationally. In seeking the antagonisms that give rise to nationalism and the construction of independent states, scholars have overlooked the commonality of experience shared by Ireland with the rest of the world. The study of the 1913 Lockout offers a different perspective. By shifting focus from nation to class, we can see events in Ireland as part of a worldwide process. The political conflict between Britain and Ireland that is usually stressed becomes nuanced by the introduction of class conflict pitting British and Irish workers against British and Irish business. By attempting to understand the project of Larkin and Connolly from their point of view, we can begin to interpret the reasons behind their revered status today and offer historians a means to re-evaluate seemingly familiar history.

JIM LARKIN AND THE ITGWU

Jim Larkin, a former Liverpool docker and trade unionist, launched the ITGWU in 1909. Prior to this, trade unions in Ireland had been mostly made up of skilled workers and were characterised by an elitist attitude. As ITGWU member James O'Shea put it, 'The Trade Unions of Dublin were at that time the most conservative narrow-minded body in Dublin. Before Larkin came there was no organisation for labourers in Dublin.'[3] The ITGWU aimed to unite the entire working class under the syndicalist slogan 'one big union'. Key to its mission was the potent weapon of the sympathetic strike. This was the idea that workers who were locked out or involved in an industrial dispute would receive support from workers in other workplaces who would refuse to deal with the company – a term called 'blacking' – and would sometimes come out on strike themselves. Workers would also refuse to handle 'tainted goods' – goods which had been created or transported by strike-breakers, commonly known as 'scabs'. The ITGWU found a ready audience for its message, and grew to 30,000 members by the summer of 1913.[4] The union set out to do much more than just improve wages however. Led by socialists, it was part of a bigger project of raising the economic, political and cultural level of the entire working class on the road to creating a socialist world. The ITGWU aimed to give the working class self-reliance and dignity. The playwright Seán O'Casey, a member of the ITGWU, summed up Larkin's mission nicely: 'here was a man who would put a flower in a vase on a table as well as a loaf on a plate.'[5] Larkin, like many socialists of his time, was an advocate of temperance, and attempted to wean the working class away from a social life that revolved around the pub. As the poet Maeve Cavanagh recalled:

> Larkin was concerned about temperance and hated the idea of the men spending their time and money in public-houses, so he started to organise concerts. He asked me would I help and we started the concerts at the time the public-houses would open. Larkin told the men to bring their wives and babies and that the babies could cry all they wanted. I used to play the piano and sometimes I got a lecturer for them and helped in any way I could.[6]

To this end, the ITGWU acquired Liberty Hall at Beresford Place in 1912 and later Croydon Park, a mansion with acres of land for the holding of leisure, cultural and educational activities for the working class. In these two venues they organised socials, dances, choral singing, children's games, the Irish Workers' Dramatic Society, and, during the Lockout, centres for the distribution of food to locked-out workers and their families. No longer would leisure and learning be the privilege of the rich, as Larkin outlined:

> I submit that the working class have as much right as any section or class in the community to enjoy all the advantages of science, art, and literature. No field of knowledge, no outlook on life, no book should be closed against the workers. They should demand their share in the effulgence of life and all that was created for the enjoyment of mankind.[7]

The central plank in this project was the creation of the *Irish Worker and People's Advocate* (later just the *Irish Worker*) in May 1911. Larkin outlined its aims:

> At present you spend your lives in sordid labour and have your abode in filthy slums; your children hunger, and your masters say your slavery must endure for ever. If you would come out of bondage yourself must forge the weapons and fight the grim battle.
>
> The written word is the most potent force in our modern world. *The Irish Worker* will be a lamp to guide your feet in the dark hours of the impending struggle; a well of truth reflecting the purity of your motives, and a weekly banquet from which you will rise strengthened in purpose to emulate the deeds of your forefathers, who died in dungeon and on scaffold in the hopes of a glorious resurrection for our beloved country.[8]

For 189 issues over forty-one months the *Irish Worker* poured forth an avalanche of articulated class anger the likes of which had not been seen in Ireland before. Week after week employers were targeted and exposed on its pages, scandals were highlighted and solutions proposed. The newspaper was largely written by Larkin himself, with regular contributors from others too, such as James Connolly and Andrew Patrick Wilson (see next chapter). Not only did it feature agitational writings, it also presented poetry, songs, plays, and prose. The writing was often raw and unpolished but it was genuine in that it reflected the concerns of the working class without condescension. It was by and for the working class and they responded to it in their thousands, the paper averaging 14-15,000 sales per week, and likely read by many more, made more impressive by the fact that many newsagents refused to stock it.[9] It would take on an important role during the Lockout, its biting satirical cartoons by Ernest Kavanagh encapsulating perfectly the scorn felt by the working class for the likes of William 'Murder' Murphy.[10]

The ITGWU was a vocal advocate of the rights of women too. Larkin, Connolly and other members of the union were strong supporters of women's suffrage, and often spoke on platforms and attended demonstrations in its favour. However, they were not just interested in suffrage but in ending inequality all round. To this end, the Irish Women Workers' Union (IWWU) was founded in 1911 under the auspices of the ITGWU, its secretary being Jim Larkin's sister Delia, who also edited a weekly column in the *Irish Worker* called the 'Women Workers' Column'. The IWWU, though small, never reaching more than 1,000 members pre-war, was a militant body, and as well as representing and organising women workers, succeeded in winning strikes, such as at Keogh's sack-makers and the Pembroke laundry in 1912. Its role cannot be overstated in overcoming prejudices among the male working class and fighting for dignity and equality among male and female workers within the workplace and in wider society.[11]

Larkin and the ITGWU thus succeeded in organising much of the Dublin working class behind a radical political vision; a vision that was not just rhetoric, but was matched by action and the example of its leaders. Its success and combative stance earned it the scorn of Dublin's employers and the admiration of its workers, and would lead to frequent clashes with the forces of the State, as eloquently expressed in the children's song quoted at the beginning of this chapter. As one witness put it many years later, 'Although you might almost say that Jim Larkin had a price on his head, he managed to hold huge meetings. He had only to put his head out of one of the windows of Liberty Hall and shout "Comrades" and Beresford Place would be thronged in a few minutes.'[12] Despite the tendency of historians to focus on the national question during these years, it was the labour movement and not advanced nationalism that was beginning to create a mass movement in Dublin and challenge the status quo. In fact, by the time the *Irish Worker* was launched, sales of Sinn Féin's weekly paper had fallen to less than 5,000.[13] This new militant working class was a threat to the entire establishment. It was clear that a major clash was bound to occur sooner or later. This came when Larkin attempted to organise the workers of one of Ireland's most successful and anti-union businessmen, William Martin Murphy. The initial strike quickly escalated out of proportion as the State clamped down harshly. After Bloody Sunday, the employers attempted to smash Larkinism once and for all. The Dublin Employers' Federation, headed by Murphy, took a leaf out of Larkin's book and declared a sympathetic lockout of over 400 employers in the city. Dublin came to a standstill. It was these actions that turned a relatively minor dispute into all-out class warfare in the capital city. Both sides had played their cards and neither side was prepared to give in. With stalemate in Dublin, attention now turned across the Irish Sea.

BRITISH AID

The development of radical, syndicalist unions was not just an Irish phenomenon, but was part of an increased militancy that gripped contemporary labour movements worldwide. Militant unions armed with the philosophy of uniting the working class under 'one big union' that could challenge capitalism at the heart of production included the Confederación Nacional del Trabajo (National Confederation of Labour – CNT) in Spain, the Confédération Générale du Travail (General Confederation of Labour

– CGT) in France, and what was probably the most famous example in the English-speaking world, the Industrial Workers of the World (IWW) in the United States, commonly referred to as the Wobblies. The IWW forged strong links with the Irish labour movement. James Connolly had been an IWW organiser while in the US; one of its leaders 'Big' Bill Haywood would speak at meetings in Liverpool, London, Manchester, Dublin and other cities in support of the locked-out workers in 1913; and Larkin would give the funeral oration of another of its organisers, Joe Hill, in Chicago in 1915.[14]

In Britain, there was no major syndicalist union, but the general ideas of syndicalism permeated the movement. In fact, labour militancy was such a facet of life in Britain between 1910 and 1914 that these years became known as the 'Great Unrest'. Mass strikes convulsed miners, dockers, railway workers, textile operatives, engineers and many more, influenced by the ideas of Tom Mann and his Industrial Syndicalist Education League. These strikes often turned violent, and developed into showdowns with the State itself. In 1911 the military were called in to a general strike of transport workers in Liverpool and, during Britain's first national rail strike in August 1911, the military opened fire on workers in Llanelli, Wales, killing two and wounding many more, provoking widespread rioting among an enraged working class. As Donal Nevin outlines, 'Altogether the number of workers involved in strikes and lock-outs in Britain and Ireland increased from 170,000 in 1909 to 1,230,000 in 1912, while the number of days lost rose from 2,800,000 to 40,900,000.'[15] Union membership had increased from 2,369,000 in 1909 to 3,987,000 at the end of 1913.[16] The leaders of the Great Unrest were often hostile to the official leadership of the labour movement, who they felt were too concerned with parliamentary reform as the most effective way to ameliorate workers lives. They instead advocated organising workers in a particular industry into one union, backed by solidarity of the entire class through alliances of unions and sympathetic strikes. These ideas led to the creation of the National Transport Workers' Federation in 1911, the amalgamation of the four rail-workers' unions into the National Union of Railwaymen in 1913, and the creation of the Triple Alliance of the aforementioned organisations with the Miners' Federation of Great Britain in 1914. Through this level of organisation, it was felt that workers could take direct action to win effective reform and ultimately control over their workplaces and daily lives. These ideas were popularised through the launch of a daily labour newspaper, the *Daily Herald*, in April 1912 headed by George Lansbury. Although open to the entire labour movement, it became in effect the organ of the 'anti-official' radical movement in the unions. It was a staunch backer of the Dublin workers in 1913, and the Herald League, which had branches throughout Britain to raise funds for the paper, organised large public meetings with Larkin and Connolly as speakers. British workers further contributed to funds for the Dublin workers through the League.[17] These workers saw themselves as part of a worldwide struggle. With this perspective, it should come as no surprise that the Irish workers received a large level of support from the British working class. Yet the international working class solidarity that was part and parcel of the time is often ignored in Irish history. The Dublin Lockout had a tremendous effect upon the British working class, and was an important event in their history too, bringing to the fore the conflict between rank-and-file trade unionists with the official union leadership.

The events of Bloody Sunday so shocked the British labour movement that the Trades Union Congress (TUC), then in session in Manchester, decided to send a delegation to investigate immediately. Their report is a very revealing document for the position of the official British trade union leadership towards the employers and their attitude towards Larkinism. While admitting that 'From the evidence obtained we are satisfied that the Irish Transport Workers' Union *had* [emphasis added] been doing good work – that it had considerably raised the wages of the various sections of industry which it had organised', the report was unfavourable in its view of Larkin and his methods:

The Irish Transport Workers' Union and its General Secretary, Mr. J. Larkin, had adopted a very aggressive policy, attacking employers individually, extending the use of the sympathetic strike, the refusal to handle what is termed 'tainted goods,' thereby involving sections of the community previously untouched by these disputes. This policy is being met by the employers with an equally aggressive policy of a sympathetic lock-out.[18]

Yet it was only through the very tactics they condemned that the improvements they applauded had come to fruition. Furthermore, while mentioning that Murphy 'was also able to apply the powers of the Press against Mr. Larkin and the union', once calling Larkin a 'mean thief', its criticism was again reserved for the union leader:

> The Irish Transport Workers' Union runs a newspaper called the 'Irish Worker,' and in this paper Mr. Larkin replied to Mr. Murphy with more vehemence than courtesy, and at the time of our arrival in Dublin the dispute had degenerated into a personal quarrel between Mr. Murphy and Mr. Larkin, and this was going on with thousands of workmen out of employment, the city of Dublin under a semi-military regime, and the whole population suffering serious inconvenience and loss.[19]

The resolution of the dispute itself was attempted through 'friendly conference between the employers and representatives of the men concerned.'[20] However, the talks broke down and they were forced to conclude that 'From information obtained since negotiations broke down, we are thoroughly convinced that the Dublin Employers' Federation Limited are not prepared to make any kind of agreement with responsible Trade Union representatives, and are determined to crush out Trade Unionism in Dublin.' Furthermore, 'there is evidence of [Dublin] Castle officials and relatives being financially interested in some of the firms in dispute.'[21]

Despite this, sympathetic action remained off the agenda. Instead, when they returned to Britain, it was decided to issue 'a strong and urgent appeal to all societies to respond generously' to a fund 'in order that the supply of provisions for the men, their wives, and families may be continued as long as necessary'.[22] The workers of Britain responded wholeheartedly to the call. The TUC report on the fund is filled with details of hundreds of donations large and small, both from organisations and individuals, with many donating multiple times and many organisations donating centrally as well as from individual branches. The largest contributions came from the Miners' Federation of Great Britain which donated £14,000 in fourteen weekly instalments.[23] Donations came from various trades councils and co-operative societies, as well as the London Society of Compositors, the Gasworkers and General Labourers' Union, the Scottish Union of Dock Labourers, the Lanarkshire Miners' Union, the gun factory workers at Woolwich, the Independent Labour Party, the British Socialist Party, the Labour Party, the Stoke Newington Socialist Society, as well as, amongst others, spinners, typographers, boilermakers, lace-makers, cigar-makers, tilers, weavers, trawlers, plumbers, clerks, tailors, coach-makers, printers, navvies, dyers, teachers, postal workers and carpenters.[24] In total £61,698 15s. 0 ¾ d. was received 'direct at the offices of the Parliamentary Committee', and a further £31,819 18s. 8 ½ d. was received 'at the offices of the "Daily Citizen," [a labour newspaper] and paid over to the Parliamentary Committee'.[25] Patrick O'Reilly, an Irishman working in Nobel's Dynamite Works in Scotland, remembered that 'through our Union we paid sixpence each per week to the strike fund in Dublin. Tom Mann was our leader in Scotland and I remember him quoting Jim Larkin when we were going on strike ourselves. He quoted, "Stand up on your hind legs and fight the capitalists, don't let your children starve any longer."'[26] It was not just money that was collected.

[T]he New Mills Co-operative Society forwarded two cases of children's clogs and boots, women and girls' coats, boys' suits, caps, and overcoats; the United Co-operative Baking Society of Glasgow sending 900 loaves of bread per week for several weeks;

some tons of biscuits being also given by the Wholesale Co-operative Society, the staff and employés [sic] of which generously raised a special fund in order that a large quantity of toys and some hundredweights of oranges, sweets, etc., might be sent to Dublin for the children's entertainment at Christmas-time.

The TUC could claim that 'it can be safely asserted that on no previous occasion had an appeal issued in the name of organised Labour met with such spontaneous, continued, and magnificent support.'[27]

The aid provided an essential lifeline to the workers in Dublin, but forced the Employers' Federation to seek its own aid overseas. With the help of the union-busting Shipping Federation, ships full of strike-breakers arrived in Dublin, the first sailing up the Liffey on 29 October. One witness would recall the hypocrisy of establishment society when comparing the reaction to the importation of strike-breakers with the 'Save The Kiddies' scheme:

The wealth of Britain could come into the city to be used against the workers without a word of protest but when gifts of food and clothes from our people in Liverpool were accepted by Larkin there was a storm of objections, and when people in Liverpool offered to take care of the children of the strikers for the period of the strike the charge was made that this was only a trick to turn them into Protestants.[28]

Connolly authorised mass picketing and the closure of the port, and also assented to the creation of the Irish Citizen Army, a workers' defence force under the direction of former British Army officer Captain Jack White. Yet all of this could only prolong the struggle, and could not definitively prevent the importation of strike-breakers and win the battle with the employers. The only hope for success lay in sympathetic action by British workers, to black all goods to and from Dublin. The huge amount of aid sent by British workers showed firmly that they were on the side of the Dublin workers, and the wave of strikes that swept over the country during the Great Unrest demonstrated a willingness to take widespread and militant strike action. Yet, as Conor McCabe has outlined in the previous chapter, all unofficial sympathetic action by British workers was promptly stopped by the intervention of union officials. As Harry Orbell, an official of the dockers' union put it:

> In all my experience I have never known a time when there has been manifested a desire to help any union in dispute as there is among dockers both in London and the provincial ports towards their Dublin comrades ... We have had to rearrange the whole of our paid officials in London, placing them in certain centres with the express purpose of preventing any disorganised move ... It has been with the greatest trouble – and some of us have received rather strong words – that we have so far been able to hold the men in check ... Should it come to a stoppage I think it will be of such magnitude as has never been equalled in any previous dispute.[29]

Larkin's 'fiery cross' campaign, despite attracting meetings with, in some cases, over 20,000 in attendance, would be too little too late. The vote of the TUC special conference on 9 December not to back sympathetic action was the final nail in the coffin for the Dublin workers. The British union leaders were unwilling to risk their funds, agreements and perhaps their positions, for the sake of the Irish union. Instead, they continued to press for negotiations. The employers, however, now had the upper hand and would never negotiate. It was only a matter of time before economic necessity would compel the trade unionists back to work.

Most had returned by February 1914, with the last workers – the women from Jacob's biscuit factory – not returning until mid-March. Despite attempts to claim a moral victory, there was no doubt that the trade union movement had been dealt a bitter defeat. The consequences were immediate.

The ITGWU lost thousands of members, and blacklisting was common. Others lost their jobs due to the economic impact of the Lockout, particularly in small businesses. Michael O'Flanagan, who worked with Dillon's Fish Mongers on Moore Street, recalled how 'With the advent of the Larkin Strike in 1913 I lost my employment because of my association with the Labour Movement. I found it very difficult to procure employment in Dublin and I emigrated to Glasgow.'[30] James Coss worked with a haulage company: 'When the strike ended I was not re-employed by the firm on the grounds that they had lost a considerable amount of business due to the strike and were only taking back the employees with the longer service.'[31] Union organiser James O'Shea recalled that the 'effect on the morale of the men was terrible. There was resentment and seething rebellion everywhere; there was also plenty of cowardice … no man could openly give you his subscription and men would not go near the Union Hall as they were afraid to be seen.'[32] The Lockout also hastened the introduction of motor transport, which required less manpower, and led to a further decline in employment. As one worker put it:

> When the strike was finished everyone was glad, but the position was not a happy one. Some of the employers never seemed to recover their lost trade. Where up to one hundred men would have been employed driving horses in the coal-yards the work was now done by three or four powerful motor lorries, and the Gas Company was now distributing gas stoves in every direction. It was very unpleasant having to work with these strike breakers, and the old comradeship of the past never returned. The old sense of security was gone.[33]

CONCLUSION

The outbreak of war in 1914 would change everything. Economic conditions during wartime entailed a remarkable recovery in union membership and political and economic strength. By 1918, the ITGWU would be the leader in a nationwide general strike against conscription and its members and branches would take militant action throughout the country, including in occupations, local general strikes and 'soviets' from 1919–23. However, the movement would lack political direction. Larkin had departed for the United States in 1914 and would not return until 1923. Connolly, exasperated with the defeat of the union and the failure of the international socialist movement to take action to prevent the war, grew ever closer to the nationalist movement. His dreams of socialist revolution were put on indefinite hold while he considered an insurrectionary blow against the British Empire the most important objective in the short term. This would lead him to play a commanding role in the Easter Rising of 1916 and his subsequent execution. With leaders of the calibre of Larkin and Connolly gone, the leadership drifted to men such as William O'Brien, Tom Johnson and others. Despite its strength, these leaders were content to let the labour movement take a back seat to the national movement in the revolutionary years from 1917–23, a place in which it would firmly stay in both states after partition. Why they did so was due to a number of reasons, some of which are discussed by Fiona Devoy McAuliffe in Chapter 5, although the influence of syndicalist ideology, which scorned parliamentary politics, is one that has not received adequate attention and is certainly a possibility deserving of further study. Although the labour movement would time and again engage in major struggles, none would ever match 1913. The formative years of the ITGWU saw the Dublin working class united in a way never seen before, led by militant leaders and equipped with a mission and method to improve its condition in every possible way. The ITGWU had provided the working class in Dublin with dignity. That is why even though 1913 ended in defeat, the struggle has taken on mythical proportions, identifying itself, much like 1916, with an entire year, and inspiring present-day workers fighting against austerity to nostalgically point to the example of Larkin and Connolly rather than anyone else. Indeed, Larkin is identified so much with this year that his subsequent history in the US and as a communist and Free State TD has been erased from popular memory.

Soon after Bloody Sunday, Augustine Birrell, the Chief Secretary for Ireland, would write to the Prime Minister, Herbert Asquith that:

> Larkin's position is a very peculiar one. All the powers that are supposed to be of importance are against him; the [Irish parliamentary] party, the whole Catholic Church, and the great body of Dublin citizens, to say nothing of the Government, and yet somehow or another he has support and is a great character and figure. The fact is that the dispute has lifted the curtain upon depths below Nationalism and the Home Rule movement...[34]

Larkin, Connolly and the ITGWU represented a vision of a just, progressive, and internationalist Ireland, taking its place in a 'co-operative commonwealth' of the world. It advocated workers self-expression and access to the highest levels of culture and education for all. What resulted after the Troubles had died down in 1923 were two insular, conservative, sectarian and monocultural states. Strident censorship made a mockery of the very idea of self-expression, and the ITGWU's advocacy of equality for women stands in stark contrast to the position of women codified in the constitution of 1937. In a society where the identity and sometimes even the very existence of the working class is elided, the Lockout takes on a central importance. The clash between the ITGWU and the Dublin Employers' Federation took on such immense proportions, affecting large swathes of Irish and British society, that it cannot be ignored. It affirms the existence of an Irish working class with its own identity, its own history and its own culture. Just as in 1913 when established society could look solely to itself and ignore a large mass of humanity until it became a threat to their way of life, so too most scholars of Ireland stand accused of this same ignorance, unintentional in most cases it must be acknowledged, yet still apparent. If scholars of Ireland 'lifted the curtain upon depths below Nationalism' they would find an unexplored wealth of existence awaited. Exploring history from the position of the working class would further offer new perspectives on familiar events, and challenge our tendency to view Ireland in isolation from the rest of the world, allowing for a more complete understanding of society and the dynamics of change in history.

Chapter Three

Andrew Patrick Wilson and the *Irish Worker*, 1912–13

James Curry

The *Irish Worker and People's Advocate*, arguably the most successful labour newspaper ever produced in Ireland, was one of its founding editor James Larkin's greatest achievements. Debuting on 27 May 1911 and soon renamed simply the *Irish Worker*, the paper was a vibrant four-page penny weekly that was circulated predominantly in Dublin and operated as an important organising tool for the Irish Transport and General Workers' Union (ITGWU). Although he was the driving force and guiding spirit of the *Irish Worker*, writing several hundred articles and mentioned on practically every page throughout its three-and-a-half-year run, ITGWU general secretary Larkin nonetheless relied on a diverse range of rotating writers in order for the paper to succeed. This helped moderate, as Robert G. Lowery has observed, 'the instability which is found in any radical paper which challenges the status quo as well as the dependence on one person in such operations.'[1] The *Irish Worker* would enjoy extremely high sales for a labour paper, regularly claiming to sell 'approximately 20,000' weekly copies, though in reality seemingly selling between 8,000–22,000 copies per week.[2] Such figures are a clear testament to Larkin's popularity within working-class circles in Ireland at that time, but also a reflection of the fact that the *Irish Worker* was far more colourful, entertaining and intellectually stimulating than earlier Irish labour journals. This chapter will outline the contributions from one of its most prolific writers, the Scottish actor and playwright Andrew Patrick Wilson (c.1886–1950). It will particularly focus on his writings of a literary nature, most of which have yet to receive any critical analysis, and demonstrate that the little-known Wilson was one of the *Irish Worker*'s most unique and important contributors during the paper's hugely successful first circulation run.

I

A curiously obscure figure despite a long and colourful theatrical career in both Ireland and Scotland, Andrew Patrick Wilson tends to be remembered, when he is remembered at all, for his later roles as General Manager of the Abbey Theatre in 1914/15 and founding member of the Scottish National Theatre in 1921. He had first arrived in Ireland in November 1911 as a travelling actor and performed at the Abbey on numerous occasions, often to some acclaim, but nonetheless soon became 'stranded with a third-rate theatrical company in Dublin'. Practically penniless, Wilson was forced to take up temporary employment as a 'workshop clerk' before landing himself 'a real honest-to-goodness job' as sub-editor, advertising canvasser and feature writer of the *Irish Worker* in May 1912. Since Wilson's prior journalistic experience seems to have amounted to little more than the odd freelance article, written in order to earn 'a few spare-time guineas', his new role must have been a fairly daunting challenge.[3] This becomes even more apparent when one considers Larkin's daily commitments as general secretary of the ITGWU and general president of the Irish Women Workers' Union (IWWU), and frequent preoccupations with campaign work in political elections and speaking duties at public meetings.[4] Yet Wilson responded well to the responsibility, and his creative fingerprints would be all over the pages of the paper for the best part of the next year.

A committed socialist at the time of his arrival in Ireland, personality-wise Wilson was apparently prone to taking 'violent dislikes to people' and 'always grousing about something or other in a rich flow of literary language', although the man who made these observations, esteemed theatre critic Joseph Holloway, was nonetheless still fond of the Scot.[5] During his time with the *Irish Worker* Wilson contributed seventy-one signed pieces, thirty-nine as 'Euchan' and thirty-two as 'Mac'.[6] Yet as sub-editor of the paper he would also have penned countless unsigned contributions as well. One such piece, 'written by Wilson partly on information supplied' by Larkin, resulted in both men having to appear in court in January 1913 to answer a charge of libel from anti-Larkinite Labour Councillor William Richardson. Richardson was angered at the following unfavourable cards-inspired comparison with ITGWU candidate Mick Brohoon, during a local election campaign which had taken place several months earlier:

> The trump card for North Dock Ward is the ace of diamonds. Mick Brohoon is a diamond, a rough diamond maybe, but still a diamond. Richardson is a knave of clubs, drinking clubs, and others of an even worse description. Not only that, but he has been put up Alfie Byrne's sleeve, and he is being played from there. There are enough tricksters and fakirs and knaves in the Corporation already without sending Richardson there. Play diamonds at the election if you want to win. Vote for Brohoon, the straight man.[7]

Wilson also attacked Richardson in two signed articles during the same 28 September 1912 issue, which additionally saw Larkin describe the former ITGWU man in his editorial column as a 'cheap tool', 'pitiful creature', 'political barnacle' (i.e. somebody who switched political allegiance based on how advantageous the circumstances involved), and 'Alfred Byrne's corner boy'.[8] Although he sought £500, Richardson had to contend himself with an award of £10 damages, which Larkin defiantly and predictably announced that he would not pay in the next issue of the *Irish Worker*, where Richardson once again found himself subjected to ridicule by the ITGWU general secretary and Wilson, the latter depicting the councillor as a 'delicate' political 'contortionist' in a brief comic 'tragedy in three acts' entitled *Bill!*.[9] Although Richardson would continue to be a legal thorn in Larkin's side over the coming years, such an outcome adequately demonstrates why so many public figures attacked in the pages of the *Irish Worker* were often reluctant to sue Larkin for libel and hence give him the subsequent additional publicity afforded by a court case, thereby making the situation even worse for themselves.

II

Based purely on his contributions as 'Euchan', a name taken from a small river running through the Dumfries–Galloway region of Scotland where he had been raised as a child,[10] Wilson has been remembered as 'one of the main propaganda mainstays' of the *Irish Worker*.[11] All of these articles, which were more often than not 'feisty, argumentative, and passionate',[12] appeared prominently on the front page of the paper and soon established Wilson as one of the paper's 'strongest writers'.[13] 'Euchan' occasionally 'engaged in written brawls' with some of the paper's readers in relation to the content of his columns, most notably with fellow *Irish Worker* contributor Sean O'Casey: the future playwright taking exception to Wilson's ridiculing of republican insurrections as outdated and advocating of a socialist Ireland achieved through the ballot box.[14] Wilson also wrote for the *Irish Worker* under the second pseudonym of 'Mac'. Indeed, it was under this guise that he actually first began contributing to the paper, upon the occasion of its first anniversary on 25 May 1912. This fact has gone completely unnoticed in existing studies of the paper as well as Wilson's 'hybrid critical study-biography' by Steven Dedalus Burch, yet that he was 'Mac' as well as 'Euchan' is clear.[15] Wilson may have chosen the pseudonym 'Mac' simply because, as a Scot, this was what his Dublin colleagues tended to call him, especially following his noteworthy turn as a character of the same name in the Abbey Theatre's production of *The Second Shepherd's Play* on 23 November 1911.[16]

What we can say with certainty is that the plays, poems and short stories which he wrote as 'Mac' have so far escaped any critical analysis. This is unfortunate, since Wilson's second pseudonymous identity was one of the *Irish Worker's* most memorable contributors.

Wilson's first contribution to the *Irish Worker* as 'Mac', 'The Sackmender', was a striking short story in which a visitor wandered into a foul, gloomy cavern to behold a 'fearful old woman' mercilessly whipping a ragged, trembling girl as she sat in a huddled heap frantically sewing hundreds of sacks:

> Still the girl worked on, rapidly plying her needle, folding a finished sack and turning to another again. Her eyes were sore and red; her whole body seemed to tremble under the drudgery and toil, but when she showed the slightest inclination to halt the cruel whip lashed again, and once more she feverishly went on with the unrelenting labour. The visitor turned on the witch with a fury. 'Why treat your slave like this?' he asked. 'She is not my slave,' the witch answered, with a horrible grin; 'she is my employee!'

A clear indictment of the cruel working conditions endured by so many unskilled Irish female workers, this was a powerful 'parable' and impressive debut. As with his following week's short story contribution, it appeared alongside an article by Delia Larkin regarding a specific Dublin employer of 'sweated' women workers with whom the IWWU, of which she was the general secretary, were in dispute.[17] Regarding 'The Sackmender', the firm in question was Keogh's Sack Factory, with a reader of the *Irish Worker* sending a letter of praise to the paper the following week, remarking that 'a more lucid and indisputable comparison' between Keogh's and the gloomy cavern in 'Mac's' story could not have been better drawn.[18]

The younger sister of James Larkin, Delia was a key figure in the social and cultural activities at Liberty Hall. In addition to organising regular excursions to the country and weekly Irish language and Irish dancing classes, she also founded a choir and drama group for ITGWU and IWWU members. The drama group, originally called the 'Irish Workers' Dramatic Club' but later re-named the 'Liberty Hall Players', was founded in early June 1912 in order to promote solidarity and build confidence among union members, as well as helping to raise awareness of labour issues by staging plays that drew attention to the plight of the working class.[19] Towards the end of the year Delia recruited Wilson as Manager and Director of the group, which debuted on stage at Liberty Hall on St Stephen's Night, 26 December 1912. The Scot was clearly a success in his new role. Certainly, the *Irish Worker* lavished him with praise, claiming that 'in a few weeks [he] took a number of men and women who had never appeared on a stage before and moulded them into players equal to, if not excelling, any company appearing in Dublin.'[20] As suggested by the subject matter of his early short stories, Wilson was deeply committed to women workers' rights. He was also a staunch supporter of female suffrage, remarking in one *Irish Worker* article, in the guise of 'Mac', that the inclusion of women in parliament would most likely have a 'humanising and beautifying effect upon politics'.[21]

On 13 July 1912, 'Mac' contributed the wonderfully surreal short story 'Wisdom' to the *Irish Worker*. The story opened as follows:

> I like St Stephens Green. Why I like it I cannot exactly say, but I have a notion that it is the duck-pond and the ducks – especially the little brown ones – that make the attraction. I simply love to sit by the pond and watch those little brown ducks swim around, dive, come up again and chase each other about in their own little ducky way; but thereby hangs a tale. Last Friday afternoon I was sitting near the pond when a little brown duck swam right up almost to the edge within a few feet of me. I looked at the duck, and she, cocking her little head on one side, looked at me. She seemed to recognise me for the

penniless scribbler I am, and knowing that there was small hope of getting any bread from me, she dived, as I thought in search of a worm. Then a strange thing happened. The duck did not rise again, but from the place where she had disappeared a little old woman dressed in a queer brown dress and green bonnet, arose, and crossing to the seat where I was, sat down beside me.

The startled 'Mac' and old woman then proceed to engage in a debate about 'Man', with the latter insisting forcefully that, no matter how many Trinity College graduates might frolic about her park with pride in their newly acquired robes, as long as 'one single child is allowed to die of starvation or disease acquired through living in some foul slum', then mankind could never truly claim to have found wisdom.[22]

In addition to his short stories, 'Mac' also contributed a number of comic poems to the *Irish Worker*. Six of these poems appeared, to great effect, alongside accompanying cartoons by Ernest Kavanagh, including the brilliantly satirical 'The Assinine Law', which ridiculed the Irish legal system:

'Tis said that the Law is an Ass, So I hear!
That it is a most vicious Ass
Is most clear
It careers around madly
And bites the poor badly
While kicking them gladly
In the rear.

It's the Classes who furnish the Law,
Do you see?
And the Masses just suffer that Law,
Oh dear me!
If the rich rob the poor,

It's quite (L)awful, I'm sure,
But it's Ass Law as pure
As can be.

A theft by the poor is a criminal act;
That's quite plain!
A rich thief is only a kleptomaniac,
Not the same.
The poor steal in their need,
But the rich rob for greed
Though the Law says, 'Indeed
That's no shame!'

Accompanying this poem Kavanagh's eye-catching illustration depicted a donkey, dressed as a judge, overseeing the enforcement of 'Law by the Classes for the Masses'.[23] Two weeks earlier Wilson and Kavanagh had collaborated to mock the wealthy visitors that flocked to Dublin each year for the city's prestigious Horse Show event, which was occurring later that same day at the Royal Dublin Stadium. 'Mac's' poem stated that:

'Tis out at Ballsbridge that the horses are seen.
And of finer gee-gees you couldn't well dream.
'Tis in Grafton Street that the donkeys parade
And sillier asses can't be found, I'm afraid.

No, nothing is new, 'tis the same old tale
That is told every year after year without fail
The horses are shown for the asses to view
And the nags have by far the most sense of the two.[24]

Poems such as these clearly reveal Wilson's talent for comic verse and why he was to jokingly refer to his 'Mac' persona as an 'irresponsible and rotten rhymster', a 'rascally rhyming buffoon' and an 'ugly word-twisting baboon'. These descriptions are all taken from 'Mac's' three-act pantomime play *Ali Martin Baba and His Forty Thieves*.[25] This effort saw a host of perceived political enemies ridiculed, telling the story of their failed efforts, under the nefarious leadership of the eponymous Baba, to kill 'Shemus', whose identity was revealed by his description as 'a lively lad, who's always "larkin"'. Ali Martin Baba was, of course, based on William Martin Murphy, one of Ireland's leading entrepreneurs and the man who would infamously lead an attempt by Dublin employers to destroy the ITGWU nine months later.

In the play Murphy was described as an 'independent ruffian' who wore 'the disguise of a respectable gentleman' and had 'a copy of the Irish Catholic' sticking out of his coat pocket. As if this was not enough to make newspaper magnate Murphy's identity clear to the audience, 'Baba' delivered the following monologue at the beginning of the play:

> I'm a ruffian bold
> Who'll do anything to get gold;
> No matter how shady the means
> Or how desperate may be the schemes;
> 'Tis gold that I'm anxious to get
> For gold is my one only pet,
> I've sunk lots of money in rails,
> In America, Ireland and Wales.
> Hotels, too, and shops I have tried
> And trams for the people supplied
> In finance I'm reckoned a king
> Indeed I'll finance anything.
> Where a high dividend can be made,
> Or directors fat salary paid.

In early August 1913, as 'Euchan', Wilson penned a withering satire based on Murphy's childhood, entitled 'The Grasping Hand', which told of how young

'Willie' was an 'unnatural child' who mortified his mother by displaying 'the born instincts of a thief from an early age' and regularly stealing his neighbours' toys. At this point in her young son's life, Mary Anne Murphy has a dream:

> She seemed to see her boy grow into a man – an old man with a scraggy white beard and hard, cruel lines marked on every feature of his face. His grasping hand hung limp and palsied by his side, and he was on the verge of his second childhood. Old and feeble-looking as he was he still stood upon the neck of a man dressed in the garments of a toiler, and as he watched the sufferings of his writhing victim an unholy smile played round his vicious mouth. The dream suddenly changed. A large red hand belonging not to one worker but to a huge army of them, had seized her son and dragged him from his prey. The man of the grasping hand had been hurled down by the red hand, and as he fell he held out one shaking appealing hand to the mother who bore him, but she turned away with a shudder of revulsion.[26]

Since the 'Red Hand' was the symbol of the ITGWU, printed on the badge of its union members, the moral of this story was clearly self-evident for the *Irish Worker*'s readers, something that Wilson himself noted wryly at its conclusion in a short postscript.

III

During his time with the paper Wilson also penned several harder-hitting plays for its readers, one of which again included a Murphy-inspired character in its cast. This effort, his earliest surviving extant play, was *Profit!*, described as 'A Modern Commercial Drama in Three Acts'. Written as 'Euchan', it was published in the *Irish Worker* during October 1912 and spread out over three successive issues.[27] Each act appeared prominently on the front page and was given the individual titles of 'Greed' (Act One), 'Tyranny' (Act Two) and 'Misery' (Act Three). Although its lack of subtlety and somewhat unconvincing dialogue and characterisation may justify Dedalus Burch's description of the play as 'a fairly infantile and clumsy piece of early twentieth century agit-prop',[28] *Profit!* nonetheless has its moments. Unashamedly written to try and convince the *Irish Worker*'s readers to play their part in rising up with 'the organised workers of the world' by joining the ITGWU, the play focuses on the traumatic effects of the decision by the high-level management and shareholders of 'Messrs Divi, Dend, Snatcher & Co., Ltd' to insist on an increased quarterly profit margin, irrespective of the impact this move has on their quality of production or the lives of their employees.

Since their 'first, last and only reason for carrying on the business is for profit' the company, led by Chairman William Martin and leading shareholder Alfred Bung (clearly based on Murphy and Dublin politician/ publican Alfred 'Alfie' Byrne respectively), consequently employ a ruthless business strategy. A young cashier is fired for seeking a pay rise due to his forthcoming marriage; a former employee named Tom Greig is blacklisted on account of his involvement with the 'confounded Transport Union' despite having a seriously ill pregnant wife; and the company's most accomplished and longest-serving employee, John Brown, is dismissed on the pretence of his disagreeing over Greig's treatment, though in reality simply because of the fact that he is now almost fifty years old. When a foreman protests against the short-sightedness and unjustness of this last decision he is angrily threatened with dismissal himself by a middle manager, Mr Gaul, unless he follows company orders and lets Brown go:

Now, if you replaced some of the older men with younger ones you would get much more work done, I think! ... Get rid of him at once. It is speed modern commerce wants and not perfection. Perfection doesn't pay and the keen competition

of to-day demands speedy work. Get rid of Brown and get a
younger man!

At first, Brown refuses to accept what has happened to him and remains
convinced that management will indignantly overturn the decision and
discipline the foreman in question. However, as the days go by and he is
continually ignored by Gaul, the devastated Brown is finally forced to face
up to the realisation that he has outstayed his usefulness in his former
employers' eyes, who clearly only want 'human machines to grind out profit,
and not men at all' on their books.

Meanwhile, Greig's inability to find employment anywhere in the city
on account of his 'new-fashioned' ideas on labour matters, inevitably
leads to the death of his wife and prematurely-born child. When the two
dismissed men meet by accident at a bar in a vain attempt to drown their
sorrows, they are contemptuously described as 'two damned loafers' by its
irritable proprietor, Alfred Bung, who unceremoniously ejects them from
his premises with the assistance of a conveniently placed policeman. The
play then ends with Bung, having closed up for the night, telling his wife
that since his shares at 'Divi, Dend, Snatcher & Co., Ltd' were up slightly
for the last quarter on account of his 'straight talk' to Chairman Murphy
at the earlier board meeting, he will now be able to buy her a new fur coat
that she has been recently requesting. The most interesting character in
the play is undoubtedly Brown's wife whom, from the outset, perceptively
recognised that her husband's dismissal was simply further proof that
'modern competition and greed of gain' has made older employees such as
he 'a nuisance that must be got rid of'. Completely ignored by her husband,
her wistful comment that his sacking 'is not the manager's fault any more
than it is the foreman's' but instead 'the fault of modern commerce and
the greed for profit', would be a theme re-iterated and expanded upon by
Wilson in his next play, the grim and powerful one-act *Victims*, which
appeared in the same 1912 *Christmas Number* of the *Irish Worker* as *Ali
Martin Baba and His Forty Thieves*, a special literary-filled issue of the

paper of which he was most likely the driving force behind and editor in practice.[29]

A gloomy and depressing play, *Victims* was 'the most brutal example of urban realism yet composed' by a playwright in Ireland.[30] Although it is usually credited as the first play 'set in a Dublin tenement',[31] it should be pointed out that Wilson never actually states that Dublin is its setting. He simply reveals in his text that the action occurs in a 'garret' of 'abject poverty'; while elsewhere the *Irish Worker* describes the play as taking place in a 'tenement room'.[32] That being said, *Victims'* primarily Dublin audience would have been under no illusions that it was their city which Wilson had in mind when he wrote. The play, which was published under Wilson's real name despite having been advertised as written by 'Euchan', tells the tragic story of the impoverished Nolan family.[33] Although he is 'known to be a good workman … punctual and steady', mechanic Jack has found himself out of work for ten weeks due to his membership of a trade union and involvement in a strike and resultant lockout two years previously. His employers, in order to 'nip the next revolt in the bud', have followed a policy of deliberately creating 'slack trade for the purpose of tossing on the scrap heap the men who they think will endanger their profits by demanding a living wage'. Finding it impossible to find work anywhere else in the city since he had been labelled a 'dangerous' man, Jack is forced to look on helplessly as his starving wife suffers and his 'wasted and worn' infant son is literally 'dying of hunger'. Disgusted at his victimisation, Jack tells Anne that 'When the employers call me a dangerous man, it is not their lives or their limbs they are thinking of, but it is their profits.'

During the course of the play, two visitors call to the Nolan household. The first, Purcell, is a pompous clerk sent by his boss Old Scott, a man whom he offhandedly describes as being 'as mean as the very devil'. Desperately seeking to earn a few shillings Anne had agreed to make alterations to a bundle of shirts for Scott. Yet when Purcell learns of her slow progress with the work she is immediately relieved of her duties. Already angered at his home having been turned into a 'sweating den', when Jack hears the news upon returning home from another fruitless search for employment, he flies into a rage. Anne quickly calms him down, echoing Mrs Brown's message in *Profit!* by declaring that Purcell 'had just to do what he was told' and should not be blamed. A second visitor, Quinn the rent collector, later calls to the home. Although three weeks behind with their rent Jack tells Quinn that his family are not in a position to pay him, refusing to vacate the premises that night since his 'child is ill, dying'. When an uncaring Quinn protests that he will be sacked by the landlord if he returns to him once more without any money, Jack echoes his wife's message about Purcell:

> What you might do if you got the sack, I do not know. Maybe you would have to be doing what I have been doing. Going round day after day looking for a job that could not be got. Coming home night after night to tell your wife how hopeless was the task of trying to get a chance of earning your living. Pawning and selling your furniture little by little to pay rent until you have to come to a miserable garret for which you have no longer any prospect of paying, and which you may be told you will be thrown out of. These are the things that may happen to you if you get the sack, my friend. You will be a victim as well as me then. We are all victims and as we cannot fight profit-mongers we fight one another. One victim tearing into another victim and all done in the sacred name of profit.

An exasperated Quinn is thus forced to leave without his landlord's money. Seconds later, Jack and Anne realise that their infant child has died. The play then abruptly ends, with the audience left assuming that the grieving couple will be evicted the next morning by their landlord to further add to their woes. Although occasionally crude and guilty of some 'fairly unsubtle bathos' at its conclusion,[34] *Victims* nevertheless 'succeeds in catching a balance between agitprop explication and grim naturalism to deliver its syndicalist moral', powerfully demonstrating 'the capacity of realism to operate polemically'.[35]

In other words, the play was a marked improvement on *Profit!*, containing a similar story and theme but displaying tighter writing and characters of greater depth. A week after its publication in the *Irish Worker*, it was one of four one-act plays staged at Liberty Hall by the 'Irish Workers' Dramatic Club', with Wilson starring as Jack Brown and Delia Larkin playing the role of his wife.[36]

IV

On 29 March 1913 Wilson finished up as sub-editor of the *Irish Worker* and temporarily returned to Scotland to work for a Glasgow repertory company. He signed off with a ringing endorsement of James Larkin, with whom he had struck up a positive working relationship during his ten-month stint with the paper:

> I leave the WORKER as I joined it, with the greatest respect and admiration for its Editor. Jim and I have got on well together, possibly because I always went straight. There is one man, and one man only, in Ireland who can ever lead the workers anywhere in an organised fighting manner, and that is Jim Larkin. As an organiser of men and fearless advocate of their rights he stands alone. The employers of Ireland know that; the Press of Ireland know that. That is why they fear and hate him, and try their dirty uttermost to work against his influence. They may go on their course, however, for all that it matters. They may hire all the thugs and political cornerboys and blackguards in Dublin to assist them, but Jim will go on undaunted to victory, for it is the great mass of the workers who are calling to him for assistance. They need him – necessity has taught them that they need him, for he is the right man. I leave Dublin then proud in the knowledge that I have had the honour of associating with Jim for so long, for Jim's name will be honoured in Ireland when

commercial giants are forgotten, and even the names of the tin
pot politicians will be recalled with an effort.

Although he would soon return to Ireland and contribute a further nine
pieces to the *Irish Worker* during the summer of 1913, the outbreak of the
Dublin Lockout on 26 August saw Wilson's involvement with the paper
seemingly come to an abrupt end. From that point on, at least, Wilson
disappears from the pages of the *Irish Worker*, even when as General Manager
of the Abbey Theatre he later wrote and directed the ground-breaking play
The Slough, which debuted in Dublin on 30 November 1914 and was clearly
influenced by Larkin's leadership of the ITGWU during the Lockout. This
has led to speculation that there may have been a falling out between Wilson
and Liberty Hall.[37] While this cannot be ruled out, it should be remembered
that by late November 1914 the world was at war, the *Irish Worker* was
shortly to be suppressed by Dublin Castle for its anti-British propaganda,
and Larkin was living in America. The fact that the *Irish Worker* had wished
Wilson 'good luck and success' in his theatre career in May 1913,[38] and that
the 'Liberty Hall Players' later performed and published two of his plays,
Victims and *Poached*, further suggests that a rift may not necessarily have
taken place.[39] Most likely, it was simply Wilson's self-confessed 'rolling stone
nature',[40] together with his desire to pursue a full-time theatre career that saw
him decide to leave the staff of the *Irish Worker*.

In his study of the *Irish Worker* Lowery has stated that those 'looking
for literary masterpieces will be disappointed', since the majority of its
contents possessed 'more historical importance than literary merit'.[41] The
truth of this statement cannot be denied, for the *Irish Worker* was never able
to attract literary contributions from illustrious writers of the day such as
James Joyce, James Stephens and W.B. Yeats (although the two latter figures
both contributed letters to the paper during the opening months of the
Dublin Lockout).[42] Yet the fact remains that short stories, plays, songs and
poetry were an important part of the paper's character, a facet that has never
adequately received the recognition it deserves. The historiographical neglect

of Andrew Patrick Wilson encapsulates this failing perfectly. Wilson may not have produced any 'literary masterpieces', but his early propaganda plays and clever and diverse range of writings, which were often characterised by great imagination and wit, were a uniquely welcome addition to the pages of the *Irish Worker*. Indeed, during his time as sub-editor the publication was well and truly at its best: free of the added bitterness occasioned by the later Dublin Lockout and outbreak of the First World War, yet firmly settled in its stride with a tried and tested format and enjoyable literary dimension. For this Wilson deserves considerable credit. Undoubtedly, the *Irish Worker* was a poorer paper following the departure of its prolific 'penniless scribbler' at a time when it needed him most.[43]

Chapter Four

'Real Irish Patriots would Scorn to Recognise the Likes of You': Larkin and Irish-America

Alan J.M. Noonan

B
ritish spies watched James Larkin step onto the deck of the steamer *St Louis* to travel to America on 24 October 1914.[1] They described the labour leader as '40 years old, 6 feet 1 inch high, clean shaven, sallow complexion, long nose, black hair turning grey, usually wears black serge suit and soft black hat.'[2] Contemporary and historical speculation about his motivations cloud Larkin's departure: emotional exhaustion 'Larkin may have been too fond of the strike'; physical exhaustion 'the Lock-out had drained his immense energy to the limit'; organisational reasons 'a leave of absence from both union and [Irish Citizen] army by going to the US allow[ed] the situation to be clarified'; and the inevitable accusations of cowardice that Big Jim's allies challenged in the *Irish Worker*:

> The Mollies and their friends are very busy, circulating a yarn here that Jim Larkin had to run to America by order of Kitchener. Ye Gods, was there ever such rot; don't Larkin's friends and enemies know that he never yet ran away from anybody. He is gone to America to let the Irish people there know the truth about the position in nationalist Ireland.[3]

While Larkin's correspondence highlighted that he had tired of union work in Dublin, this sentiment related less to exhaustion and more to the direction of his energies towards the Irish Citizen Army (ICA) and garnering support for it abroad, an often neglected aspect of his legacy.[4]

Irish leaders often organised speaking tours in the United States to collect funds for their cause in Ireland. Irish-America had responded generously to earlier arrivals such as Charles Stewart Parnell, Michael Davitt, and James Connolly, who had only returned to Ireland in 1910 after a seven-year visit.[5] Larkin's journey at this time made sense given his leadership of the ICA, whose membership had expanded into the hundreds in his brief five months in command.[6] In travelling to the US Larkin aimed to arm the workers' army he had built and he explained to an Irish-American audience in New York soon after his arrival that the arming of the Ulster Volunteers justified the arming of the Citizen Army; 'if Carson has the right to arm in Ulster, we have the right to arm in Dublin.'[7] Larkin pleaded more explicitly to another crowd, 'Men and women, give us money to buy guns, and by the living God who gave us life we will not fail you', while the *New York Tribune* reported that Larkin 'hinted vaguely at an uprising in Ireland against England'.[8] British intelligence confirm this determination to arm the ICA and after closely observing his movements and speeches wrote, 'Larkin went to America in 1914 as a messenger from the Irish Transport Union and the Citizen Army to raise money with which to purchase arms for Ireland from Hamburg.'[9]

CATHOLIC AND SOCIALIST

In the US Larkin found himself detached, not from Irish-America, but from his socialist brethren who were unwilling to embrace their new ally because they remained unable to reconcile his devoutly Catholic, devoutly Irish and devoutly Socialist positions. Most members of the American Socialist Party saw the socialistic elements of Christianity in the purely secularist vein of Eugene V. Debs, with Jesus portrayed as a proletarian social prophet. Furthermore, the Catholic Church earned the same rancour from Debs as from Protestant nativists, who called it 'Vampire of the centuries'.[10] (Nativism is defined as seeking to protect the interests of native-born against those of immigrants and in the nineteenth century this included hostility towards Irish Catholics.) Socialists fundamentally failed to understand the uniqueness of Irish Catholicism, generalising that the Church in Italy, Spain, Mexico, and the Philippines was the same Church that existed in Ireland, and writing that in each it had 'ruled for centuries in holy partnership with the robber kings, barons, plutocrats and other ruling and exploiting classes'.[11] Socialists further ignored the bridge Pope Leo XIII's encyclical *Rerum Novarum* 'On the Condition of Labour' offered them. It decried capitalism as forcefully as socialism and stated in one part that 'a small number of very rich men have been able to lay upon the teeming masses of the laboring [*sic*] poor a yoke that is little better than slavery'.[12] However, socialists found it difficult to recognise that the Catholic Church could hold views similar to their own and, unable to look beyond their deep-seated hatred, many, like Debs, alienated working-class Catholics.

Conservative Irish-Americans based in the north-east dominated the highest echelons of the Catholic hierarchy in America and they were triumphant after the intervention of Rome against their liberal and progressive clerical foes. Prelates used elements of *Rerum Novarum* to justify the enmity of their sermons and tracts against socialists.[13] Cardinal Gibbons argued against socialism's egalitarianism stating it 'would bring all men down to a dead level, would paralyze industry and destroy all healthy competition … this varied condition of society must result from a law of life established by an overruling Providence', and Cardinal Farley argued at the annual Confraternity of Christian Doctrine that socialism was 'the heresy of the hour – a rampant heresy'.[14] Cardinal O'Connell was the most direct; 'There is not and cannot be a Catholic Socialist'.[15] Earlier individual efforts by Irish-American priests Thomas Hagerty and Thomas McGrady to unify the two had met with censure from the hierarchy. The former had helped establish the radical Industrial Workers of the World (IWW) and created the group's insignia the 'wheel of labour', representing their goal of 'One Big Union'.[16]

Not long after his arrival in the US Larkin spoke to a meeting of socialists and tried to explain the apparent contradiction of his dual Catholic and socialist identities to them. He opened his shirt, showed the audience his gold cross and told them, 'There is no antagonism between the Cross and socialism. A man can pray to Jesus and be a better militant Socialist for it. I stand by the Cross and I stand by Karl Marx.'[17] Larkin may have touched a nerve amongst the crowd by going so far as to suggest prayer makes for better socialists, but more important was his effort to explain that Irish Catholics in America and elsewhere saw their religion more as a belief and identity and less as a monochromatic institution with clergy as the solitary voice. Indeed, Larkin himself openly criticised the clergy.[18]

Contrary to Larkin's usual adversarial tone when faced with opposition, his comments towards other socialists appear a genuine attempt to offer constructive criticism to the Socialist Party and early in 1915 he repeated his 'pleads' for a tolerant and inclusive party in the socialist paper the *New York Call*.[19] Debs's anti-Catholic sentiments seemed to be widespread within the party, which hampered efforts to recruit Irish-Americans probably as much as tirades from the Catholic prelates. Nativists and socialists used the same language when condemning Catholicism and its followers and it was obvious that the Socialist Party ignored the poor example set earlier in the century when anti-Catholic bigotry from leaders of both the Populist Party and the People Party had alienated Irish support for those movements.[20]

Larkin was exposed to this hostile strain soon after his call for tolerance as party members let him know their feelings on the matter. Three days later he wrote, 'I have never found more bigotry and intolerance than I have found among a certain wing of the Socialist party … for I have been made to suffer for this intolerance as an Irishman and a Catholic.'[21] His mention of ethnic insults highlights that the ideological inclusivity of the movement often fell prey to a degree of sectarianism and intellectual snobbery within the party. Despite this, Larkin again called for tolerance: 'there are Jews, Protestants, agnostics and secularists, sectarians of all kinds within the ranks of the party. If we are to have a real international movement, there must be room in it for the Catholic worker as well'.[22] Larkin recounted that he inquired of one party member why subway workers were not organised and received the reply that they were all Irish and Catholic. He at first dismissed this excuse, offering statistics showing subway workers were a mixture of ethnicities, but he went further and laid a firm challenge at the door of the movement. He continued 'But suppose they were all Irish and Catholic? Aren't you going to organise them? … I deny that it is any harder to organise Irish Catholics than any other people, and I know because that has been my work'.[23]

The decreasing popularity of the Socialist Party amongst the Irish-American and wider American population is illustrated by the sharp decline in the numbers of Socialist Party mayors throughout the US from seventy-four in 1911 to eighteen in 1917.[24] The squeezing of socialism out of Irish-American identity by both Catholicism and nationalism marked a double defeat. If Larkin's time in the United States offered an opportunity for the Socialist Party to engender itself to a broader demographic it remained unexploited, at least on the east coast where he concentrated his efforts.[25] Although some historians credit the Catholic Church as a reason for the weakness of socialism in the early twentieth century, the alienation of Irish-America perhaps played as great a part as any Catholic encyclical or homily.[26]

Larkin made further conciliatory pronouncements at a meeting of the American Irish Society in New York where he 'urged all Irishmen to be tolerant, and remember that thousands differed, and that differences in opinion must be respected'.[27] He also clarified that the most important role of the Irish in America was not tied up in Irish nationalism. He was reported as saying 'The fight for Ireland's future must be fought by the people on the soil' and that, more importantly, they should 'endeavor [sic] to impress their best characteristics on the future Americans'.[28] Larkin's early life in Lancashire seems to have taught him vital lessons on the long-term accommodation of ethnic identity with other peoples in other countries.

In America the most difficult aspect of the *Rerum Novarum* challenged this inclusivity. This was not the criticisms of socialism or capitalism or the remedies of labour (mediation between worker, owner, state, and church), but the warning that Catholics had two options: to 'either join associations in which their religion *will be exposed to peril* [emphasis added], or form associations among themselves' to stop 'intolerable oppression'.[29] While the Irish across the US had already proven adept at organising exclusively Irish cultural and nationalist organisations in the multiracial, multicultural workforces they lived in, by the early twentieth century the only path to secure their rights as workers lay in allying with different ethnic and religious groups, particularly in the scattered towns of the American West, thus contradicting the guidelines expressed in *Rerum Novarum*.[30]

Within the largest trade union in America at the time, the American Federation of Labor (AFL), Catholic workers formed a slight majority of the membership, largely by virtue of the strong Irish presence. Irish-American Catholics were also well represented in its leadership positions and over fifty occupied the position of president in the affiliated AFL unions in the years 1900–1918.[31] Even the most stringently Catholic members who formed the Militia of Christ for Social Services (later absorbed into the American Federation of Catholic Societies) remained within the AFL with their non-Catholic working brethren and as such ignored the papal warnings of their 'exposure to peril'.[32]

The AFL president, Samuel Gompers, saw that the First World War had critically undermined socialism; '[Patriotism] was stronger than the fundamental tenet of socialism, stronger than ideals of international peace, stronger than love of life and family'.[33] In contrast to the Irish- and German-American ethnic organisations and the Socialist Party organisations that furiously opposed American entry to the war, Gompers attempted to place the union within the war mobilisation effort, and was rewarded for his efforts when President Wilson appointed him to a position on the Council of National Defense as chair of the Labor Advisory Board.[34] Despite this collaboration the AFL never gave a 'no strike pledge' during the First World War and perhaps more surprising was the tumultuous wave of strikes in industries dominated by AFL membership in 1917. This constituted the largest strike wave in American history up to that point, with sixty-seven of the strikes involving over ten thousand workers each, demonstrating the vast mobilisation of discontent that rose after a spike in the cost of living.[35] The number and size of these actions highlighted the degree of local autonomy within large unions, the scale of labour dissatisfaction and the limitations of Gompers's conservative strategy.

Meanwhile, the radical IWW, the Wobblies, were responsible for one-sixth of lost workdays, especially in the northwest timber fields and in mines across the American West.[36] Larkin was drawn to the IWW, the movement reflecting him in both their fiery rhetoric and determination for radical change. One of his prouder moments was giving the graveside oration at the funeral of the IWW organiser, Joe Hill, whom the state of Utah executed after a blatantly unfair trial. However, it was in Butte, Montana that Larkin's railing against corrupt business, nationalist and political leaders resonated most.

IRISH LABOUR IN BUTTE

In 1900 Butte was the most Irish city in the US with one in every four of its 30,470 residents Irish-born or second generation.[37] Ninety per cent of Irishmen in the city earned a reliably high wage in the copper mines.[38] While other mining regions frequently convulsed with intense bouts of labour protest and violence, the main union in the town – the Butte Miners' Union (BMU) – had never led its workers on strike simply because there was no need. Cavan-born Marcus Daly operated his Anaconda Company sympathetically towards the Irish, 'He did not care for any man but an Irishman.'[39] At the start of the First World War the Anaconda Company were the dominant copper mining and smelting company in Montana but by then the company had changed. The accession of the Irish-American John A. Ryan to the head of the company after Daly's death prompted the gradual transformation of the company from ethnic paternalist to pure corporation. Ryan's loyalty was primarily to the business rather than the Butte Irish. The old structures binding company to union to community fell apart as the BMU could no longer guarantee work and security to newer Irish arrivals. This led to the literal destruction of the BMU culminating in the demolition of their main office in mid-1914 by a 'progressive' cohort of members who soon after established a new union, the Butte Mine Workers' Union.[40]

The moderate nationalist and Catholic Ancient Order of Hibernians (AOH) encapsulated the last bastion of the old Butte Irish. Their decade-old alliance with the Germans in the town climaxed in the 1915 St Patrick's Day festival where three nations' flags flew in the parade; Irish, German and American.[41] If the Irish-German alliance represented the inclusive aspect of the Irish, they were equally able to demonstrate exclusive tendencies. The lyrics for the famous William Jerome and Jean Schwartz song 'My Irish Molly O' were changed in the following way in Butte:

> Oh Maggie dear, and did you hear
> the news that's goin' round;
> They're firin' all the Corkies
> That are workin' underground.
> I've rustled at the High Ore,
> And I've rustled at the Con,
> And the dirty blackguard Bohunks
> Is all they're putting on.[42]

The specific reference to 'Corkies' – Corkonians – and the strikebreaking Hungarians – 'dirty blackguard Bohunks' – indicates the song was intended for an Irish audience. Other ethnic groups participated in a similar rewriting of songs, even Irish ones. Another version of the above song contains the third line 'They're canning all the savages', meaning Irish, and the last lines 'But the dagoes [Italians] are the only ones / That they are putting on.' The deprecation of the Irish suggests that this version was meant for a Cornish audience, who had on another occasion referred to the Irish as 'savage'.[43]

The presence of two Irish poets, Seamus Ó Muircheartaigh and Seán Ruiséal highlights the Irishness of this community and they lived and worked in Butte during this tumultuous time. In the poem 'Mo chiach mar a thána' ('Alas that I ever came'), Ó Muircheartaigh grieved over his emigration and urged others to return to Ireland or not to leave at all:

> Is mór mór go mb'fhearra bheith in Éirinn an ghrinn,
> Ag éisteacht le ceolta na n-éanlaithe ró-bhinn,
> Ná ag lorg lá oibre ar spriúndlóir beag cam,
> Gur dhóigh leis gur asal tú a bhuailfí le feam.

> It's far far better to be in Ireland where there's cheer,
> Listening to the melodious bird songs,
> Than looking for work from a crooked little miser
> Who thinks you're only an ass to be beaten with a stick.[44]

The poem vividly details feelings of exile and regret, even in one of the most densely Irish places in the US, and highlights the dislocation felt by the newer Irish, both from the established community and from its fraternal networks (BMU and the AOH) that provided security.

Ruiséal wrote in a similarly negative fashion about his Butte experiences in the poem 'Amhrán na Mianach' ('Song of the Mines').

> Beidh an saoiste ansúd ann 'na sheasamh,
> Is i n-aice dho an foreman caol,
> Is iad a' fógairt gach stróile chun taisce,
> Ar maidin le fáinne 'n lae.

> The bosses will be standing there
> And next to him the lean foreman,
> Driving all the wretches to work
> At the break of day.[45]

An aspect often overlooked in these poems is the sharp definition of the position of labour in Butte. As David Emmons observes, Ó Muircheartaigh's poem depicts him at the stage of still searching for the work that would lead to him being beaten.[46] Likewise, Ruiséal had not reached the point of submission but he saw workers in that position, wretches driven into the mines while the bosses stood tall with the foreman above the workers, complicit in their exploitation. The insult 'crooked little miser' was probably a barb directed at the Anaconda Company's John Ryan, showing divisions within the ethnic group. The poems echo the tenets of Larkinism, though Larkin might have added that there was little point in fleeing to Ireland where the same struggle existed.

If the Irish themselves viewed their leaders in such a cynical light Larkin's second visit to Butte in June 1916 must have struck a deep chord with them as he spoke on the topic of the Irish Rebellion.[47] In a fiery oration he explained that the Easter Rising was 'a working-class rising to keep Irish boys out of the British army' and he localised the conflict, 'You forget that the struggle you have here is the same you knew in Ireland – the struggle against economic and political tyranny.'[48] His comments bore the weight of the Rising and execution of its leaders that followed. He castigated local nationalists as 'mercenary phrase mongers' for manipulating the cause for their own ends. The Irish-American leaders in Butte listening to the speech could not ignore such brazen insults and James B. Mulcahy, editor of the *Butte Independent*, stood up to challenge Larkin. Larkin screamed at him 'Real Irish patriots would scorn to recognize the likes of you' and a mortified Mulcahy sat down again.[49] Larkin finished his speech advising Irish miners that to 'be true to the spirit which inspires the rebellion in Ireland, you must do your own thinking and not delegate it to any judge, lawyer, editor or priest.'[50] The two poets, had they heard Larkin, would have intimately understood his rhetoric and, as importantly, Larkin tapped into the deepest emotions of the Butte Irish while disarming his targets of their greatest defence, their cultural identity.

His third visit in January 1917 highlighted this theme again when he gave a speech railing against the 'parish pump form of patriotism' and 'the malignant beasts in human form … gombeens in their relations with their fellow Irish, shoneens in their slavish servility'.[51] The use of the Irish words gombeen and shoneen are particularly interesting as they illustrate the two-faced nature of Irish sedition, the gombeen – someone who worked for the British, an economic traitor – and the shoneen – someone who adopted English customs, a cultural traitor. Shortly before this visit the Pearse–Connolly Irish Independence Club was founded to adopt Larkin's recent efforts to equate the cause of Ireland with the cause of labour and to reassert Connolly's position as a hero of labour rather than of nationalism. The AOH, humiliated by their German alliance and their endorsement of John Redmond, appeared to the younger Irish like a branch of the conservative Knights of Columbus, and weakly responded to the Pearse–Connolly Club stating too many Irish organisations already existed in Butte.[52]

Efforts to slander them by association either with socialism or the IWW were equally doomed to failure as Father Hannan, in addition to being a co-founder of the Pearse–Connolly Club allowed it to hold meetings in his church, St Mary's, and prominent republican Liam Mellows described him as a 'tower of strength to the movement'.[53] This local clerical support existed despite the sentiments of the Irish-American Bishop of Montana and national chaplain of the AOH, John Carroll, who condemned the IWW as 'a purely Socialistic organization' and thanked 'the miners of Butte for voting them down' in 1912, referring to when the Anaconda Company fired five hundred Finnish workers because the Finns made up the bulk of IWW support in Butte and formed a growing threat to Irish control of the mines.[54] The Finns appealed to their fellow miners in the BMU to strike hoping they might see wisdom in the IWW and Larkin motto, 'an injury to one is an injury to all' but their request was denied after a ballot of its members.[55] In the minds of their enemies the IWW and the Pearse–Connolly Club were one and the same, primarily because their loyalty to the US was in question.[56] They were certainly sympathetic to one another; when the IWW radical Frank Little was murdered more than a thousand Pearse–Connolly Club members with their distinctive green sashes marched in the funeral procession. When the Pearse–Connolly Club offered to join with the AOH for the 1917 St Patrick's Day parade the AOH abdicated their traditional leadership of the event replying 'we are going to Mass'.[57] Mayor Charles Lane refused the Pearse–Connolly Club their parade permit, labelling it an 'IWW affair' but it went ahead regardless.[58] Even before the American declaration of war, support for the Irish rebellion was seen as being anti-Allies and thereby anti-American. Once the US declared war in 1917 the contradiction at the heart of Irish-American identity opened like a chasm where once there had been a mere hyphen.

On 5 June 1917, two months after the American entry to the war, leading members of the Pearse–Connolly Club organised a new union called the Metal Mine Workers' Union (MMWU).[59] Prompted by opposition to the draft and the Speculator mine disaster in which 165 men died, the union led Butte miners out on strike from 11 June until 28 December of that year. Production of copper, a vital wartime commodity, fell to a trickle with Daniel Kelly, a counsel for the Anaconda Company, stating that the mines were 'absolutely crippled and shut down'.[60] Another counsel for the company, L.O. Evans, further told one Chamber of Commerce in Montana that the MMWU was a front for the IWW and that 'the Kaiser had found one of his most effective allies' in the IWW and the Pearse–Connolly Club.[61]

No other population centre had remained so solidly Irish and so peaceful for labour for so long as Butte. For those that believed their city to be a Gibraltar of unionism to finally see the arrival of large-scale strikes, dynamiting and the deployment of the military on the streets in 1917 must have seemed like the war itself had arrived, or if not the war then radical labour, long kept at bay by the strength of the BMU. Rather than reflect the loyalty of German-Americans to their homeland or the hatred of Irish-Americans for the British, the Butte strikes demonstrated a sharp disconnect between the region's local politics and the American national mood. Whatever the hope for a strike, to do so against an industry critical for the war-machine at one of the largest copper mines in the US meant only a response of treason from the government. War and the associated hysteria over the loyalty of hyphenated ethnic groups obfuscated the real cause of destabilisation in the peaceable mining city: the Anaconda Company was changing from benefactor to corporation. No longer would it act as the patron saint of the Irish in Butte through the proxy of the BMU and with the BMU's raison d'être gone it rapidly disintegrated, unable to offer jobs and unwilling to ally with newer Irish migrants and others.

Strikes in Butte continued after the war and the observations by one military officer during a strike in 1919 identified its leaders as 'Finnlanders, Sinn Feiners, and members of the Pearse–Connolly Club and IWW', and further suggested that the 'situation could only be solved by the prompt deportation of undesirable aliens, mostly Finns and Irish'.[62] The ethnic-orientated exclusionary tendencies witnessed by the BMU's rejection of the Finns had been wholly upended and many Irish now favoured the radical, socialist and nationalist Pearse–Connolly Club, rather than the moderate nationalist AOH or militant Clan na Gael fraternities.[63] Larkin certainly played a part in this development and there remains the possibility that the strike of 1917 represented Larkinism writ large in America and a triple blow against the war, against Britain, and against the exploitation of the workers.

LEAVING AMERICA AND A LEGACY

During Larkin's time in the US his need for funding and arms drew him to collude with the Germans. This led to an embarrassing episode when he travelled to the German embassy in Mexico, they tried to recruit him as a saboteur, and he refused.[64] He was robbed the following day and had to wire for funds to pay his hotel bill and return to the US.[65] Larkin made his first serious effort to leave the US in 1915 after German agents persuaded him to join Roger Casement in Germany to recruit an Irish brigade among prisoners of war, but he found his requests for a passport thwarted by the British.[66] When he had first arrived in the US the British authorities, still fearful of his popularity and firebrand speeches, watched him closely and hoped for his arrest when he returned to Ireland.[67] However, this plan changed by December 1914 when the authorities in Dublin saw an opportunity present itself through the passage of the Defence of the Realm Act and instead of arresting Larkin when he returned they decided to deny him entry to Ireland.[68] These efforts should not be underestimated: in August 1919 the Directorate of Intelligence warned that 'his influence in Ireland would still be great', and to fully appreciate this potential danger they contextualised the threat, stating in the same report that the Irish Transport Union 'is probably a far more dangerous menace to the future of Ireland than Sinn Fein itself'.[69]

Larkin applied for a passport at the San Francisco consulate to travel to Shanghai on 5 September 1916 and throughout 1917 circulars were repeatedly dispatched to the British embassy and consulates throughout the US specifying that he should not be issued a passport to return to Ireland or to travel anywhere in the Commonwealth.[70] In 1919 the Dublin Metropolitan Police felt convinced by rumours circulating Dublin 'that James Larkin may at any moment turn up at Liberty Hall', while the Royal Irish Constabulary warned officers that if he appeared in Ireland 'it would be most objectionable to leave Larkin at liberty a moment longer than necessary'.[71] US authorities arrested Larkin on 9 November 1919 during the anti-communist 'Red Scare' and New York State's Lusk Committee raids directed at people suspected of sedition. He used the three-and-a-half hour summation at his trial the following January to lecture the American people on values such as truth, freedom and tyranny, after which the unsympathetic jury quickly declared him guilty of 'criminal anarchy'.[72] According to the FBI Larkin did not attempt to escape the trial as 'he considers himself a Martyr to the cause'.[73] Despite much condemnation and the creation of a 'Larkin Defence Committee' it was only in 1923 that Al Smith, newly-elected Democratic Governor of New York pardoned Larkin and, after a failed effort to organise a food ship to accompany his return, the authorities unceremoniously deported him.[74]

Historians have tended to portray Larkin's time in the US in terms of failure, partially reflecting disappointment that he did not live up to their high expectations after the Lockout, but they fail to specify the requirements that would have made it a success.[75] Bertram Wolfe, one-time communist and labour organiser, in his aptly named *Strange Communists I Have Known*, wrote that 'America proved Jim Larkin's undoing. Like Antaeus his strength was great as long as he was in touch with his mother earth. In America, he was out of his element.'[76] Within the increasingly fractured socialist and communist movements on the east coast this held true; the movements themselves grew increasingly out of touch as Larkin himself noted and tried to change, but in western states, such as the Irish mining community of Butte, he proved wholly in his element. Nonetheless, his eight-and-a-half years there were not by choice. He applied repeatedly for passports and permission to travel and when arrested during the post-war 'Red Scare' he possessed a fake passport. Obviously he was preparing to return in the immediate future and stated as much to his followers in his messages home.[77] Larkin's inability to return, rather than being a moot point, highlighted the British and American governments' increased fear of workers' political awareness, agitation, and radicalisation. Larkin inevitably tried to transform his incarceration into martyrdom, Connolly effectively having taken his place in history during the Easter Rising. His effort failed in the minds of his Irish opponents who lambasted him as a coward for his time spent in America and two flyers, probably printed in the 1920s, testify to these accusations. The first by the OBU [One Big Union] Defence League that read:

> The Run-away Chief [Larkin] has run away again as he did in 1914, leaving his dupes to face the storm which is brewing amongst the workers who have been betrayed by him that 'Big Noise' (The Run-away Chief) remained out of this Country for eight and a half years while the workers were fighting for 'improved' conditions, and facing the Black and Tans.[78]

Another notice reads 'Why is Larkin attacking the Transport Union Executive? Because he ran away in 1914 and returned in 1923 to find the Union a powerful and nation-wide organisation, with its members enjoying better conditions than those enjoyed by members of any other organisation. Larkin cannot bear to think that the Union survived his absence.'[79] Even his friends thought of his time in the US as wasted: when Jack Carney wrote to Larkin in 1946 he urged him to dictate a memoir in three volumes, the first covering 1907 to 1910, the second volume on 1911 to 1914 and the third from 1923 on, omitting the American years completely.[80]

In terms of integrating the diaspora within the framework of national history, Irish history has been poorly served. Labour history points to a different way and as historian Larry Peterson wrote in 1981:

> The national focus of virtually all previous studies tends to obscure the general nature of the movement and makes a cross-national comparison all the more urgent if one is to understand the full dimensions and significance of revolutionary industrial unionism in the early twentieth century.[81]

Irish history should not be an island unto itself and British fear of Larkinism seems more comprehensible given the contemporary international context of strikes in Ireland and the US, the Russian Revolution, failed socialist revolutions in Germany, and factory occupations in Italy. While it can be implied that Larkin had a limited influence on the period of Irish revolution because he was outside of Ireland, records suggest a greater impact, and the belief in his imminent return remained considerable until his arrest. The sense of abandonment many Irish shared at this development seems to have altered the historiography of Larkin's entire career, especially his early years in the US, but this is part of a larger problem with Irish historiography. Irish-American identity survived the tumultuous period intact but its influence on the Irish nationalist and socialist movements remains largely maligned by historians writing Irish history or brushed off in brief as a source of funds, a trend borne out by Larkin's own legacy. Possibly this marginalisation of Irish-America highlights a subconscious effort to limit the extent of the Irish diaspora and its importance in Irish history, an effort we must continually strive to overcome if we are to develop a fully-rounded history.[82]

Chapter Five

Workers Show Their Strength:
The 1918 Conscription Crisis

Fiona Devoy McAuliffe

While the 1913 Lockout demoralised and depleted the trade union movement, the First World War provided an opportunity to revitalise working-class struggle in Ireland. The period was key in awakening class consciousness as workers realised their potential to control their circumstances and influence the course of history. This chapter seeks to demonstrate how their vital role in providing munitions and food afforded workers a bargaining chip to demand improvements. The years 1914–18 consequently saw a significant revival of the class struggle as progress was made in winning wage increases and trade union organisation. The 1918 Conscription Crisis reignited the Irish left as male and female workers refused to be pawns in a war that would ultimately defend the prevailing capitalist and imperialist system. They demonstrated their power in organised campaigns against both economic and military conscription. This culminated in the General Strike on 23 April 1918, a spontaneous national work stoppage that the *Nationalist and Leinster Times* declared paralysed the government of Ireland and illustrated that national control rested on the consent and good will of the people.[1] While the threat of conscription gave Irish workers the outlet to express their power and presence, it also dominated the minds of the Irish people and prioritised the struggle for national independence, ultimately stilting the awakening of the working classes. This was demonstrated as women workers declined to assert themselves in the employment market created during the war by refusing to take the places of men forced to enlist. It was also evident in the Labour Party's decision to step aside during the 1918 General Election as the Crisis had helped bring Sinn Féin and the question of independence to the forefront of Irish politics, overshadowing the working-class movement. With the resulting Sinn Féin victory, Irish workers' recovery from the 1913 Lockout remains a side note in the existing narrative. This chapter uses the Conscription Crisis as a vehicle to reinterpret this period, illustrating how the conscription menace encouraged labour militancy, assisting growth and re-organisation and emulating international trends in workers' struggle for equality while also impeding the progress of the Irish left.

THE FIRST WORLD WAR – AWAKENING CLASS CONSCIOUSNESS

At the outbreak of the First World War, Emmet O'Connor sums up the state of organised labour:

> From a position of unprecedented power on the brink of the 1913 lock-out, trade unionism had become a demoralised and declining force a year later; reduced to strongholds in Dublin, Belfast, and a few other provincial towns, with a slim presence among general workers and none at all on the land.[2]

Many lost their jobs due to the 1913 Lockout and the demand for linen and textiles reduced while non-essential industrials including brewing and distilling were curtailed leading to increased unemployment and falling wages, although the cost of living soared.[3] The fear of starvation gripped Ireland's working class as enlistment took vital labourers to gather the harvest, while considerable amounts of food were exported to feed the troops and British population. While industrial munitions jobs were created by the war, only 5,000 materialised in the south of Ireland in comparison to 6,000 in the north, creating significant resentment.[4] As war conditions caused hardship and discontent amongst workers, it also provided workers with an opportunity to improve their circumstances.

Although British labour leaders agreed not to use strike action during wartime and the government banned stoppages in July 1915, Irish workers took advantage of their position, leading industrial struggles throughout the war.[5] The threat of stoppages forced the government to set up tribunals to arbitrate industrial disputes and enforce claims against reluctant employers, ultimately encouraging trade unionism.[6] What John Newsinger describes as 'second wave syndicalism' took place from 1917–1923 nationally, as working-class militancy made significant progress winning wage increases and organising unskilled labourers.[7] Ireland's largest trade union, the Irish Transport and General Workers' Union (ITGWU), particularly grew in influence and numbers. By 1916, the best branches were found in Dublin, Belfast and Sligo.[8] The ITGWU expanded in Cork and Kerry, with a branch re-established in Waterford. By the end of 1917, the union had significantly regained lost ground and membership was in excess of 25,000, although Belfast saw little progress.[9] Organisation depended on whether the war created good employment conditions, and good business in Ulster somewhat negated these workers' need for union membership.[10] The ITGWU broke ground in organisation with agricultural labourers in the 1917 land struggle.[11] The union became so strong in Limerick that the Trades Council published a periodical, *Bottom Dog*, which ran from 20 October 1917 until August 1918.[12]

There was an unprecedented upsurge in working-class activism during 1918. The Irish Trade Union Congress (ITUC) with its affiliated unions and the Irish Labour Party (ITUCLP) increased in membership from c.110,000 in 1914 to 250,000 in 1918,[13] and the number of strikes and lockouts went from approximately fifty-eight in 1914 to over 200 in 1918. ITGWU membership grew to 68,000.[14] In 1918, judicial intelligence reports for the south show that the labour movement grew in Dublin, Wexford, Westmeath, Meath, Queen's County, Longford, Kerry, Limerick, Clare, Galway, Tipperary, Kilkenny, and Mayo.[15] By March 1918, the ITGWU acquired a weekly journal called *Irish Opinion: the Voice of Irish Labour*.[16] There was also an influx of women workers into the movement. By spring 1918, membership of the Irish Women Workers' Union (IWWU) was over 5,000.[17] IWWU branches were established in Dublin, Bray, Limerick and Cork.[18] These developments in the Irish labour movement were accelerated by the strain the war was placing on the working classes. Class consciousness and militancy was also encouraged by international events, particularly the 1917 Bolshevik revolution in Russia and the Peace demonstrations throughout Europe. But the 1918 Conscription Crisis was a crucial milestone in the revitalisation of the Irish labour movement, providing activists with a focus for organisation and militant action. As workers demonstrated their determined opposition to compulsory military service in a General Strike on 23 April 1918, the Crisis heralded the re-birth of the Irish left.

IRISH WORKERS AND THE THREAT OF CONSCRIPTION

Many labour activists throughout the world opposed the war from the outset. In Ireland, labour leaders including James Connolly and Jim Larkin advocated Irish neutrality, viewing the war as an economic battle between capitalists that should not be supported by sacrificing workers' lives.[19] In July 1916, Larkin insisted that each member of the Irish Citizen Army take an oath 'that he would take no orders from King, Kaiser nor any capitalist government, but would march and fight only by instruction of the common people and to preserve the rights of the common people.'[20] In the *Irish Worker*, Connolly questioned whether the Allies were really friends of small nationalities as they claimed, noting that their own oppression of races was forgotten.[21] But the real opposition came from militant workers themselves who, amongst a diverse group of radical nationalists, pacifists and suffragists, became essential in resisting recruitment and conscription. They laid the precedent for the resistance campaign in the 1918 Conscription Crisis, which allowed Irish workers to demonstrate their strength and renewed determination after the 1913 Lockout.

The earliest rumours of military conscription emerged in October 1914 when Dublin newspapers implied that compulsion would soon be imposed. In response, the ITGWU and the Irish Citizen Army resolved to resist any form of conscription and to begin preparing their resistance including 'barricades in the streets, guerrilla warfare in the country'.[22] Authorities denied the rumours but the threat persisted throughout 1915 as dwindling recruitment figures fuelled government attempts to find further sources of manpower. In July the national registration of men of military age perpetuated the rumours. The conscription threat awoke anger and indignation amongst Irish workers. Listowel Rural District Trades Council argued that the working classes should not be conscripted when there were 12,000 armed police in Ireland performing 'slight duties that could be done by pensioners, with the help of the public'.[23] In the *Workers' Republic*, Connolly asserted that conscriptionists were merely aristocrats whose fortunes were endangered prompting their demands to 'send out the slaves who eke out a hand-to-mouth existence, to ward off the evil days!' But he contended that 'the slaves are waking up and will not be fooled any longer'.[24] Dublin Trades Council members condemned conscription as an action akin to Prussian militarism, urging men to get guns and to enlist in either the Citizen Army or the Irish Volunteers to effectively resist compulsion.[25] The police sought to suppress dissident activities, arresting people like Patrick Dyer, a bookkeeper and foreman, for counselling resistance to compulsory service proposals.[26]

In Britain, Lord Derby's campaign practically destroyed the voluntary recruiting system by implementing persuasive measures to ensure men joined up. A document in Thomas Johnson's papers entitled 'Some notes on the persuasive aspect of voluntary recruiting' reports how the War

Office increasingly placed pressure on workers to enlist. In October 1915, recruiting authorities were instructed 'to take whatever steps you consider most effective' to induce men in non-essential industries to join the army. Some employers were directed against appointing eligible men and even to dismiss those who would not enlist. The National Patriotic Association urged employers to persuade men to enlist by promising to re-engage them (if fit) after the war, and refusing to engage any man of military age unless he had exemption. Men were also personally canvassed and often shamed or ridiculed into enlisting.[27] Some Irish employers cooperated with recruiters attempting to replace men of military age with women who were a cheap source of labour or men who were ineligible for recruitment.[28] On 2 September 1914, the executive of the ITUC identified the phenomenon, passing a resolution denouncing the compulsion of dismissed men 'by a process of starvation, to enlist as Volunteers'.[29] Many cases were reported in the *Workers' Republic*. Fifteen men working for Messrs. J.P. Corry & Co., Timber Merchants were invited to join the army. On refusing, they were handed typewritten slips stating their services were no longer required.[30] The Manager of the Belfast City Tramways issued a manifesto to conductors and motormen calling upon them to enlist and stating that their services would be 'dispensed with' on a certain date mentioned.[31] Arthur Ascott claimed that on applying for a job at Jacob's biscuit factory, he and other men were told that 'they would not give us a job unless we had army rejection papers.'[32] A District Circular from Joseph Pike, Chairman of Cork, Bandon and South Coast Railway, encouraged enlistment asserting that 'every man who can possibly be spared will, consistent with the efficient working of the Railway, be liberated to join His Majesty's forces.' The *Workers' Republic* identified this as a threat that men considered dispensable would be forced to join up, dismissing Pike's assurances that when discharged and 'if physically fit' they would be found employment.[33] Cork employers' enlistment methods aroused much comment and on 13 November 1915 Cork United Trades Council members claimed that 'Nearly all the employers are doing it.'[34] Councillors passed a resolution declaring that dismissing men of military age 'and endeavouring to starve themselves and their families, is a very obnoxious form of Conscription'.[35] Labour activists particularly objected to Lord Wimbourne's letter to Dublin employers inviting them to a meeting on 23 November 1915 and requesting that they bring a full list of employees of military age that could be replaced.[36] On 18 December 1915, a *Workers' Republic* writer officially defined the phrase 'Economic Conscription' as 'the policy of forcing men into the army by depriving them of the means of earning a livelihood.' This was called hunger-scription in Canada. The paper asserted that economic conscription had been used against trade unionists in 1913, and declared sympathetic strike the only tool powerful enough to save the victims.[37]

THE CRISIS

A Military Service Bill was introduced in January 1916 conscripting bachelors in England, Scotland and Wales. Military leaders continued to demand a more extensive conscription measure[38] and, with increasing manpower losses, the issue of Irish inclusion was a prominent topic of discussion. The bill was repeatedly extended during 1916 and 1917 with persistent calls for Ireland to share the burden despite the manpower it would take to impose such a measure in an increasingly defiant and radicalised nation.[39] However, when Germany launched its largest attack on the Western Front in March 1918, the British cabinet took the risk and sought to include Irishmen in the April Manpower Bill resulting in the Conscription Crisis. The growing strength of workers was decisively demonstrated during the 1918 anti-conscription campaign. The bill engendered an immediate and militant response from the Irish labour movement, and throughout the campaign trade union activists even achieved moments of trade union cohesion that resembled the one big union advocated by Connolly.

The executive committee of the ITGWU met in Dublin and resolved that 'Absolute solidarity of all grades and trades is necessary ... it is their duty to act in unity with their fellows. An injury to one is an injury to all.'[40] The Dublin branch of the Socialist Party of Ireland declared its determined opposition to conscription imposed by any government.[41] In Thurles, County Tipperary, 106 members of the National Union of Railwaymen declared conscription imposed by an alien government on Ireland 'contrary to all laws of civilisation'.[42] In Fermanagh, Enniskillen Labour Union resolved against the bill as a whole, but particularly the conscription of Irish workers claiming that the war was 'waged solely in the interests of the large capitalists at the expense of the lives of hundreds of thousands of Irish and British working men'. They pledged to 'passively and actively' resist the measure.[43] Cork trade unionists resolved 'that any attempt to apply either military or industrial conscription to Ireland will be resisted by the workers of this country regardless of the consequences that such resistance may entail'.[44] At a mass meeting in Limerick led by Arthur Griffith and the President of the Limerick Trades and Labour Council, John Cronin,[45] P. Walshe proposed a general strike throughout Ireland if the government persisted with the measure.[46] On the steps of Belfast's Custom House, approximately 8–10,000 workers protested against conscription on 14 April, led by Thomas Johnson (trade unionist and Irish Labour Party leader) and D.R. Campbell (Secretary of Belfast Trades Council).[47] Thousands of handbills were distributed urging resistance to a bill it asserted would be used to weaken labour organisation, 'The Capitalists, Bankers, and landlords of England fear Social Revolution after the war, they fear the rising discontent of the workers, the coming into power of the people, and they mean to save their property and privileges. The iron heel has begun to work! That is the real purpose of the bill'.[48] A Railwaymen's Emergency Committee was formed in Dublin representing all twenty-two railway trade unions. Chairman of the Dublin Engineers Society, Dunne, asserted that in welding together the Irish workers, Lloyd George had saved Ireland from ruin.[49]

An All-Ireland Labour Convention was held on the 20 April to consider the most effective opposition to conscription. Johnson described it as 'the largest and most representative assembly of labour delegates ever held in this country'.[50] Approximately 1,500 delegates attended comprising of skilled artisans, transport workers, drapers' assistants, and all classes associated with the trade union movement. The convention also included 'many ladies'.[51] Secretary of the IWWU, Louie Bennett pledged on behalf of their workers that they would not take the jobs of men liable for conscription.[52] In addition, the IWWU organised a concurrent demonstration at Dublin city hall where women signed the pledge to support the men in their resistance.[53] Delegates declared their intention to resist the measure, claiming the Irish population's 'right of self-determination as a nation as to what action or actions our people should take on questions of political or economic issues,' before fellow-workers within the international labour movement.[54] The resolution stated that organised labour would equally reject compulsory service imposed by Ireland's own parliament, indicating how labour differed from many nationalists who may have accepted the measure from an elected Irish government.[55] The resolution appealed to their contemporaries for support, hoping that their example would encourage workers of the world to resist capitalism. In a letter to Thomas Johnson before the trades conference, Shán Ó Cuiv, a journalist with the Irish labour newspaper *Irish Opinion*, pointed out that Irish labour were fighting against conscription 'not only the battle of the Irish nation but of the British worker as well'. He sserted that Irish labour was ultimately seeking a victory 'for democracy in England and all over the world'.[56] The labour movement repeatedly called on their British counterparts for support in resisting conscription and at the convention, Alderman Kelleher of Cork criticised the British Labour Party's lack of opposition to conscription or support of Ireland, declaring that the industrial classes should be united.[57] Within the international socialist community, the Irish workers looked to the Russian Soviets for inspiration. *Irish Opinion* claimed that Irish labour's convention 'had no parallel outside Russia since the All-Russian Congress of the Soviets ... The Irish working class can, without fear or shame, clasp the hand of its Russian brother and with just pride and righteous fervour claim, in this anniversary week of the Republic, that it is following James Connolly'.[58] The Conscription Crisis was an important moment in which the Irish labour movement intended to show its strength and identify with the workers of the world.

THE GENERAL STRIKE

On 23 April Irish workers made their most significant contribution to the anti-conscription campaign in a General Strike. This was generally acknowledged as a well-organised, passive demonstration of Irish workers' strength and determination to defeat conscription.[59] A report by strike participant John Brennan claimed that, with the exception of Belfast, everything stopped including factories, shops, and transport, showing 'most effectively what would happen if conscription was enforced'.[60] *Irish Opinion* praised it as an example to everyone that when the workers 'all fold their arms and stand idly by, the world is theirs for the taking'.[61] In Dublin, the *Freeman's Journal* reported that the strike 'was of the most absolute as well as impressive character', as every trade and industrial activity in the city was stopped, although the strike had been almost organised on the spur of the moment.[62] The *Evening Telegraph* reported that the city's twenty-four hour cessation of work 'was so complete that it was not possible to buy a box of matches'.[63] Theatres, cinemas, public houses, tobacconists and even public lavatories closed.[64] Most shops closed, 'not only in the principal streets but in every by-street and lane. Small shops in the suburb and back streets closed their doors as rigidly as the big establishments in the main thorough-fares'.[65] The *Freeman's Journal* reported that the hungry could not get food from restaurants and the thirsty, 'a still more formidable body', could not get drink 'even though they were willing to pay more than war rates'.[66] While the majority of restaurants were shut, *Irish News* reported some endeavouring to remain open in view of large numbers in Dublin who would find it hard to get meals, or vehicles to return home.[67] Trains stopped at midnight at which time the whistles of various trains arriving at the Dublin termini reportedly sounded a prolonged blast. The engines were taken to the sheds, the fires drawn, and the men left.[68] While the Great Northern Company maintained a service, 'not a wheel was turned on the Great Southern and Western route, nor on the Great Southern and Eastern lines'.[69] Britain's *Daily Mail* described the capital as a 'city of stagnation', where there was 'No work, no play and no disorder,' but a 'holiday atmosphere' amongst the work-free populace.[70] Dublin's work-free population thronged the streets, where anti-conscription badges and flags were sold. The most favoured reportedly bore the inscription 'Conscription – Not D-n [Damn] Likely.'[71] In conjunction with the labour movement's General Strike on 23 April, Cumann na mBan organised a national women's day supported by the IWWU whose members carried banners saying 'Women won't blackleg'. A flag was hung from the Irish Women's Franchise League (IWFL) office reading, 'Conscription! No Woman Must Take A Man's Job.'[72] Throughout nationalist Ireland, the *Freeman's Journal* asserted that the state of affairs in the capital 'was practically reproduced'.[73] The *Cork Examiner* reported an entire suspension of business, 'the commercial and industrial lie of the city was for one whole day at a standstill.'[74] The big event of the day was the monster demonstration of an estimated 20,000–30,000 people held under the auspices of the Cork District Trades and Labour Council on the Grand Parade.[75] Speakers included Father Thomas who declared that it would be the power of the workers that would be the 'deciding factor,' since they were the force that controlled the nation's prosperity.[76] Although there was some dissent to the strike in Belfast, labour newspapers proclaimed the strike an outright success: 'No work was Good Work' in *Irish Opinion*.[77] *Bottom Dog* journalists claimed that 'Labour has found its feet at last and now that it knows its strength let us hope it will use it to the full not alone to beat the conscription ideas of the capitalists but also to remedy the many ills imposed on it by the same capitalist class.'[78] Surprisingly, the *Irish Times* best described its implications for Irish labour:

> The Roman Catholic Church and the Nationalist leaders have united Nationalist Ireland against conscription, but … It was the voice of Labour not the voice of religion or of politics, which yesterday stopped the wheels of industry in Dublin, made a desert of the quays, turned trams off the streets, extinguished for twelve hours the existence of three great railway companies.

> Yesterday witnessed the first general strike of Labour in Ireland,
> and it was a notable success ... We think that April 23 will be
> chiefly remembered, not as the day when Nationalist Ireland
> proclaimed her spiritual and moral isolation, but as the day
> when Irish Labour found itself.[79]

The militancy of the anti-conscription campaign instilled a fresh confidence
in Irish workers after the humiliation of the 1913 Lockout and led to an
unprecedented strike wave from 1918–20.[80]

In August, Lord Decies acknowledged the leading role taken by labour
activists in the anti-conscription campaign writing that 'Nothing during the
past few months has been more noteworthy than the growth of labour as a
force in national politics.'[81] As the immediate Crisis passed, Desmond Greaves
writes that the ITGWU returned to organising workers and grew in success.
On 30 June 1918 there were reported to be 43,788 members of the ITGWU
and General President, Tom Foran declared the day of the one big union had
come.[82] While the industrial wing strengthened, the Irish labour movement
avoided asserting their growing strength within the political sphere. On 27
April, *Irish Opinion* called on workers to 'Let no humbugging about politics
and parties, no question of ancient foes and new friends, divert them from
the path the most supreme of duties dictates. To the work, then, brave
hearts. You have only your chains to lose, have a world to win.'[83] This sums
up labour leaders' wish to avoid divisions caused by party politics, which
were already evident in Ulster's general abstinence during the General Strike.
With the exception of some nationalist shopkeepers and Roman Catholic
schools closing for the day, Ulster was unaffected. In Belfast, industry carried
on as usual and train services were maintained with Dublin trains worked
by special staff sent from Belfast.[84] While some Protestant, unionist workers
may have been willing to co-operate, their leaders refused to participate,
limiting action.[85] The *Belfast Telegraph* published sarcastic descriptions of the
strike. One journalist reported that 'In a truly marvellous spirit of self-denial
the thousands of its labouring classes refrained from all forms of toil.' On a

serious note, the writer declared the dislocation of trade and industry to be a 'monstrous crime' and an 'inexplicable disgrace' when the war was at its most critical point.[86] Although the labour movement's appeal to resist conscription was part of a greater socialist struggle for independence from capitalist employers, the anti-conscription campaign was primarily led by Catholic radical nationalists who were focused on asserting Irish self-determination and resisting British rule. The Conscription Crisis consequently highlighted the division amongst Irish workers on the faultline of the national question.

CLASS VERSUS NATION

Labour activists contributed significantly to the anti-conscription campaign, which in turn reinvigorated working-class militancy and revealed the potential strength of the labour movement. Many commentators have argued that labour came into its own as a political movement during the Crisis.[87] Yet while its contribution impressed many, the Irish labour movement failed to harness credit for its role in resisting conscription. A letter to prominent trade unionist William O'Brien from a labour activist asserts that although organised labour was a distinct element in the community, it had 'escaped notice as a factor of some importance in the present crisis' concluding that the 'absence of outstanding leaders like Larkin and Connolly has perhaps blinded the general public to the real power of trade unionism in Ireland.'[88] The labour movement increasingly became politically subordinate to Sinn Féin as the Crisis ultimately prioritised gaining Irish self-determination over other current issues including class and gender equality. Intelligence reports observed that anti-conscription platforms were believed to be 'in reality Sinn Féin' stages, and after the Crisis, 'the great bulk of those who identified themselves with [the] anti-conscription movement continued to give their support to Sinn Féin.'[89] Labour leaders' emerging auxiliary political position was evident as they abstained from contesting the 1918 by-elections, arguably waiting to assert their power until the national question was decided.[90] As the General Election approached, Irish workers faced a choice between asserting their rights through an independent Labour Party and supporting the Sinn Féin agenda to achieve national self-determination. John Horne surveys the tension between class and nationalism internationally during this period, placing Irish workers' dilemma in a wider context. He observes that labour movements and socialist politics emerged stronger in Britain, France, Germany, Italy, Russia, the USA, Poland, Bulgaria and the Balkans; however, where nationalist and class struggles coincided, 'Usually nation preceded class as a political cause.'[91]

Despite initial preparations to contest the election and objections from labour leaders including Tom Farren and Cathal O'Shannon,[92] the Labour Party abstained from the 1918 General Election. Explaining their decision, Johnson claimed that 'A call comes from all parts of Ireland for a demonstration of unity on this question [of self-determination] such as was witnessed on the Conscription issue.'[93] Numerous opinions have been put forward to explain Labour's decision not to contest the election. In retrospect, D.R. O'Connor Lysaght asserts that Labour leaders primarily withdrew fearing to split nationalist and unionist workers 'by making too open a commitment to one form of that struggle, even to what was becoming obviously its majority expression.'[94] David Fitzpatrick writes that while preparing for the election, certain leaders believed it was of little use to lay down any detailed programme of reform until the war had ended and self-determination had been won.[95] C. Desmond Greaves contends that labour activists were content in the knowledge that at least Sinn Féin's republic could be converted into a workers' republic without England's permission.[96] A combination of reasons resulted in the decision to abstain from the election. Primarily, it would have forced Labour Party leaders to take a position on the national question, both causing dissension within the labour movement and undermining Ireland's bid for self-determination by splitting the nationalist vote between Labour and Sinn Féin candidates. With the negative consequences seemingly outweighing the benefits, it is easy to see why labour leaders chose to stand back and wait to assert their strength. However, they failed to see the long-term need for the Labour Party to take a lead in the national struggle. This decision left the Labour Party seriously underdeveloped, shackled to the ITUC and in second place next to trade union organisation. Newsinger writes that labour leaders arguably 'handed political leadership in Ireland over to the Sinn Féin alliance, a surrender from which the Irish labour movement never really recovered.'[97]

WOMEN WORKERS

While undermining the political growth of the labour movement, the conscription threat also proved detrimental to women workers' struggle for class and sex equality. As the most significant alternative workforce to men of military age, women workers were vital in opposing economic conscription by refusing to take the jobs of men forced to enlist. At a public meeting of women under the Cork District Trades and Labour Council on 28 April 1918, Alderman Kelleher expressed the hope that when the time came to do their duty, 'women would also take their place and refuse to accept industrial conscription.' John Good T.C. declared that they could 'rely on the women of the Industrial World to do their duty', and Miss O'Doherty of Blarney and Miss Barrett of Pouladuff proposed: 'We warn our fellow Irishwomen of the danger of conscription being introduced indirectly and we pledge ourselves not to accept any position from which a man has been discharged.'[98] The labour movement's campaign relied on women to refuse to take the places of dismissed men. On 1 June, an *Irish Opinion* journalist praised women workers' involvement in resisting conscription, declaring that 'women have taken their part and are getting ready to do more.'[99] The following week, the newspaper again praised the women's determined refusal 'to play the grabber, the blackleg, or the scab!'[100] As editor of the *Irish Citizen*, Louie Bennett also acclaimed women workers for nobly answering the call to refuse the posts vacated through the enforced military service of their countrymen.[101] Questioning why employers were keen on employing women, James Connolly's *Workers' Republic* concluded that they believed female workers would be cheap and obedient while 'Dublin men are too well organised.' From reading capitalist newspapers, the author asserted that 'one would think that women were cabbages capable of being bought and sold and thrown here and there without their own consent!' He challenged Irishwomen to protect themselves and not 'whine about men protecting you. If men wanted to protect you there would be no wars and no prostitution.' The journalist reminded women that they were now in a position of power because if men go, employers must take them on or shut up shop. From this position of power he asserted that women workers could impose their own form of compulsion by organising and compelling employers to pay them decent wages.[102] However, for the time being women workers declined to assert themselves in the employment market, prioritising the fight against conscription. Considering the impact of the Crisis on women workers, Charlotte Fallon questions whether this policy ultimately kept women out of male-dominated workplaces in the long term.[103]

The Conscription Crisis further undermined women workers by overshadowing feminist concerns that were often shared and interlinked with the socialist movement. In 1918, Margaret Connery of the IWFL wrote that while 'suffrage agitation used to be described as the "woman's question" not so long ago. There is another woman's question in Ireland to-day … The woman question for us to-day is Conscription or no Conscription?'[104] She observed that 'The political ferment in this country has, in the nature of things, largely overshadowed – indeed, almost eclipsed – every other movement in the popular mind.'[105] Connery contended that while 'The average Irishwoman needs no instruction in national politics … but when it comes to sex consciousness or social consciousness her mind is virgin soil.'[106] As a national plebiscite on Irish freedom dawned, Maria Luddy asserts that it was natural to give the national question precedence before women could focus on social reform.[107] Although Sinn Féin put forward two female candidates in the General Election and most women were granted the vote, only Constance Markievicz was elected and the feminist movement struggled to convince Irishwomen that their campaign for equal rights was not concluded with the 1918 Representation of the People Act.[108]

CONCLUSION

The Conscription Crisis is a useful vehicle to examine the recovery and growing class consciousness of Irish workers following the 1913 Lockout. Labour activists contributed significantly to the anti-conscription campaign, which in turn reinvigorated working-class militancy and revealed the potential strength of the labour movement. In November 1918, the *Irish Citizen* declared that 'The enthusiasm which blazes in the labour movement in Ireland is a revelation to people whose causes are for their spare moments.'[109] However, the Crisis also illustrates how the national question came to dominate Irish politics and overshadow other reform movements, particularly stifling the Irish left. Resistance to conscription was indicative of the international rise of nationalism and break from established authority and empire. Yet while revolutionary as regards imperialism, Ireland's break for freedom was primarily about ousting foreign control rather than being socially or politically innovative. The Crisis ultimately foreshadowed the character of the Irish state, helping to create a conservative government that was intent upon achieving and demonstrating national independence. Asserting independence dominated subsequent domestic and foreign policies including efforts to become economically self-sufficient, gaining international recognition, and military neutrality. The political legacy of the conscription threat, and this entire revolutionary era, was an insular focus on Irish nationalism that arguably overshadowed the country's social and economic development.

Chapter Six

Newsboys and the 'Animal Gang' in 1930s Dublin

Donal Fallon

The so-called 'Animal Gangs' of Dublin in the 1930s have historically been portrayed as reactionary street mobs who engaged in violence against left-wing organisations in the capital. In reality, the first 'Animal Gang' consisted primarily of young newsboys, described by Gardaí as being mainly 'of the corner boy type', who had banded together for the purpose of carrying out a private feud against various publications and other youths in the city.[1] A series of high-profile court cases would arise when young members of this self-titled gang appeared before the courts in September and October 1934 on charges of assaulting other youths across the city, and by the mid-1930s the name 'Animal Gang' had been adopted by the media and those in authority as almost short-hand for youth criminality or gang violence. This chapter aims to examine the origins of the term 'Animal Gang' in Dublin, pinpointing the newspaper strike of 1934 as the moment the term is first used in the mainstream media and Garda intelligence reports. Examining the historic poverty and politicised nature of Dublin's newsboys in the early twentieth century is crucial, as it was among that group of youngsters that the term would be born. This chapter also intends to place the 'Animal Gangs' in the context of anti-communist violence in 1930s Dublin, and examine just what role, if any, 'Animal Gangs' played in that violence. As Brian Hanley has noted, the so-called 'Animal Gangs' have entered 'Irish left-wing folklore', being held responsible for almost every attack on the organised left in Dublin in the 1930s.[2]

'QUICK WITTED URCHINS': DUBLIN'S NEWSBOYS HISTORICALLY

While street selling is an ancient tradition, the idea of the 'newsboy' came to prominence in the British Isles only in the 1850s, with the arrival of cheap daily and evening newspapers. Writing in *The Journal of the Royal Society of Antiquaries of Ireland* in 1924, George William Panter noted that the practice of hiring young newsboys dated back to 1855, with the hiring of 240 boys by the *Daily Telegraph* for the purpose of selling that paper on the streets of London.[3] This theory that the practice originated with the *Daily Telegraph* is found also in Alan J. Lee's study of the popular press in England, in which he notes that 'The *Daily Telegraph* was, perhaps, the first to use uniformed boys', and that 'by 1874 similar clad sellers were to be found everywhere.'[4]

References to young newsboys operating in Dublin can be found in the pages of the *Irish Times* from the early 1880s, with a letter signed 'Pro Bono Public' in 1882 noting the 'many trials and hardships which the majority of the newsboys of Dublin have to contend with' and asking 'would it not be a truly charitable and benevolent undertaking for the citizens of Dublin to provide a newsboys home in a central place' for these young Dublin workers.[5] Dublin newsboys were presented from the 1880s onwards in newspaper reports as being typically ragged and barefoot, with the *Irish Times* for example producing a shocking 1884 illustration titled 'The Tired Newsboys!' showing two young, ragged-dressed youths asleep in the doorway of a bank, with a poem underneath noting that 'they may perish! Of cold or some worse fate!'[6]

Evidently, newsboys had long been a presence on the streets of the capital before the 1930s, and as Pádraig Yeates has noted the boys had a history of militancy in Dublin in the early twentieth century. In 1911, the trade unionist Jim Larkin set about attempting to organise Dublin's newsboys politically, and in his attempts to do so Larkin also benefited. As Yeates has noted, 'by organising the newsboys, Larkin also ensured that his own newspaper had an effective distribution network', establishing a working relationship with boys who took a higher commission on the trade union papers they sold than copies of mainstream publications like the *Irish Independent*.[7] A newsboy strike in 1911 had shown the militancy of the youths, with youngsters striking against the terms on which the *Evening Herald* was provided to them. During this dispute there were wild scenes, and on one occasion a gang of newsboys numbering 200 attacked an *Evening Herald* van on O'Connell Bridge.[8] Republican Ernie O'Malley would recall in his memoirs seeing newsboys at this time clash with police, writing that he witnessed a scene where 'mounted police were charging quick-witted urchins who scattered and lured the attackers into narrow by-lanes. There the boys used stones and pieces of brick with accuracy and rapidity.'[9] The links between the boys and the union movement remained strong throughout the great labour dispute of 1913, and as Emmet O'Connor has noted, even a generation on to the young newsboys of the city 'Larkin was a champion. He had organised them in 1911 and they reminded him of the two glorious years that stretched between the summers of 1911 and 1913.'[10]

In addition to the interest shown in Dublin newsboys by the labour movement, there were also attempts by charitable organisations to engage with them. Of these, the most successful was the Belvedere Newsboys' Club, of which Dr William Lombard Murphy was a founding member. Murphy, rather ironically, was the son of William Martin Murphy, with whom Jim Larkin had clashed in 1913. By 1928 the Belvedere Newsboys' Club was operating from impressive premises on Pearse Street, and Dr Murphy noted at the opening of that club that 'Everyone who knows the Dublin newsboy knows what good qualities are to be found in him. He might not posses the greater civic virtues such as thrift and order and regularity, but he has immense loyalty to parents and an innate and essential decency of mind.'[11]

The club continued to grow throughout the late 1920s and early 1930s, and by 1931 a team of volunteer workers were responsible for the welfare of 150 young Dublin newsboys.[12] Not only did the institution provide food and shelter for young boys, it also argued on their behalf. At the club's Annual General Meeting in 1931, it was reported that the board of the club put forward its belief that it would be a great advantage if there existed 'a special court for children under 14, far removed from the ordinary courts, and presided over, perhaps, by a lady.'[13]

Dublin newsboys enjoyed mixed relations with the various political movements active in 1930s Dublin. A strong working relationship with the republican movement is evident from the praise *An Phoblacht* heaped onto the youngsters in 1931, following the outlawing of that publication by the State. Newsboys continued to sell *Republican File*, which was a publication produced by the movement while its main organ was banned. Hanna Sheehy-Skeffington, co-editor of the paper at that point in time with Frank Ryan, would later remark that through the days of State repression against the paper, the young newsboys stood by *An Phoblacht*:

> The newsboys were our best friends. It was cheerful to hear their defiant shout 'Stop Press! *An Phoblacht*!' in Grafton Street and round the Pillar through the darkest days. Every issue become a 'Stop Press!' The moral effect of that newsboy stand was great. I remember once when the C.I.D held up an issue how the boys mobbed our office, with its guard of the attendant C.I.D men, yelling 'We want *An Phoblacht*!'[14]

Upon her release from prison in February 1933 following a stint in Armagh Jail, newspaper reports noted that among the crowds who greeted her in Dublin at a mass-rally in College Green were a significant number of Dublin newsboys.[15]

Less successful in appealing to the youngsters was the League of Youth, who publicly courted young Dublin newsboys in 1934. This organisation had emerged following the suppression of the right-wing Young Ireland Association, and a meeting it organised exclusively for young interested newsboys on 9 April 1934 at Parnell Square ended in a near riot, with the media reporting that between fifty and sixty young newsboys attended the meeting which was addressed by Richard Mulcahy, and that when Mulcahy spoke, the lights were switched off, cries of 'Up The Republic!' were raised, and the boys marched out of the building, before breaking windows.[16] Unknown to the youngsters at this point was the fact that they were only weeks from facing into one of the longest running newspaper strikes in Dublin's history. On 26 July 1934, the Irish Transport and General Workers' Union (ITGWU) withdrew its members from the offices of the *Irish Times*, the *Irish Independent* and the *Irish Press*, beginning a devastating labour dispute in the capital.

THE 1934 DUBLIN NEWSPAPER STRIKE

Out of the 1934 newspaper strike in Dublin, the term 'Animal Gang' would first emerge in the national media and in Garda intelligence reports. This strike, which lasted for several months, led to great hardship for Dublin newsboys and confrontation with several publications in the city. The strike, according to the ITGWU, had its origins in 'the refusal of the proprietors to meet a demand for higher wages, shorter hours of work and longer holidays.'[17] Initially 300 ITGWU members were involved in a dispute which involved eleven firms, and the strike affected every aspect of newspaper production and distribution in Dublin. The strike escalated when printers followed the ITGWU workers onto strike action, even refusing to set in type the statement from the managers of Dublin newspapers on the grounds it was 'anti-worker propaganda'.[18]

An Phoblacht gave vocal and consistent support to the striking workers. As Brian Hanley has noted, the Print Unions' Strike Committee allowed production of *An Phoblacht* to continue.[19] *An Phoblacht* would note that 'This strike is more than a dispute between the newspaper owners and the employees. It is a challenge to the workers and it must be taken up by every citizen who has the interests of a free Ireland and a free people at heart.'[20]

The scarcity of newspapers in the capital was crippling for young newsboys. On paper, there actually existed very few 'official' newsboys or juvenile street traders. When the matter of newsboys was raised in the Dáil in May 1934, it was noted that there were officially only thirty-four boys and thirteen girls between the ages of 14 and 16 entitled to sell on the streets, but it was acknowledged that in reality there were 'five times that number of juveniles trading on the street.'[21] With their primary source of income removed, the newsboys found themselves in economic dire straits, and as the *Irish Independent* would later note, the dispute 'hit none as badly as it hit the newsboys.'[22] The Belvedere Newsboys' Club found itself having to open nightly, and providing more meals to more newsboys than at any point prior.[23]

CONFRONTATION BETWEEN NEWSBOYS AND REPUBLICANS

Despite the sympathies of the republican press being on the side of the striking workers, one group of workers were about to clash with the movement. With the republican press remaining as the only papers printed with regularity in a city deprived of news, young newsboys would clash with the proprietors of *An Phoblacht* and *Republican Congress* (the newspaper of the socialist-republican organisation of the same name) seeking cheaper wholesale costs for the publications. The 'Strike Editions' of *An Phoblacht* were widely read in Dublin, and in seeking a cheaper rate for this publication young Dublin newsboys would physically confront republicans. Details of this confrontation are contained within the file 'Disturbances created by newsboys at Frederick's Lane, Dublin City' (JUS 8/67) within the National Archives of Ireland. The file, dated 14 September 1934, reports that at about 4.50pm on 12 September Gardaí were alerted to the fact that 'there was a row by newsboys in Frederick Lane and that some windows had been broken'. Gardaí noted that upon attending the scene, they found 'about fifty' newsboys, that were 'going away from the place at the time, having refused to pay an extra 3d [pence] per dozen [bringing the cost up to one shilling] that was demanded of them.' Later, at about 8.50pm, 'about fifty young men were observed marching four deep along Parnell Square, North, towards Frederick Street.' These young men made for the distribution offices of *An Phoblacht*, where it was reported they 'at once drew sticks from under their coats and lined across the street'. The republican movement had taken it upon itself to protect the offices of the paper, rather than notify Gardaí, and as the Garda report noted, the presence of these vigilante protectors only served to draw the attention of young newsboys who 'collected in North Frederick Street from various directions and scuffles took place between them and the men who had assembled previously'.[24]

This newsboy gang clashed not alone with *An Phoblacht*, but also with the left-wing Republican Congress. Gardaí noted that prior to the incident at Frederick's Lane, newsboys had gone to the offices of the Republican Congress at 112 Marlborough Street to demand they be supplied with copies of that organisation's paper at a cheaper rate. When this request was refused, Gardaí noted that the boys attacked Frank Ryan and Michael Price. The intelligence report on the incident noted that 'Mr. Frank Ryan informed them that they were little better than animals in their behaviour and by this remark he unconsciously christened the gang who thereafter adopted the name "Animal Gang".'[25] This theory is interesting, as in most Dublin folklore the name is believed to be derived from either the viciousness of the gangs, or to folklore tales that the 'Animal Gang' were supposedly dockers, who acquired their name from the fact they worked alongside real animals and livestock.[26]

An Phoblacht wasted no time in condemning the youths, and its front page of 15 September 1934 noted that a gang, known as 'the Animals', had not only smashed windows at the offices of the newspaper but had made 'several abortive attempts to enter the offices'.[27] The newspaper claimed that some of the newsboys who returned later in the day were 'wearing blueshirts' and noted that 'bottles and iron bars were flung'.[28] The Garda report on the incident makes no reference whatsoever to boys wearing blue shirts, and while it is possible Gardaí missed the presence of such shirts, it is likely to be propaganda from a republican perspective, aimed at linking the boys with the right-wing of street politics. The paper claimed that the 'outrage was an anti-strike move by agents of the employers',[29] and in a follow-up edition of the paper the IRA would pledge itself to 'clean up city gangs'.[30]

On the night of 25 September 1934, the IRA would attempt to speak to the leaders of the young newsboy gang by carrying out raids in the north-inner city community it believed they had come from. Garda intelligence reports show that at least two such raids were carried out by the IRA. The first involved an armed hold-up at the Ardee Hall on Talbot Street, which Gardaí believed to be 'the outcome of recent friction between the newsboys and members of the IRA organisation concerning the distribution of the periodical *An Phoblacht*.'[31] This club was popular with inner-city newsboys, and the IRA sought out two men named McAuley and Lawless who it blamed for the recent attack. The hall was, according to one 1932 newspaper report, 'not a registered club'[32] and Gardaí believed that as far as they knew these two 'were the leaders of the newsboys who clashed with the IRA in Frederick Lane'.[33] When the IRA called to the club, they failed to locate the men. One youth who had been in the club at the time described the republicans who called as 'about 20 to 30 years, medium height and build, dressed in black trench belt coats, but one appeared to have a tweed coat'.[34] One youngster was informed to 'tell McAuley if Lawless was not got they would shoot McAuley'.[35]

The following night, the IRA once again attempted to locate the two. This time, the organisation approached men in the area seeking information, namely Denis Byrne (19, of 113 Foley Street) and Christopher Kenny (34, of 57 Corporation Street).[36] These men later went to Gardaí to report the incident, and in turn the Gardaí informed McAuley and Lawless that they were in danger. Both men refused police protection. Gardaí visited McAuley at home at 57A Corporation Street, and Lawless at 26 Cumberland Street.

In the case of McAuley, they noted that 'He is aware he is being sought by members of the IRA but appears to be determined to continue his activities against *An Phoblacht*.'[37]

The *An Phoblacht* reporting on these raids was sensationalist, writing that men, armed with revolvers, had 'taken possession of Ardee Hall', which it described as 'the Animals [*sic*] hide out'.[38] The paper warned that 'more exciting incidents are likely to happen should "Animal Gang" activities continue'.[39] Only two days after this threat, the newspaper strike of 1934 came to an end. *The Times* of London noted that 'the losses which have been sustained by the City of Dublin are incalculable',[40] but Gardaí believed that at least the 'principal cause of conflict between the newsvendors and the proprietors of *An Phoblacht* had been removed, and that future conflict was unlikely.' The Gardaí believed that there had been no political motivations to the attacks upon the IRA and *An Phoblacht*, and that the members of the gang were 'hooligans, pure and simple'.[41]

OTHER ACTIVITIES OF THE
NORTH INNER-CITY 'ANIMAL GANG'

Evidence shows, however, that this young gang had other targets in mind beyond merely attacking the offices of political newspapers. The first appearance of the term 'Animal Gang' in the mainstream press was within the pages of the *Cork Examiner* (unaffected by the Dublin strike) in September, in a report which was reprinted within the 22 September issue of *An Phoblacht*. The *Cork Examiner* wrote that 'as a result of the activities of what is called the "Animal Gang", five youths have been arrested, and upwards of eighteen people have been treated in hospital for ugly wounds inflicted by weapons or sharp instruments.'[42] While Gardaí believed the report to be highly exaggerated, there was truth in the *Cork Examiner* report that five youths were arrested for their role in street violence in Dublin. They were Michael Dunne (20, 99 Foley Street), Patrick Ryan (28, no fixed address), William Dunne (22, 6 Railway Street), Robert Weller (21, 45 Corporation Buildings) and Robert Lyons (22, no address).[43] Of those who provided addresses, all were based in the same inner-city area as McAuley and Lawless. It was clear that the so-called 'Animal Gang' had their base around Corporation Buildings and Foley Street in the heart of the inner-city, an area long-scarred by poverty. Corporation Buildings, which dated back to 1904, have been described by Murray Fraser as 'a blatant attempt to house the very poor: 80 per cent of the 460 flats had only a single room' and the estate 'earned such an unrivalled reputation for vice and squalor that loss making rents, some as low as 1s per week, had to be set'.[44] Corporation Buildings had long been considered one of the most troubled housing projects in the inner-city by authorities, and during the 1913 Lockout the complex witnessed intense scenes of violence, with local residents attacked by the Dublin Metropolitan Police following a raid. One resident, John McDonagh, already paralysed, died following an attack on him in his sickbed by police officers.[45] In the years following Independence, life was little better inside Corporation Buildings. Writing about the gang problem of 1930s Dublin in a 1942 edition of *The Bell*, the anonymous 'Crime Reporter' asked if it was any mystery the 'Animals' had emerged from the north-inner city, noting that:

> Born to squalor, unemployment and ennui, remembering perhaps the unconcealed viciousness that flourished all about them in their childhood days, the open and relatively unpunished flouting of the laws of God and man, how could one expect them to be otherwise than anti-social?[46]

Throughout September and October more 'Animal Gang' cases emerged in the national media. Several youths were imprisoned for their role in 'Animal Gang' violence. There appeared to be no political significance to these attacks. John Ryan, the victim of an assault on Henry Street, claimed that the youths who attacked him had claimed to be from the 'Animal Gang'.[47] On 13 October 1934, Peter McAuley, who the IRA had earlier sought, was arrested at home. Newspapers noted that McAuley's father shouted at Gardaí 'you will not take my son, although he is the leader of the Animal Gang!'[48] In the scuffle that followed his son's arrest, one Garda was hospitalised, and McAuley's parents themselves arrested. During their court case, the judge would remark that he 'was informed by charitable organisations that Corporation Buildings should never have been built'.[49]

THE SPREAD OF THE TERM 'ANIMAL GANG'

Any attempt to form a coherent picture of the make-up, ideology and activity of the so-called 'Animal Gang' is seriously complicated by the fact the initial gang, and the publicity given to their exploits, appears to have quickly inspired several others. In the eyes of the national media and the Gardaí, there was not one 'Animal Gang' but several from 1935. In a 1936 media report on a gang battle in Donnybrook, the *Irish Times* noted that a 'Tiger Gang' from Ringsend and a self-titled 'Animal Gang' from Donnybrook had clashed, leading to 'twenty-seven youths, some with discoloured eyes, and others wearing sticking plaster' appearing in the courts.[50] These gangs were geographically far-removed from the initial territory of the newsboy gang. To make matters more confusing, the north inner-city 'Animal Gang' who had clashed with the IRA in 1934 appears to have remained active into 1935, as in September 1935 Peter McAuley was again in court, sentenced to six months' hard labour for assaulting a Garda with an iron bar on Talbot Street.[51] Yet another 'Animal Gang', based around Golden Lane and the Iveagh Trust Buildings emerged too, with Gardaí labelling 19-year-old Herbert Genockey as its leader.[52] 'Animal Gang' appears to have become shorthand for youth gang violence by 1935.

WHAT ROLE DID THE 'ANIMAL GANGS' PLAY IN THE ANTI-COMMUNIST VIOLENCE OF THE PERIOD?

Dublin witnessed intense anti-communist disturbances on its streets in the early 1930s, motivated primarily by strong religious feeling. The hosting of the Eucharistic Congress in the city in 1932, coupled with international issues such as the decline of church–power in republican Spain, nurtured a spirit of militant Catholicism among significant sections of the population. Catholicism and communism were presented as being inherently incompatible, and yet there existed a belief that the obscene poverty of inner-city Dublin could potentially *create* communists. In a city where 4,840 tenement homes sheltered 25,320 families, the *Irish Times* wrote in October 1931 that it was 'almost a miracle that hitherto communism has not flourished aggressively in that hideous soil.'[53]

March 1933 would see severe anti-communist violence on the streets of the capital, violence that R.M. Douglas has noted in his study of the fascist movement Ailtirí na hAiséirghe was among the most serious disturbances in the city since the Civil War.[54] The most dramatic attacks of the period were carried out against Connolly House, the headquarters of the Revolutionary Workers' Groups (the predecessor of the Communist Party of Ireland (CPI)) on Great Strand Street. These attacks had been the result of a particularly heated sermon at the Pro-Cathedral on 27 March 1933, during which a Jesuit preacher allegedly informed the congregation that 'Here in this Holy Catholic city of Dublin, these vile creatures of communism are within our midst.'[55] Over three nights Connolly House was besieged, while a small number of socialist activists attempted to defend the building. The blame for this attack has often been laid on the 'Animal Gang'. Charlie Gilmore, then active within the IRA, recalled in a 1983 interview with the *Irish Times* that the 'Animal Gang' had led this attack. In the interview, journalist Michael Farrell wrote that 'the backbone of that mob, he says, came from the "Animal Gang", a vicious street gang drawn from the worst of the Dublin slums.'[56] In a 2003 obituary for Eugene Downing, another socialist who had defended Connolly House, the *Irish Times* wrote that 'he took part in the defence of Connolly House … when it was attacked by a mob led by members of the notorious "Animal Gang."'[57] The length of time between the events and these references to the involvement of the so-called 'Animal Gang' should be noted. No reference to such a gang at this siege appears in media or Garda reports from the time. Gardaí compiled a detailed report on the siege of Connolly House, and actually noted that 'the crowd who assembled in Strand Street last night was made up of persons of different walks of life in the city, including a very large percentage of respectfully dressed young women.'[58] The term 'Animal Gang' was not on the Garda radar until 1934, yet some historians have placed this gang at the centre of earlier anti-communist violence.[59]

While it is easy to debunk any claim that the 'Animal Gang' spearheaded the assault on Connolly House in 1933, it must be noted that many protagonists of the period active within left-wing politics have spoken of a self-styled 'Animal Gang' who did assault demonstrations and meetings of the left in the years following 1934. Bob Doyle has noted that he recalled a gang he knew as the 'Animal Gang' who were made up not of criminals, but rather 'they were toughs, and used bicycle chains.'[60] Doyle wrote that this gang would fight republicans with frequency on O'Connell Street, and even claimed that this gang would 'wear British Legion poppies in their lapels.'[61] Doyle believed they fought for the Blueshirts, and 'always thought a priest organised them', going on to claim 'they'd attack anyone on the Left, targeting meetings, marches and demonstrations.'[62] These claims were made by Doyle in his 2006 memoirs. I have not found the poppy claim made in any other account of anti-communist gang violence in Dublin.

Bob Doyle's claims were made decades on, but some figures close to the events blamed a so-called 'Animal Gang' for attacking the left in contemporary written accounts too. Peadar O'Donnell made the claim in 1937 in the pages of his work *Salud! An Irishman in Spain*. O'Donnell wrote that the 'Animal Gang' were made up of 'very fine fighting material in the slum basements', and were 'the most effective of the terrorist gangs who ruled there.'[63] O'Donnell told of how the 'Animal Gang' had supposedly been mobilised in an inner-city hall and told by a young woman that the 'fight in Spain was only a preliminary to a war against religion in Ireland, and the churches in Dublin would be the first to suffer.'[64] This woman supposedly went on to inform the gang that the Pro-Cathedral would be turned into an 'anti-God museum'.[65] I have been unable to find any reference to such a meeting beyond

O'Donnell's text, though he is not alone in labelling this gang a right-wing auxiliary. Another contemporary example is the song 'O'Duffy's Ironsides', penned by 'Somhairle Macalastair', the alias of Diarmuid Fitzpatrick. First published in the *Worker* in October 1936, the song notes that 'On Badajoz's red ramparts, the Spanish workers died. And O'Duffy's bellowing Animal Gang, sang hymns of hate with pride.'[66]

Attacks on the left were plentiful in the latter half of the 1930s in Dublin. Rosamond Jacob, a republican-socialist activist in the period who was close to Frank Ryan and the Republican Congress claimed to have received a letter in the post in May 1936 which warned her, in relation to her printed letters in the *Irish Press*, that she would 'want to be very careful what you say in your letters, as you are a marked man. Beware of yourself. The Animal Gang.'[67] On one occasion, in April 1936, an Easter Rising commemoration was repeatedly attacked in the city centre and at Glasnevin Cemetery by an anti-communist mob. Donal Ó Drisceoil has noted that 'the CPI and [Republican] Congress contingents were attacked by the animal gangs at the Easter Sunday parade to Glasnevin Cemetery.'[68] Jack White, a founding member of the Irish Citizen Army during the revolutionary period, was one of those attacked. He later blamed 'Catholic actionists' for the assault, writing that:

> Last Easter Sunday, I had myself to fight for three kilometres against the Catholic actionists, who attacked us on the streets as we were marching to honour the memory of the Republican dead who fell in Easter week 1916. The pious hooligans actually came inside the cemetery and tore up the grave rails to attack us.[69]

When coupled with a violent assault on a public meeting at College Green on 13 April 1936, when Gardaí estimated 'about 98% of the people present were opposed to the meeting',[70] it is evident there did exist a militantly anti-communist street force in Dublin. In addition to attacking the left-wing demonstration on 13 April, the crowds also attacked Trinity College Dublin and the Masonic Hall, which indicated a spirit of militant Catholicism.[71] Trinity College Dublin would have been regarded as a Protestant institution by many Catholics, and the Catholic Church itself forbade its followers attending the institution, without the permission of their bishop, until 1970. The Republican Congress organisation quickly blamed the 'Animal Gang' and 'other such defenders of faith and morals'[72] for these assaults, but was 'Animal Gang' just shorthand for violent mob? Certainly, the anti-communist violence of April 1936 was far removed from the gang of newsboys who clashed with republicans two years previous.

CONCLUSION

The 1930s was a period of intense political street confrontations in Dublin, and separating the actions of the 'Animal Gang' or 'Animal Gangs' from the general political violence of the period is in many ways impossible. The sheer scale of anti-communist violence is evident from Garda reports of the period, and it is evident that those in authority believed that the hostility of the general public had made it impossible to hold meetings or communist demonstrations in the city. Much of what has been attributed to the 'Animal Gang' in this period appears to be folklore, and fails to capture the widespread anti-communist feeling of the public at the time, evident, for example, in the support enjoyed by groups like the Saint Patrick's Anti-Communist League.[73] 'Animal Gang' has become an almost 'one size fits all' labelling for those who engaged in anti left-wing violence.

The story of the 'Animal Gangs' dragged into the 1940s, but they were no longer seen as a political issue but rather a social one. As Kevin Kearns has noted, the 'Animal Gangs' were perceived then to be involved 'in mercenary money-lending or outright extortion of shop-owners'.[74] It would appear the media and Garda frenzy around the clashes of young newsboys and republicans, and indeed youth-on-youth violence in 1934, gave birth to a term which would enter Dublin lingo for decades to come, a term which became fluid and could apply to all violent gangs. While an initial band of young, working-class newsboys may have clashed with other youths, the IRA and even Gardaí in late 1934 at the time of a newspaper dispute, their name appears to have outlived their exploits.

Chapter Seven

'The Problem is One Not of Criminal Tendencies, But of Poverty'[1]: The NSPCC, John Byrne and the Industrial School System in Ireland

Sarah-Anne Buckley

'The State shall endeavour to ensure that the strength and health of men and women, and the tender age of children shall not be abused and that citizens shall not be forced by economic necessity to enter avocations unsuited to their sex, age or strength.'

–Article 45.4 Bunreacht na hÉireann

The story of Ireland's industrial schools in the twentieth century has received much attention from the media and a small number of historians and sociologists over the past fifteen years. In 1996, the documentary *Dear Daughter*, which described Christine Buckley's experiences in Goldenbridge industrial school, represented a first look at the abuse suffered by past residents in Ireland. Following on from this in April 1999, the Irish television station RTÉ aired a three-part series, *States of Fear*, documenting the experiences of former residents of the industrial school system in Ireland.[2] The programme caused widespread debate on the schools, and in the weeks that followed the media was filled with stories from former residents. On 11 May 1999, the Taoiseach Bertie Ahern issued a public apology on behalf of the victims of childhood abuse, while also announcing the formation of a commission to investigate allegations made by victims. In May 2009, the Report of the Commission to Inquire into Child Abuse (the Ryan Report) described the emotional, physical and sexual abuse that occurred in the industrial schools as 'systematic' and 'endemic'.[3] Unfortunately for most, the ethos of article 45.4 of Bunreacht na hÉireann was far from the reality.

While the establishment of industrial schools and reformatories was a British initiative, and one that was followed in many other Western societies in the nineteenth century,[4] from the 1920s institutionalisation was progressively criticised in Britain, other European states and the US, with alternatives such as boarding-out and adoption increasingly preferred.[5] This chapter will look at two issues that have previously been neglected with regard to the historiography of the industrial schools – the involvement of the National Society for the Prevention of Cruelty to Children (NSPCC), and the deaths of children in care, in particular that of John Byrne in 1935.[6]

THE NSPCC AND THE INDUSTRIAL SCHOOLS

During the year we have had to arrange for the placing of a large number of children in industrial schools chiefly because their parents were unable to maintain them … The whole question of the treatment of 'deprived' children in this country calls for investigation, such as it has received recently in England … It is not surprising that many of our more experienced officers try to avoid the easy course of committal, even when the task of bringing about suitable home conditions seems almost insuperable.[7]

–*Annual Report Dublin Branch NSPCC*, 1948–49

This statement from the NSPCC is revealing for a number of reasons. First, the recognition children were being committed to industrial schools due to their parents' poverty; second, the lack of alternatives to the industrial schools; and third, the recognition that England had moved far from institutionalisation as the answer to poverty in families while in Ireland this had remained fixed. This was not the first time the NSPCC had discussed the schools in their reports. From the early 1890s, the Dublin reports contain numerous discussions of the 'controversy surrounding industrial schools' with the Society denouncing their use unconditionally in 1894. However, it appears that it was forced to roll back on this in subsequent years. In 1895, the Society reiterated that while it did not endorse the sending of children to industrial schools, in cases where provision was not available in the form of relatives (particularly when parents were convicted and imprisoned) they could be sent temporarily. In 1900, their report stated that:

> ...they fully understand that there are circumstances under which it is better for the child to be removed from the influence of the parents, and under such circumstances they are prepared to avail themselves of the Industrial School System, or of any other suitable one that presents itself. We do not wish to enter into the controversy that has been raised over the Industrial Schools question. Our position in regard to the system is a simple one. We believe in the absolute responsibility of enforcing parental responsibility. We do not think that it is good for the individual, or just to the public who are taxed, that any persons should be lightly relieved of the duty of supporting his children in order that they should be brought up at the public expense. That this has been too often done in the past we know from experience.[8]

Initially, the Society's principal arguments against industrial schools were that children should not be maintained at public expense, and should where at all possible be kept within the home. This argument benefited the Society in a number of ways: in the first instance, by emphasising that the Society kept children within the home, it was tactically gaining public approval, and maximising its influence. This also was related to issues of class reform, as in order for the Society to inculcate middle-class ideals of domesticity, children needed to remain in the home (the removal of illegitimate children was obviously outside this remit as one-parent families were not the nuclear ideal and the removal of children from 'immoral surroundings' was widely accepted). Louise A. Jackson's examination of child sexual abuse in Victorian England discusses the involvement of the Society in removing children from the home and placing them in institutions in the late-nineteenth century. Examining cases of sexual abuse or 'immorality', she acknowledges the Society's awareness of the controversy surrounding child custody from the beginning of the twentieth century and argues that welfare workers in schools and homes, 'were more than simple cogs in a bourgeois mechanism that aimed to mould the lower orders into humble and obedient servants.'[9] Taking a similar stance in her study of industrial schools and children's homes in nineteenth-century Scotland, Linda Mahood maintains that historians should break away from the 'social control' paradigm influenced by Foucault's work on institutions and focus on issues of initiative, agency and resistance on the part of child clients and their parents.[10] However, in the Irish context, it is difficult to view the widespread neglect, physical and sexual abuse that occurred in industrial schools in the twentieth century without focusing on the 'social control paradigm'. Families in poverty were rarely in a position to pay for legal representation (as the case of John Byrne will demonstrate), and if a justice was faced with a testimony from an NSPCC inspector, school attendance officer or Garda, it is likely that opposition from a parent would not have been successful. This is not to diminish the role of families and society in the committal of children to schools, but to emphasise the lack of choice and power for many families in poverty. Integral to this discussion is how much society knew about the industrial schools and other similar institutions. Oral testimony from the period 1930–1970, for example in Kevin Kearns's excellent study of Dublin's 'Mammies and Grannies', demonstrates that people knew institutions were not places to which children should be sent. The following quote from Margaret Byrne demonstrates this:

> I remember this one family's mother and father dies of T.B. and there was eight or nine children. The eldest girl, she was about twelve years of age and the baby was about twelve months old. And that elder girl well, she was called a 'little mother' cause she was looking after all her little brothers and sisters. She *reared* those children and they *never* had to be sent away to a home...[11]

Officially, from 1922 until 1940, the NSPCC in Ireland did not involve itself in discussions of the industrial schools, or the need to protect the family and support alternatives such as fostering and legal adoption. This is one of the starkest contrasts between the Irish and British branches in the 1920s and 1930s, and the conclusion must be drawn that as a pressure group its influence was greatly decreased in independent Ireland. In fact, it appears in the reports to be appeasing the State throughout the 1920s and 1930s. In 1951 all branches cited Article 42, Section 1 of the 1937 Constitution at the beginning of their annual reports – 'The State acknowledges that the primary and natural educator of the child is the Family and guarantees to respect the inalienable right and duty of parents to provide, according to their means, for the religious and moral, intellectual, physical and social education of their children.'[12] In 1952, Article 41 was quoted – 'The State recognises the Family as the natural primary and fundamental unit group of Society, and as a moral institution possessing inalienable and imprescriptible rights, antecedent and superior to all positive law.'[13] When looking at the State's control and interference in families from the 1920s, both articles seem almost farcical. Far from recognising or protecting the family, the removal of children to industrial schools, and the lack of financial support for families jeopardised the family, in all its forms. While the extent to which the NSPCC inspector was involved in removing children to industrial schools and reformatories in the twentieth century may never be known due to insufficient documentation, observations can be made from the existing files and the testimonies of residents in the Ryan Report. In 1937 alone, 11 per cent of the neglect cases investigated in the Wexford District Branch resulted in removals.[14] Similarly, in the Waterford and District Branch in 1939, thirty-four of the 490 children dealt with were placed in industrial schools, while in 1940 this figure was forty-three out of 527 children involved in cases with the NSPCC.[15] While this is not a criticism of the Society in isolation, as it was enforcing a policy supported by the State, an examination of the files reveals much about the families involved in these situations and the biases of the inspector. In 1929, a Sister in St Michael's Industrial School, Wexford wrote to the inspector regarding a mother 'who had turned up at her doorstep' looking for her daughter:

> ...the mother of K is here, just crossed from Wales – wants to take K back this evening. She, the mother has not seen her husband. What is to be done? Would it be well to ask one of the Guards to call up and explain the law to her? She seems reasonable but wants the child.[16]

The police were called and the mother was told her rights by the police and the convent. It was a clear case in which, upon signing the committal form, a parent had not considered or perhaps been coerced into thinking that this was the best place for their child.

It was, however, not always the convents and schools which did not agree to the return of children. In 1930, a sister in St Michael's Industrial School, Wexford, wrote to the local NSPCC inspector requesting advice regarding the release of a young girl in the school – 'I should not regret this child's departure from the School but *there is a soul in question* [emphasis added].' The inspector replied:

The parents of M detained in your school are well known to me. The father is a man of very low mental standard and has neglected his family for years. The mother is not morally good. In my opinion it would be a grave error to discharge or release on licence the said client.[17]

In an even more revealing case, the following extract divulges not only the inspector's distrust of the boy's parents and relatives, but the idea of the child being a commodity of the State:

The boy, who is now 10 years old, is due to be transferred to Carriglea Industrial School and with the necessary training at the end of six years he will be an asset to the State. In view of the information disclosed by the inquiry I cannot recommend that the boy be discharged from School (at this stage) and returned to the relatives ... who are said to be mentally deficient.[18]

The extent to which the Church, the State and the NSPCC collaborated in the removal of children is difficult to assess. However, the following letter reveals one particular aspect and attitude to the placement of children in religious institutions. The letter, written by Sister X in St Michael's, Wexford to the local inspector demonstrates not only her attitude to the welfare of destitute children, but to their religious denomination and faith:

My messenger, *** had some business in the County Home Enniscorthy on Monday last. She said something of the women and children of that institution and from her description of the place and inhabitants, I could not think of sending the little *** children there – if permitted to keep them we shall keep them in the school without any renummeration [sic]. The Almighty will provide the means. A few years ago we took in two English Protestant children who were abandoned by their step-mother, the father being dead. They were brought over from Wales and left in an old shed near Wexford – We were asked to admit them. We did so and kept them for some years. They are now Catholics and work in a Convent Laundry ... Since that time we have not known want in this Institution so we shall trust to the Grand God to help us in the *** case also – Thanking you very much for many favours and for your letter of Thursday.[19]

While many institutions expected donations from the parents of the children being admitted, and legally justices could enforce this, if a school was not filled to capacity this 'donation' was not a necessity as the following passage reveals: 'A few lines to let you know that we would be glad to get the Browne children you mentioned some time ago. We could take them anytime I would defray any expenses with them.'[20] Dated two days after the arrival of the children, the same Sister wrote to the inspector stating that one of the children who 'was let out to her aunt for the day' had not returned. Unfortunately this is where the file ends so it is not possible to know whether the child was found and brought back to the school, although it is highly likely that this was the case.

Although the policy of maintaining children within the home was reiterated by the NSPCC in its annual reports, the correspondence in the case files reveals another side to the issue and perhaps, as the 1948 Dublin report addressed, it was easier for inspectors to partake in the incarceration of children in the schools. In numerous letters from those in charge at St Aidan's Industrial School for Girls, Wexford; St Michael's Industrial School for Girls, Wexford, and St Michael's Industrial School for Boys, Waterford, references are made to the need to protect the souls of Catholic children and maintain the numbers of children in the schools. Overall, the language used by both the inspector and those working in the institutions is instructive, and at times detached. In 1938, one Sister of Charity wrote to the inspector regarding a child that was to be committed: 'I hope she is healthy and normal.'[21]

The NSPCC, John Byrne and the Industrial School System in Ireland

In the NSPCC files, three separate letters from the Mother Superior in St Michael's, Wexford to the NSPCC inspector reveal the personal relationships that existed between these institutions of influence in cases of child welfare. In the first in 1928, the Sister wrote to the inspector: 'If Mr. "X" is not presiding at Court on the 24th I shall not send the "Connor" children down but defer committal to another day.' In a subsequent letter in 1929 regarding the committal of a young brother and sister, there is a small note to the inspector with the following scribbled on the bottom: 'I mentioned the other matter to Mr "X" and he was not at all pleased as like myself he appreciates all the help you always give in children's cases.'[22] In a final letter in 1928, she includes a note from the local priest to the inspector stating that a particular mother had consented to the committal of her child if the inspector would like to follow up the case. The familiarity that existed between the inspector, the local clergy, the managers of the religious orders, the courts and the Gardaí is very complex and difficult to assess. However, with a capitation system in place in industrial schools in Ireland, a child living in a home deemed 'immoral' by the inspector could quite easily be placed in a school if the incentive was there. The lack of regulation of inspectors, and the class of the mostly male inspectors who were in place must also be considered in this context. It appears from the documentation available, NSPCC inspectors did not conduct follow-up investigations on the children placed in institutions. This may also have been the case for those boarded out – but it is an area worthy of further investigation. Finally, from the reports of the Society it appears the NSPCC inspector was receiving on average £250–300 a year. This was quite a substantial figure when one considers that the assistance the inspector was sometimes able to acquire for families was 6s per week.

The relationship between the courts, the inspector and the religious can be further seen in the following two notes. In the first the Sister mentions a particular family to be investigated, asserting that 'both cases are cases that should pass in court I think'.[23] In another case sent on a Tuesday morning

to the inspector, the hastiness of the sister is apparent: 'regarding the three
*** children, would it be too late now for application to Next Wednesday's
court?'[24] The following letter is significant as it was written in 1920, prior to
independence.

> Dear Inspector L.,
>
> Many thanks for kind letter. I am happy to say the two children
> arrived today. The Police were busy. Thanking you most sincerely for
> your kindness to us. If you have any more children you won't forget
> St. Aidans.
>
> I am dear ***
>
> > Yours gratefully,
> > Mother Superior.[25]

THE DEATH OF JOHN BYRNE

> 'I saw my boy on Holy Thursday, when he was lying dead at
> the Mater Hospital. I lifted the shroud. His ribs and whole side
> were black and blue and his jaw was discoloured.'
>
> > *—Workers' Voice*, 4 May 1935

In 1935, 15-year-old John Byrne died in the Mater Hospital, Dublin. This
statement is from his father, Patrick and was printed on the front page
of the *Workers' Voice*, the paper of the Communist Party of Ireland. John
Byrne had been a resident in Artane Industrial School for three years prior
to his death – a death which from the available evidence was not sufficiently
accounted for in this author's assertion. The story of John Byrne's death was
not only referred to in the *Workers' Voice*, but also the *Irish Times*, the *Irish*

Press and the *Irish Independent*.[26] In 1930s Ireland, this may be surprising. In the Dáil and Seanad, there are no references to the case, and as the Commission to Inquire into Child Abuse looked at the period from 1936, his case was outside the remit of the investigation. Aside from the press, the case was recorded in a letter to Hanna Sheehy-Skeffington in 1935. At this time, the Irish Labour Defence League had begun a petition to support John Byrne's parents, after the inquest had found John Byrne had died from 'natural causes, but the origins may have been unnatural'. The letter was a plea for help:

> A few weeks ago a boy named John Byrne lost his life in Artane Industrial School following a beating by a teacher named Lynch. This terrible tragedy calls for an investigation. There is every reason to believe that the authorities intend to let the matter pass and take no action. The boy's parents (he was their only son) are endeavouring to take the matter into the Courts and to make a claim for compensation for the death of their son. But this cannot be done without financial help. £5 is needed at once to enable the solicitor to proceed. All just minded people are asked to come to the assistance of the parents of the dead boy and enable them to make a fight for justice to ensure that such inhuman recurrences will no longer happen in these institutions.[27]

Both the letter and *Workers' Voice* article attribute the boy's death to a beating from a brother in the school. The article records the following statement from Patrick Byrne – 'When I saw my boy before he died … he said to me: "the master kicked me, but don't say anything daddy, or he will kill me when I go back."' The paper states that the following are the 'facts' that were revealed in the inquest: 'Dr Murphy, Medical Officer to Artane, was unable to diagnose the cause of the boy's illness … James Doran, a pupil at Artane stated "Mr Lynch punched Byrne in a joke. Byrne fell to the ground and Mr Lynch kicked him for a couple of minutes on the soles. Byrne kept wriggling and received a kick in the thigh.'" In response to this account, the brother involved, Cornelius Lynch, changed his earlier description of events – 'I admit I was flurried when I made the previous statement, which was not right, that I ran at Byrne as he was about to throw himself on the ground.' To which Mr McCarthy for the family asked, 'So the first thing you did when asked for an explanation by your superior was to tell a lie?' – 'Yes'.

As previously stated, the inquest was recorded in the *Irish Times*, the *Irish Press* and the *Irish Independent*. Held in the Mater Hospital on 26 April 1935, chaired by De MacEarlean and with a jury in place, the coroner told the court that the boy had received a kick while playing football, and was admitted to the hospital with a pain in his leg five days later. The coroner stated that the boy's death was due to 'abscesses in the lungs, heart and hip, and to septicaemia', but there were no signs of violence – yet he goes on to state that the abscesses 'could have been caused if the skin was broken but unlikely to be caused if the skin was unbroken'.[28] What is interesting in the case is the lack of discussion about the boy's medical treatment or medical records. Dr Murphy, the medical officer at Artane stated 'there were no signs of bruises or other injuries, but he showed signs of pain on pressure' upon examination. The *Irish Times* reported 'on going there, the boy, who was ill, told him that while playing football he happened to strike the master, who then kicked him. When the witness asked the Sister if that were true she replied "He keeps saying that."'[29] He is recorded as having a temperature of 102–104 Fahrenheit throughout the five days he was kept in Artane, 104.8 upon hospitalisation, yet they did not think this was enough to admit the boy?[30] As he died from septicaemia this could have been prevented or made apparent. With reference to his medical records, the Artane Manager was obliged by law to keep these, particularly in the case of any long-standing illnesses, yet they are not mentioned in the inquest and John's father stated that his son had never had a serious illness in his life. With regard to the family, it is recorded that they only heard of their son's illness when his sister called to the school with a parcel and was informed he was in hospital. It is also very unrealistic to believe the boy died from a small kick, and James Doran's evidence that he received a punch and a few minutes of kicking is more probable. What is not probable is that there were no marks – or perhaps they had been lessened as the boy was kept for over five days in the school, not admitted to hospital. Aside from these issues, the *Workers' Voice* reported that there was also a question surrounding his removal. The paper reports that the Coroner told Patrick Byrne 'You can see him again, but he must be boxed up tonight', yet later he was told that the undertaker was not allowed to coffin the boy and the hospital did it instead. 'I am not even sure I buried my own son', he told the paper. The paper ended its report with the following:

> Every worker will agree with the sorrow stricken parent. Unless this tragedy is properly investigated workers will have no other option but to believe that conditions in Artane are being deliberately covered up by responsible people. This is not the first death there in suspicious circumstances: there have been others in recent years. In the name of the whole working class we demand:
>
> **Put Lynch into the dock and hold a public inquiry into the conduct in Artane!**
>
> **Proper working class representation on the inquiry!**
>
> **No whitewashing, but a free and full inquiry to reveal all the facts!**

The events surrounding John Byrne's death can only be speculated upon here – but from the newspaper reports and the lack of questioning at the inquest, it is difficult to accept all the facts as laid out in the inquest report. John

Byrne was one of twenty children to die that year alone in Ireland's industrial school system, or at least one of twenty recorded.[31] Even registering the rate of deaths in younger people, this figure was much higher than that of the general population – an unfortunate commonality with many State and voluntary institutions at this time.

CONCLUSION

'We are overcrowded with applications and I must keep vacancies for children whose faith is in danger as this is the object for which we were founded.'[32]

–Letter to the NSPCC inspector from a Sister of Mercy,
St Michael's Industrial School Wexford, 1929

The industrial school system was a nineteenth-century British construction endorsed by successive Irish governments until the late-twentieth century. Representing one of a myriad of institutions kept in place to deal with perceived social problems, it was accepted then and now that the principal reason for children's removal to industrial schools was poverty in families, as the quote from the title of this chapter highlights. While from the 1920s, Britain, the United States and most other western countries had begun to move towards developing a welfare state to deal with this poverty, in Ireland, the Church and State retained control of families through the continued use of institutions. This was not the only option, nor was it the cheapest option, yet even a cursory glance at the other alternatives (social welfare, single mothers allowance, legal adoption, nurseries, fostering, and more generally, the legalisation of contraceptives and abortion) demonstrates the tension that would have existed between the Catholic Church and the State if they had been pursued. Maintaining a structure of 'charity' as opposed to one of social welfare set Ireland apart internationally, yet it enabled the Church and State to retain an enormous amount of social control. This control spread past the separation of undesirable families and the reluctance to support families through welfare. Both the industrial schools and Magdalen laundries provided the Church and State with an unpaid workforce. That this did not emerge in debates at the time demonstrates the State's lack of inspection of the schools and the class and gender bias towards those placed. Yet the State did not act alone, and the role of the NSPCC was central to the maintenance of the industrial schools. Not only did inspectors choose the families that would be subject to investigation, they acted as a semi-State workforce in bringing children to court, accompanying them to the schools and corresponding with all the actors involved in the industrial school system. Nothing represented a greater move away from the motto of 'protecting children within the home'. In the case of John Byrne, the lack of attention or care placed on those who died within the industrial school system remains, to this day, the biggest stain on its history.

Chapter Eight

Pro-Hitler or Anti-Management?: War on the Industrial Front, Belfast, October 1942[1]

Christopher J.V. Loughlin

In October 1942 Belfast industry was crippled by two simultaneous strikes: one at the engineering firm James Mackie & Sons; the other at the aeroplane manufacturer Short and Harland. The strikers were subjected to a barrage of criticism from the Northern Ireland government, employers, press and politicians. The *Northern Whig* stated 'they are in the wrong. They are being misled, and should return to work at once.'[2] W.H. McCullough, Secretary of the Belfast Communist Party claimed 'strike action … only benefits the enemies of the working class.'[3] However, strike action was comparatively common in Northern Ireland during the Second World War. The region recorded 10 per cent of the total working days lost in strike action across the UK, 1939–45, yet only had 2 per cent of the total workforce.[4] The strikes of October 1942 exemplify the industrial experience of Northern Ireland during the Second World War and remain a relatively under-researched area of labour historiography. This chapter will investigate why the strikes took place, and will use them as a case study to investigate how the three components of local industrial relations – government, employers and employees – performed in conditions of 'total war'.

NORTHERN IRELAND:
'HALF-INVOLVED' IN THE WAR?

Northern Ireland had a poor war-production record prior to 1942 although it 'improved as the war went on'.[5] Nevertheless, the conduct of the province would remain troublesome for the British government for the duration of the war. The British government refused to introduce conscription in Northern Ireland during the war because of political and security concerns. Harold Wilson visited the province in December 1940 on behalf of the War Cabinet and was astonished by what he saw.[6] He was concerned that 'not enough was being done to mobilise Northern Ireland's resources for war and to bring its full workforce into employment'.[7] There was unused capacity at this critical stage and officially 72,000 remained unemployed. By contrast, the British unemployment rate was significantly lower throughout the war than Northern Ireland's. This was despite the emigration of 14,000 people to work in British factories.[8] Harold Wilson also reported that there were other serious problems in the province: local management was deemed conservative, the trade unions uncooperative and the Northern Ireland government, headed by John Millar Andrews between 1940 and 1943, was ineffective.[9] The gerontocracy which ruled the province shared much in common with Neville Chamberlain's premiership at the beginning of the war. The anaemic Northern Ireland government failed to prepare for the Blitz in Easter 1941 and the region only witnessed significant expansion of war-related production from mid-1941. These differences resulted in an accurate perception that Northern Ireland was only 'half-involved' in the war.[10]

Northern Ireland's different experience is, however, only partially true. In many respects the province had a similar war-time experience to Britain. For example, politics and society shifted to the left.[11] The Communist Party became a significant presence in the province between 1941 and 1945. The Northern Ireland Labour Party (NILP) also expanded considerably in Belfast. The ruling Ulster Unionist Party (UUP) lost a number of by-elections in the province, such as Harry Midgley's victory for the NILP in the Willowfield constituency in December 1941. Midgley won election on a strong 'win-the-war' stance and his victory has been described as 'the biggest electoral upset in Northern Ireland's political history'.[12] Despite the region's poor early war record there was significant industrial expansion. Shipbuilding and engineering expanded substantially between 1939 and 1945: shipbuilding employment approximately trebled to over 20,000, engineering increased from 14,000 to 26,000 and the aircraft industry from 5,800 to 23,500 employed.[13] A significant consequence was that the wage differential narrowed between Britain and Northern Ireland.[14] The 5 per cent unemployment rate achieved during the war was also the lowest since the inception of the State in 1921. In Britain a serious public debate in 1941 and 1942 occurred on war-related production.[15] A similar discussion took place in Northern Ireland during this period of the war. The level of war-related production was a significant concern for those who struck in Belfast in 1942. The province did have a distinctive experience of the Second World War, but it would be a mistake to see it as exceptional.

Northern Irish wartime industrial legislation fits this pattern of similar but different. The Conditions of Employment and National Arbitration Order introduced by the British government in 1940, made strike action and lockouts illegal.[16] Other legislation, such as Regulation 58A of the Emergency Powers (Defence) Act, gave the British Minister of Labour 'the authority to require individuals to register for war work and then to direct them to work under terms and conditions laid down by the Ministry'.[17] The Northern Ireland Minister of Labour was delegated the powers of Regulation 58A.[18] However, other industrial legislation did not apply in Northern Ireland, such as the Essential Work Order, 1941,[19] introduced by the British government to keep workers in jobs considered vital for war-production, such as engineering, coal, shipbuilding and steel.[20] Industrial legislation in Northern Ireland during the Second World War was, therefore, similar but different to Britain's.

Industrial relations in Belfast industry were severely strained during the war and proved to be crisis-prone. One strain was caused by the need to expand war-related production. Production at industrial establishments in Belfast in 1939 was dominated by skilled labour. Skilled employees controlled the entry of new labour into the workforce through long apprenticeships, and had considerable control over the work process. One of the methods devised to circumvent such constrictions was 'dilution'. This involved the division of complex tasks, which were usually performed by skilled labour, into simpler tasks which could be carried out by semi- and unskilled workers.[21] Trade unions did not positively endorse the process of dilution. For example, in July 1941 the Amalgamated Engineering Union (AEU) in Northern Ireland had adamantly maintained that dilution was 'unacceptable' whilst skilled workers remained unemployed throughout Ireland.[22] The Electricians' Trade Union (ETU) accepted dilution in the Belfast shipyards only in May 1942.[23] Dilution, however, also caused a number of other frictions. The entry of women into engineering and shipbuilding challenged prevalent gender conceptions about the workplace. Dilutees could be trained in one month, while other trainees continued to serve long apprenticeships. Differences in pay were another source of disquiet because of both gender and generational disparities. By 1942 dilution had progressed in Belfast industry but it had contributed to a number of frictions in the workplace.

Problems on the labour side were compounded by the poor performance of local management. Trade union officials complained of intransigent and out-dated management techniques in Belfast. Harold MacMillan visited the province in April 1941 on behalf of the British Ministry of Supply. Local trade union officials protested to MacMillan that 'employers in Northern Ireland did not cooperate with the workers or trade unions'.[24] A visit of Scottish labour inspectors in January 1942 noted the 'suspicion' which existed between employers and employees in Belfast. They noted that supervisors in industry were technically good but lacked 'the aptitude for handling manpower efficiently'. The Scottish inspectors, however, also criticised 'over-zealous trade union representatives' as a negative influence in the work place. Strident unions and poor manpower supervision were exacerbated by the inept interventions of the Northern Ireland government.[25]

The Northern Ireland government was slow to respond to negative assessments of the performance of local industry. Andrews' administration demonstrated a tendency to prioritise the claims of local management at the expense of trade unions. An internal Northern Ireland government document on 'Factors affecting production' claimed that workmen 'practically rule the roost'.[26] W.P. Kemp, the general manager of Short and Harland Belfast, claimed there was 'mob law' in the workplace and such assertions were taken at face value by the Northern Ireland government.[27] However, employees interpreted industrial relations differently. They construed legislation as unduly protective of the employer. A shop stewards' public meeting in Belfast in August 1942 complained 'in practically every instance where workers have been punished the employers have provoked the workers'.[28] The shop stewards' claim is reinforced by figures for the number of workers prosecuted for taking industrial action. Comparatively, Northern Irish workers were more likely to be prosecuted than British workers: by November 1942, 2,271 persons had been prosecuted for strike action in Northern Ireland and 2,068 persons in Britain.[29] Industrial legislation and prosecution were significant contributory factors to the October 1942 strikes. The undue weight Andrews' administration gave to employers' claims led it to dangerously under-estimate the anger of workers in Belfast in October 1942.

BELFAST, OCTOBER 1942: 'THESE STRIKES ARE A GRAVE DISCREDIT TO THE "HOME FRONT"'[30]

In October 1942 two strikes shook Belfast industry: a dispute at Mackies engineering firm and another at the Balmoral dispersal unit of Short and Harland. The Mackies dispute began on 24 September 1942 because of a decision to employ a non-trade union foreman. The ETU claimed Mackies was a 'closed shop' and refused to work with the non-trade unionist.[31] The dispute appears to have centred on the issue of trade union power to enforce a 'closed shop' in the workplace. Mackies informed the Northern Ireland Ministry of Commerce a day after the dispute began that they were not concerned and refuted the ETU's claim that the firm was a 'closed' shop.[32] The national origins of the worker, who was from Éire, may have played a contributory role in the dispute. The 'Éire worker question' was a problematic issue for the Northern Ireland government. The Stormont administration was concerned at being portrayed as drafting Southern Irish labour into the province while sending people to Britain for war work. There were scare stories in the press on the issue.[33] However, there is not enough evidence to definitively state the strike at Mackies was either solely about nationality or trade unionism. Those involved were probably motivated to some extent by both issues.

The dispute at Short and Harland was caused by the attendance at work of approximately 100 female workers on Sunday 4 October 1942 at the Balmoral dispersal unit when they were not scheduled to work. Those who attended work disagreed with the implementation of a government directive to cut back on overtime work on Sundays. The works superintendent, Herbert H. Whittaker, felt that two shop stewards who belonged to the AEU, McBrinn and McAteer, had organised the workers and fired both men on the spot. Workers responded by going on strike on 5 October 1942. The employees at Balmoral took unofficial and, therefore, illegal strike action. The strike spread to other Short and Harland factories and workplaces across Belfast. Short and Harland insisted that negotiation with the AEU would only occur once those on strike had returned to work. The firm argued that negotiating machinery – which had been legislated for by the Conditions of Employment and National Arbitration Order, 1940 – should be used to resolve the dispute.

Both strikes originated amongst a small number of workers: under 100 at Mackies and just over 100 at Balmoral. Both strikes were resolved by early November 1942: approximately 10,000 workers had been involved in industrial action and 165,000 working days had been lost.[34] Winston

Churchill was 'shocked' by the strike wave.[35] The War Cabinet felt the Northern Ireland government demonstrated weakness in dealing with the disputes.[36] The strikes took place in defiance of government, the press, the vast majority of politicians and national trade union structures. The Northern Ireland government adopted a stance of strong public support for both Mackies and Short and Harland. Privately, however, Northern Ireland government ministers upset Mackies by suggesting the foreman should be suspended from employment.[37] The Ministry of Commerce also informed the British government on 8 October 1942 that 'all those charged with the responsibility here feel that there should be no compromise.'[38] At a meeting on the same day between Northern Ireland ministers and Short and Harland it was 'definitely decided that the two shop stewards who had created the strike should not be reinstated.'[39] The danger of such an intransigent position was highlighted on 12 October 1942. A shop stewards' meeting threatened an entire closure of the port of Belfast within forty-eight hours unless some step was taken to resolve the disputes in the city.[40]

The disputes were debated at Stormont on 13 October 1942 and all those who took part in the discussion deplored the strikes.[41] Harry Midgley, NILP MP, for example, claimed that losses in production were 'wittingly or unwittingly assisting Hitler and the Nazis'. Major Robinson, a UUP MP, also claimed that 99 per cent of Northern Irish workers were loyal but that the strikes were caused by 'a lot of disloyal people trying to prevent more production intended to win the war'. The maverick independent Unionist MP J.W. Nixon responded that he and the 'men concerned' needed 'no lessons in loyalty from anyone who shook hands with or entertained [Joachim von] Ribbentrop'. However, during the debate members of the Northern Ireland government called for the employees to return to work and use negotiating machinery to resolve the issues involved. This demand was a sign of the general refusal of the Northern Ireland government to take an interventionist approach to industrial relations. J.F. Gordon, Northern Ireland Minister of Labour between 1938 and 1943, claimed he could not intervene in either strike because they were both illegal. Government refusal to intervene was given short-shrift by some MPs and the impotent reaction of the Stormont government was a significant criticism the press made at the end of the disputes.[42]

By mid-October 1942 a serious situation had developed in Belfast industry. Two separate, unofficial and illegal strikes had occurred simultaneously. The Northern Ireland government and the two firms involved adopted an intransigent attitude towards the workers' demands. Poor handling of the disputes by the government and employers inflamed the disputes. The workers, however, had also adopted a hard-line position. A joint Strike Committee was formed and issued a set of five demands. The formation of this committee marked a serious escalation of the strikes.

The five-point list of minimum demands, on which basis work would be resumed, was adopted by a mass meeting of strikers on 15 October 1942.[43] These demands were: the unconditional return of workers at Short and Harland, including the two dismissed shop stewards; the removal of the non-trade unionist from Mackies; 'the cancellation of all fines incurred by workers in recent disputes'; a response on the organisation of a committee 'to inquire into production in Northern Ireland'; and a joint committee of workers and employers representatives, under an impartial chairman, to 'settle all disputes which may arise in the future'.[44] A suggestion to march on Stormont to demand the resignation of Sir Basil Brooke, Northern Ireland Minister of Commerce, 1940 to 1943, and J.F. Gordon was 'at first greeted with enthusiasm'.[45] The Strike Committee, however, convinced the meeting against this course of action.[46] In response to the strikers' demands a *Belfast Telegraph* editorial claimed they were 'not a helpful contribution' to settlement of the dispute.[47] The editorial asserted that 'the signs multiply to show that an industrial dispute, which is illegal and unauthorised, is being made the excuse for an attack on the Northern Ireland government.'[48] Short and Harland remained adamant that it would not re-employ the two dismissed shop stewards.[49] There was no change at Mackies by 16 October. Workers at the shipyard on the same date passed a resolution which strongly condemned 'the attitude taken up by the [Northern Ireland] government in the present strike crisis.'[50] At this stage, however, the local administration began to distance itself publicly from uncritical support for the firms involved. Minister of Labour J.F. Gordon announced on 16 October 1942 that a Court of Inquiry would be appointed to ascertain the 'exact facts' in the dispute at Short and Harland.[51] It was also noted in the *Northern Whig* that an approach would be made to re-instate the two shop stewards at Short and Harland and the suspension of the non-trade unionist at Mackies, pending negotiations.[52] The Northern Ireland government may well have been split by the issue: Sir Basil Brooke noted in his diary that 'the papers unofficially say that [J.F.] Gordon has offered reinstatement [to the shop stewards]. If this is so, I feel it is a mistake.'[53]

The Court of Inquiry appointed by the Minister of Labour met on 19 and 20 October 1942.[54] The testimony of both management and employees demonstrates how bitter industrial relations were at Short and Harland. Each side blamed the other for production problems. The trade unionists, for example, claimed that management did not know the applicability of industrial legislation in the workplace. The Blitz of April and May 1941, according to the trade unionists, resulted in the 'panic dispersal' of factories, such as Balmoral, which contributed later to production problems. Management replied that shop stewards were responsible for industrial problems. Walter Browning, general works manager for Short and Harland Belfast, claimed he was made aware that for a 'considerable time' there had been increasing trouble 'caused by either inefficient or over-zealous shop stewards'. However, Samuel Gibson, senior foreman at the Balmoral unit did admit that 'yes, there are some occasions when a shop steward can be and is of assistance to a foreman and there are other occasions when they definitely are not.' Acrimonious division between management and employees at Short and Harland was not a conducive context to maximising war production.

There were also important political and social divisions between each side at Short and Harland. It was claimed, for example, that management called staff 'Irish pigs'. It was also alleged that individuals in the management of Short and Harland were members of a pro-Nazi organisation 'The Link'.

Management, in response, stated that shop stewards at Short and Harland acted in a 'domineering' fashion. A foreman maintained that he was intimidated by a shop steward who told him 'after the war the likes of you and thousands of others like you will be slaughtered by the thousand.' Sibald Treacy, who worked in the planning office of Short and Harland, refused to accept a request from shop stewards for a higher price for a set amount of work and stated 'any man who require[s] any more incentive to produce to assist the nation to victory in time of war is a lousy bastard.' Sloan, a shop steward, responded to Treacy during the Inquiry that 'I happen to have a brother-in-law seriously wounded and three brothers wounded, and [all] fought in the last war a much younger man than Mr Treacy. I suggest that if he wants to call anybody a lousy bastard that he was one if he didn't fight in 1914–18.' The testimony at the Court of Inquiry demonstrates a workplace seriously and acrimoniously divided.

The Court of Inquiry concluded that the strike was unofficial, therefore, illegal and deplorable. It recommended a works conference and if this was done all the workers – excluding the two shop stewards – should be re-employed without victimisation. Trade union officials at the Court were not impressed. James Morrow (AEU shop steward at Short and Harland and chair of the Strike Committee) warned that if the two shop stewards were not re-instated then the shipyard would be shut down. W.P. Kemp, local manager of Short and Harland Belfast, eventually relented and offered to re-employ the two shop stewards in another section of the firm as long as they guaranteed to refrain from union activities. The union officials agreed to put this offer to those on strike. However, James Morrow pertinently warned that 'I am chairman of the [Strike] Committee and as such it will be my duty to conduct a meeting when it is held. I have no reason to believe that even the suggested arrangement will be agreed to.'

On 22 October a mass meeting of those on strike in Belfast passed a resolution 'by an overwhelming majority' to reject the employers offer 'in toto'.[55] The decision of the strikers was greeted with astonishment and condemnation. The *Belfast Newsletter* called it a 'deplorable decision'.[56] The

Belfast Telegraph unconvincingly argued that 'every step they have taken, from the calling of the strike to the formulation of dictatorial demands, has argued a weak case.'[57] The workers' threat to shut down Belfast now seemed imminent and the strikes spread. On 27 October men 'at an important establishment' and maintenance engineers on the trams and buses in Belfast took strike action.[58] The 'important establishment' is probably a reference to Harland and Wolff. As the escalation developed further the management of each firm relented. Both shop stewards at Short and Harland were re-employed.[59] A few days later it was reported that agreement was reached at Mackies on the non-trade unionist employee and 'machinery had been laid down for dealing with any future problems.'[60] By 30 October 1942 workers began to return to work.[61] Those who struck had won an important industrial struggle and during the course of the disputes a shop stewards' movement was organised across Belfast.[62]

THE SIGNIFICANCE OF THE BELFAST DISPUTES: INDUSTRIAL RELATIONS, TRADE UNIONS AND GENDER

The October 1942 disputes demonstrate that local management, at times, handled labour problems poorly. Employees claimed at the Court of Inquiry that the employers were applying 1922 conditions to 1942.[63] Employers and management felt they retained the managerial prerogative in the workplace. In a strictly legal sense this was true, but the supervisory functions of management were qualified during the Second World War. There were, for example, substantial legal restrictions on the uninhibited right of management in the workplace. Government legislation to direct labour meant firms could be forced to employ labour. The new industrial strength of employees also meant management prerogatives were circumscribed. Similarly, the necessity for all-out war production meant that the profit-motive was impinged by another objective. David Edgerton has stated that the war killed laissez-faire as a policy, but that capitalism was maintained.[64] The Second World War meant employees and their representatives also had to be kept informed of production decisions. Liaison between management and employees occurred through works conferences and Joint Production Committees (JPC). The small number of JPCs in Northern Irish industry by 1942 is indicative of the lack of priority given by unions or management to cooperative industrial relations.[65]

The poor performance of local management was matched by a Northern Ireland government which lacked an accurate understanding of industrial relations in Belfast. The Andrews' administration displayed an inability to correctly judge the mood of industrial workers during these disputes. Early in the disputes Sir Basil Brooke, Northern Ireland Minister of Commerce, and the Minister of Labour J.F. Gordon both adopted an intransigent public position of support for the employers. On 14 October 1942 Brooke described the disputes as in 'defiance of all constituted authority, including the trade unions, and it will have to be fought out'.[66] The disputes could conceivably have been settled earlier had the Northern Ireland government been more sensitive to the employee side. J.W. Nixon, independent Unionist MP, commented at Stormont 'when that report [on the Balmoral dispute] is read no fair-minded man will have any difficulty in coming to the conclusion that tactful handling of the situation on the first day would have prevented any strike'.[67] The government's role was also highlighted by W.P. Kemp at the Court of Inquiry. The general manager, after offering to re-employ the two shop stewards, stated 'I have had to weigh things up with great deliberation to make sure I am not contravening their [the British and Northern Ireland government] wishes, and I almost might say their instructions'.[68] Evidence from Sir Basil Brooke's diary reinforces Kemp's contention.[69] The Stormont administration lacked a figure, such as Ernest Bevin in the British Cabinet, who wielded significant clout amongst trade unionists. The appointment of Harry Midgley as Minister of Public Security in May 1943 by the new Northern Ireland Prime Minister Sir Basil Brooke was an attempt to address such weakness.[70]

Trade unions in Belfast at this time were in a strong position. For example, by 1943 the number of trade unionists in Northern Ireland had doubled since 1938.[71] Unions across Britain and Ireland were invigorated by government legislation which encouraged collective bargaining. Skilled unions, such as the AEU, were changed by growth of membership and the relaxation of pre-war work practices. The strength of the workers' position is attested to by the decision to adjourn the prosecution of sixty-four strikers from a prior dispute, at the end of October 1942.[72] There was, however, no automatic correlation between stronger unions and left-wing politics. J.W. Nixon, independent Unionist MP, strongly supported the workers' actions. Similarly, the nationality of the non-trade unionist at Mackies implies a heightened sense of British national identity in Belfast. The evidence from October 1942 is ambiguous: there is strong evidence of both a 'militant economistic'[73] understanding in the workplace and, also, increased British national consciousness.

The men and women who struck faced a barrage of criticism: at Stormont they were described as 'disloyal' and 'wittingly or unwittingly assisting Hitler'.[74] In mid-October Harry Midgley condemned the extension of the strikes as motivated by 'a degree of irresponsibility, almost criminal'.[75] These condemnations do not, however, fit with the available evidence about why workers took strike action in Belfast. For example, a public meeting organised by shop stewards was advertised in the local press with the exhortation 'God save the King'.[76] Two of the trade union representatives were highly critical of managers at Short and Harland for their failure to serve militarily during the First World War. Similarly, the role of the independent Unionist MP J.W. Nixon as the most important advocate for those on strike does not point to a 'subversive' motivation amongst strikers. Moderate criticism of the Northern Ireland government was often enough to imply 'subversive' intention.

The disputes also highlight ambiguities about the 'People's war'. This concept was deployed both to describe the international fight against the Axis powers and how the Second World War was waged by the Allied nations. 'People's war' facilitated the co-operation of widely disparate groups in society during the war: for example, Sir Basil Brooke and Communists.[77] The term assisted an armistice in domestic politics but it did not fundamentally resolve social and political divisions. Different social groups and actors interpreted the term in different ways. At the Court of Inquiry some employees demonstrated a clear commitment to the war on the basis of their identity as trade unionists.[78] The waging of 'People's war' also resulted in a form of British patriotism that was class conscious and this was reflected politically and industrially in Northern Ireland.[79] This interpretation helps contextualise how an extreme Unionist politician like J.W. Nixon could be more supportive of strike action than Harry Midgley of the NILP.

The participation of female workers in the disputes is also important. One hundred female workers were involved in initiating the strike at Short and Harland. Significantly, however, the role of women is not displayed explicitly throughout the strike. The vast majority of evidence mentions only men being involved in the dispute: a single female worker gave evidence at the Court of Inquiry; all other participants were men.[80] Female employment went up absolutely during the war. For example, in 1939 there were 250 female engineering workers in Northern Ireland, by 1943 12,300.[81] A concomitant was increased numbers of female trade unionists. In 1936 there were 11,372 female trade unionists in Northern Ireland (in British and Northern Irish-based unions); by 1945 there were 23,588 female trade unionists.[82] Unions, especially those rooted in craft-based production such as the AEU, did not allow female members until the Second World War. The AEU allowed female membership in January 1943.[83] It was admitted at the Court of Inquiry that no union officially represented the female workers, but the AEU at Balmoral agreed to act on their behalf.[84] Workers' representatives at the Court of Inquiry raised issues of welfare facilities, contraception in the workplace and language around female employees. The above evidence suggests heavily-gendered conceptions of the workplace still dominated amongst unions and employees. Due to the impact of the Second World War these views were under challenge socially, politically and industrially. For example, Communists in Belfast campaigned for equal pay for women during 1942.[85] Tom Boyd, a trade union activist, claimed that the Second World War liberated women from attitudes which had been prevalent pre-

1939.[86] The subject, however, of female trade unionism in Northern Ireland during the Second World War awaits a definitive study.

CONCLUSION

Industrial relations in Belfast during the Second World War were severely strained. Local management and the Northern Ireland government were unable to deal with a newly assertive workforce. It is reasonable to conclude that those involved in the disputes in 1942 felt that strike action was a way to *both* improve production for the war-effort and assert employee power in the workplace. Despite the claim of contemporaries there is no evidence to suggest that those who struck in October 1942 were 'wittingly' assisting Hitler. Industrial legislation was used as a solution to workplace trouble and this was a significant contributory factor to the disputes. However, the strikes highlighted serious deficiencies in such an approach. J.C. MacDermott, Northern Ireland Attorney-General, in the aftermath of the October 1942 disputes felt that the Conditions of Employment and National Arbitration Order, 1940 should be repealed because it had failed to deter mass strike action.[87] The constituents of Northern Irish industrial relations – government, employers and employees – failed to resolve the strains caused by the Second World War. Sir Basil Brooke's new Northern Ireland government from mid-1943 did not fare much better and this is demonstrated by the May 1944 Belfast munitions strike which dwarfed the disputes of October 1942.[88]

1. 'Freedom's Martyrs. Members of the Irish Women Workers' Union who suffered terms of imprisonment in the cause of Labour'. Taken at Liberty Hall, c. 1914. Delia Larkin seated front row, centre. This image is reproduced courtesy of the National Library of Ireland, KE 204.

2. The National Executive of the Irish Trades Union Congress, 1914. Back row, standing L-R: James Connolly, William O'Brien, Michael J. Egan, Thomas Cassidy, W.E. Hill, Richard O'Carroll. Front row, seated, L-R: Thomas MacPartlin, David R. Campbell, Patrick T. Daly, James Larkin, Michael J. O'Lehane. Thomas Johnson, not pictured, was also part of the National Executive.

3. Proclamation banning proposed demonstration on Sackville Street, Dublin, 31 August 1913. The baton charge that ensued on that day earned it the name 'Bloody Sunday'. This image is reproduced courtesy of the National Library of Ireland, EPH L.

4. 'The Assinine Law'. Illustration by Ernest Kavanagh in the *Irish Worker*, 14 September 1912. This image is reproduced courtesy of the National Library of Ireland.

5. 'We Serve Neither King Nor Kaiser, But Ireland!' The Irish Citizen Army outside Liberty Hall. This image is reproduced courtesy of the National Library of Ireland, KE 198.

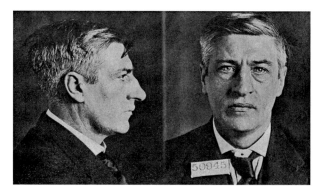

6. New York State Police photo of Jim Larkin, arrested 8 November 1919 on a charge of 'criminal anarchy'.

7. Miners in Butte, Montana.

ANTI-CONSCRIPTION PLEDGE.

The following is a copy of the Pledge:—

"Denying the right of the British Government to enforce Compulsory Service in this Country *we pledge ourselves solemnly to one another to resist Conscription* by the most effective means at our disposal."

8. Irish Anti-Conscription Pledge during the First World War. This image is reproduced courtesy of the National Library of Ireland, EPH E103.

9. 'We Demand Open Inquiry Into Scandal Of Artane Tragedy'. The *Workers' Voice*, newspaper of the Communist Party of Ireland, highlights the death of John Byrne in an industrial school in 1935.

10. Corporation Buildings, 'a blatant attempt to house the very poor'. The scene of police brutality during a raid in 1913 which resulted in the death of John McDonagh, they also gave rise to the 'Animal Gang' in the 1930s.

11. Female munitions workers in Belfast, 1941. The war resulted in increased opportunities for women, helping to redefine traditional gender roles.

12. Munster Bar, the winners of the Waterford Pubs League, 1971. L-R: John Toms (Captain, Munster Bar), Jimmy Searson (Chairman, Waterford Junior Football League), Carl Bowe (Guinness representative, Waterford).

13. Female textile workers in Cork's Sunbeam-Wolsey factory, 1940s.

14. Joe Heaney, one of Ireland's most accomplished seán-nos singers. 'The Rocks of Bawn' was one of his many recordings.

15. Robert Noonan, better known under his pen-name Robert Tressell, author of *The Ragged Trousered Philanthropists*. His work, though widely acclaimed in Britain, has been neglected along with other working-class writers in Ireland.

Chapter Nine

'The Brightest Couple of Hours': The Factory, Inter-House, Inter-Firm and Pubs Leagues of Ireland, 1922–73[1]

David Toms

During a 1930 Dáil debate on the Gaelic Athletic Association's (GAA)[2] exemption from Entertainments Tax, Thomas O'Higgins, Cumann na nGaedhael TD for Dublin North since the previous year, was compelled to state:

> [The exemption] to a very slight extent, betters the position of other forms of football and we cannot forget ... that the very poorest people in our cities are followers of Association football, that possibly the brightest couple of hours or the only bright couple of hours, that they have in the whole week are when they get off on Saturday afternoon to see an Association football match.[3]

Association football, or 'soccer' in many countries, is the most widely-played ball-game of the past 150 years. Reflecting the dominance of industrial towns and cities in the game's formative years in Britain 'the map of the Football League', writes Eric Hobsbawm, 'was virtually identical with the map of industrial England'.[4] Teams were often founded from the workplace, such as the Thames Ironworks from which developed West Ham United, and the munitions works at Woolwich from which came Arsenal. These teams would compete with each other in leagues often created, initially at least, around the workplace. These practices were mirrored in Ireland, and would encompass not just soccer, but also Gaelic games, athletics, table tennis, basketball and even pitch and putt.[5] The 'brightest couple of hours' extends not just as a metaphor; for working people in Ireland, it is an indicator of the stretching summer evenings when they could play sports, when the hours were indeed brightest. This chapter will consider what were variously called factory, inter-firm or inter-house leagues; all three terms denoting the same thing: sports leagues based around the place of work, usually the factory. More often than not, these leagues were played during the summer, when the 'regular' sporting season was in recess.

The main focus of this chapter will be soccer and GAA leagues of this kind. They will be presented side by side, rather than discretely as they shared many similarities in their founding, running and function. These leagues were an important social outlet and engendered a collective spirit of fun and solidarity among workers, as the following quote from a 1978 commemorative booklet on the history of the Galway Inter-Firm Hurling League illustrates:

> Gone are the frustrations of the working day. It is very much a case of all for one and one for all and as the competition gets on its way the results and performances are largely the topic of conversation as workers commute or at tea-break or just any place on the factory floor. The whole business engenders solidarity and breeds happiness instead of dissension.[6]

This chapter will provide an overview of the development of these leagues, as well as other important related competitions such as pub leagues and the 'Tops of the Towns', using Waterford as a case study for much of the chapter.

WORKS TEAMS AT THE NATIONAL LEVEL

Many of the earliest soccer clubs in the Irish League (founded in 1890) and the subsequent League of Ireland (founded in 1921) had their roots in factories – Lisburn Distillery in Antrim, St James' Gate, Jacobs, and Transport in Dublin, and Fordson's in Cork for example.[7] Naturally, not everyone was capable or interested in playing the game to this high level but the popularity and success of these factory teams at the highest level is crucial for understanding the subsequent popularity of soccer in these places. Soccer was especially connected to the working class of Dublin, the most industrialised city in the Free State. In his autobiography, the politician Todd Andrews noted of Dublin's social classes that 'at the bottom of the heap were the have-nots of the city, consisting of labourers, dockers, coal heavers, shop attendants, messenger boys and domestic servants … they had scarcely any amusement outside the pubs or an occasional soccer match at Dalymount Park [home of Bohemians FC] or Shelbourne Park [home of Shelbourne FC].'[8] As well as their League of Ireland teams, Dublin clubs like Jacobs and St James' Gate also had teams playing soccer in the Leinster Senior League.

Beyond Dublin – in Cork, Waterford and Limerick where there was a growing working class, soccer's development continued. Between 1922 and 1939, all three cities went from having no representatives in the League of Ireland to one each. Of the three, Fordson's of Cork was organised around a factory. The club, founded five years after the Ford marina plant was established in 1917, had joined the League of Ireland at the beginning of the 1924/25 season on the back of their impressive displays in local leagues and national competitions; they went on to beat Shamrock Rovers in the Free State Challenge Cup in March of 1926.[9] Named for the tractor model which was the plant's main output they were known as the 'Tractor Boys' extending their association, not just to Ford, but the output of local workers. In four short years they went from playing locally to winning the blue riband of Irish soccer. Similarly, Waterford Celtic's success saw them transforming into Waterford FC in 1930. Attempts in Waterford to organise the game on a work-based footing were put in place just as Waterford FC began establishing themselves in the League of Ireland.[10] Those looking for something more informal had competition between workers from individual factories, like at Ford in Cork where an in-house tournament of several teams competing for a set of medals developed.[11] The success of local teams at national level enhanced the popularity of the game among the working class and encouraged the development of local factory leagues.

1931–1946: BEGINNINGS OF THE LOCAL FACTORY LEAGUES – A MUNSTER CASE STUDY

Despite the failed attempt in 1931 to establish an Employers' League for soccer in Waterford to supplement the existing competitions of the Waterford and District Football League, soccer flourished there, a factory league eventually starting in 1936.[12] The first mention of the factory league in the local newspaper in 1938 relates that the League was set up in the 1936/37 season. At that time there were ten teams involved including the Foundry and John Hearne's. When the new Waterford and North Munster Football League was established in 1937 it also included a factory section.[13] In Cork, the GAA had an inter-house league, essentially the same as a factory league with teams from different factories competing, in 1936, and in one report of a game, former All-Ireland winning captain Eudie Coughlan felt that if more interest was taken in the league, it would greatly improve Cork's chances in the coming All-Ireland Hurling and Gaelic Football Championships.[14] In Tralee by 1938 there was also a Gaelic football factory league, the final won that year by the Tile Yard when they beat the Boot Factory team 2-2 to 1-3 at Austin Stack Park.[15] Limerick GAA had its factory league too which was 'arousing remarkable interest and arousing good crowds for every match. Enthusiasm has reached a high pitch in the various city establishments' with the chance of seeing inter-county players in action forming a large part of the attraction for the public attending the matches. According to the report in *The Kerryman* some nineteen teams were competing, split into three divisions.[16] Many of these were the major employers in the city of Limerick at the time, so there was considerable public interest.

Soccer was growing in Limerick with a team playing in the League of Ireland from 1937; that a factory league followed is not surprising. One round of fixtures in the *Limerick Leader* from 1939 show a similar interest in soccer in workplaces with Gaelic football teams.[17] By August of 1939, the Limerick Gaelic football factory league was being wrapped up too with the section B final taking place between Ranks and the ESB (Electricity Supply Board).[18]

The outbreak of the Second World War – known in independent Ireland as 'The Emergency' – did not stop factory leagues from continuing on their business in the first half of the 1940s, with some even expanding. In Waterford in 1940, Waterford and North Munster Football League secretary Willie Toms noted that some forty-six clubs were affiliated for the coming season of which eleven were for the factory league.[19] In Limerick, the return of the factory league season in 1942 was promoted with a match between Cannocks and Todds, which played heavily on the declining living conditions experienced during the Second World War:

> The inter-house league is beginning to stir again. To stimulate interest, Cannocks have accepted the challenge of Todds, and the 'elevens' will appear at the Markets Field on to-morrow week. The 'goods' in the soccer line, from these monster houses, will be on view, and the attendance should be large. They won't 'ration' the football and no 'coupons' are required.[20]

The worsening economic situation of the country was taking its toll on the inter-house league in Limerick, with one round-up noting in 1944 that

> The Committee has a grievance! It has come to their notice that objections have been raised to collections at inter-house

games. Despite this, they have no other option but to continue their appeal for funds. The welfare of the competitions depends primarily on the support from the spectators, but it should be realised that their appeal is not a demand. It is a well-known fact that many of the fans cannot spare a copper or two, but at the same time there is a hearty welcome for them at Caledonian Park.[21]

Such a state of affairs amongst Limerick's working class is not surprising, given the conditions of the time.

1946–1959: EXPANSION

Interest expanded after the Second World War as factory-based team sports diversified in the 1950s. In part this may at least be explained by the fact that there were relatively few private pursuits at the end of the working day and so people passed their time with a greater variety of public amusements. This was still an Ireland that was as yet unchanged by the coming of television, and an era marked in some places by high emigration.[22] For all that, across the country, there was an explosion in the organisation of the factory leagues in one sport or another. As well as the establishment of a hurling factory league in Galway in 1954,[23] factory league GAA began to make its mark in Meath, Westmeath and Cavan thanks to the Leinster Factory League during the 1950s, a sign that the platform for the economic success of the 1960s was being built as industry expanded out from its traditional centres.[24] Another important development for inter-firm sport in Ireland was the establishment of Córas Iompar Éireann (CIÉ) in 1945 which amalgamated all the major railway and omnibus companies in the country. This huge workforce soon took to organising sport on both a local and national level in GAA. Such were the numbers employed in CIÉ that in the Inter-Depot GAA Competition, Cork was able to field eight teams in 1950.[25] The same went for Limerick, where CIÉ-man Ned Fitzgibbon was a founder of the GAA Inter-Firm

League in that city in 1954.[26] Although it fell away in Waterford's soccer calendar during 'The Emergency', the factory league was back on the agenda by 1947, with the *Munster Express* noting that in Waterford the factory league was a somewhat misleading name for the competition since various trades and professions also competed.[27] The new league would commence with seventeen teams, which as one report noted would cause 'a pretty jam' in the fixture list.[28]

The inter-house league, as it was called in this period, was going from strength to strength in Waterford, with the Printers side inviting the team of The Irish Press Ltd to a challenge match to be played in 1949.[29] In total for the 1950 inter-house league, there were fifteen teams in the top two divisions, one of eight and the other of seven, out of a total of sixty affiliated sides across five divisions according to the secretary of the Waterford and District Football League at their annual general meeting that year.[30] This, along with the possibility of a football ground for the newly-formed football club of Henry Denny & Sons, bringing the total of soccer pitches in Waterford to five, was a considerable indication of the game's popularity in the south-east as well as the interest and impact of the inter-house league.[31] In 1952, there were some twenty-two entrants into the league, in two divisions of ten teams and twelve. Most of the city's major employers were represented in both divisions.[32] One fixture, between Denny's and Clover Meats was referred to tongue-in-cheek by the *Munster Express* as 'the clash of the ham slashers'.[33] Denny's were beaten in the final that year by Snowcream United, but this was not the end of their season. Less than a week later they were in action against a Denny's side from Cork as part of a double-bill of challenge matches. The Denny's side from Cork included Florrie Burke, then captain of League of Ireland side Cork Athletic and an Irish international. The other game on that bill was Waterford Bohemians taking on a selected CIÉ side which included players from League of Ireland side Transport FC.[34]

The success of the Leinster Factory Hurling League saw feelers put out for a similar league by the Waterford GAA county board, after a match was played between a Printers side and a CIÉ side.[35] Some thirteen sides were involved that summer in the new hurling league, and there was a considerable cross-over between the workplaces represented in this new league with those in the soccer league. Split into three divisions of four, four and five, the teams competing in the new hurling league were as follows: Printers, Glass Factory, Denny's, CIÉ, Clover Meats, Paper Mills, Foundry, Graves', Commercials, Builders, Mental Hospital, Goodbody's Jute Factory, and Local Authorities.[36] The inaugural final was between Clover Meats and the Builders team.[37] The success of the hurling league in Waterford ensured that it would carry on for another year, with a balance in hand of £33 14s 9 ½d.[38] Waterford teams also took part in the Munster hurling league, created in 1953.[39]

The Showband era was just kicking off, a development born of infatuation with the glamour of post-war rock 'n' roll music emanating from the United States which captivated young Irish men and women, and the continued success of Waterford's factory soccer league was boosted when it was announced that popular Showband musician Chick Smith would play the factory league dinner dance later that summer.[40] There were no such musical delights for Portlaw Tanners who were barred from being in the soccer league in 1953 because travelling to play them was proving too costly for other teams, while their hurling team were sweeping all before them in the hurling league.[41] The Waterford Builders were the ones with the most success in hurling, reaching the Munster final of the new Munster Factory League, playing against Ranks' of Limerick on 1 November. It was a struggle for the Builders to even get to the match since many of the team had been recently unemployed and were in need of financial aid from the county board to help pay for their travel expenses.[42] These factory teams were not funded by their management as a way of promoting the workplaces like those in the League of Ireland had been. Largely independent, they had to pay their own subscriptions to the leagues they competed in (the soccer league in Waterford was 3 guineas a team) and as with the Builders, their own travel expenses. Nevertheless, the overall success of the hurling league encouraged the creation of a Gaelic football league also and both would compete in 1954's Munster Factory League.[43]

The Waterford soccer factory league was also going from strength to strength, as some thirty sides submitted their names for 1954's summer competition.[44] Despite this, rancour developed within the Waterford and District Football League over the season's extended length with so many competitions – the usual local, provincial and national league and cup fixtures in the traditional winter season followed by the factory league, and so the factory league fell victim to this congestion.[45] The differences in popularity between the soccer and GAA factory leagues were significant; even though in 1955 the soccer league in Waterford was dispensed with, the previous year some thirty teams took part while the Waterford hurling Factory League only had twelve teams in 1955. The hurling league too however, was dispensed with and both soccer and hurling fans had to contend themselves with short-lived cup tournaments until the re-launch of a factory football league for the 1956/57 season, and a hurling factory league in the summer of 1958.[46] That same summer, plans were made to restrict entry to the soccer tournament to just twenty teams to ensure the competition did not run on with meaningless matches.[47] In the end, twenty-four teams in four groups of six teams each competed.[48] The teams in the league changed little from previous years. The stability of the workplace and the fact that people remained in their jobs longer meant that factory league teams could enter year after year without much change.[49]

1960–1973: THE PUBS LEAGUE AND THE TOPS OF THE TOWN

The 1960s have gained a reputation for being something of a golden period in Irish economic and social life. The huge number of people then employed in industrial work is reflected in the increasingly large numbers taking part in the factory leagues during the period. The GAA, a body with considerable organisational nous had by this time county, provincial as well as All-Ireland structures for factory leagues. For soccer, things were more ad-hoc, being the product of local impetus rather than a nationally organised competition.

In-west Cork, a Gaelic football factory league established itself and in 1962 it was won by the Ballyclough Creamery who beat Mallow Sugar Factory by a score of 4-9 to 0-5.[50] For the factories of Roscrea, County Tipperary, the Munster Factory Hurling League remained the main competition throughout the 1960s with the bacon factory, Antigen, and Meat Products all variously beating teams throughout the province including Ford's of Cork, Waterford Glass, Shannon Diamond Co., the Chipboard factory from Scariff, County Clare, and Rippon amongst many others.[51] Another inter-firms league was established in Listowel, County Kerry in 1969 with the local Shops, Jowika, Farmers, and a Combined Garages, ESB and Creamery side all competing with proceeds of the matches and league going towards funds for the North Kerry Old Folks Home.[52] Surprisingly for Kerry, there was even inter-firms competition organised in soccer with teams from Knitwear, Kingdom Tubes, Kerryman, Dennys, CWS, CBS, Abbey Inn, Merchants, Sean O'Connor's, and Clerks.[53] Killarney also had its own inter-firms league,[54] while the Tralee soccer inter-firms league was continuing to grow, with some fifteen teams entering in the summer of 1970.[55] At the same time as that tournament was kicking off in Tralee, Scariff's Chipboard factory in County Clare were making waves in the Munster Factory League, getting to the final after betting E.I. Shannon on top of their victory over the Waterford Glass in the first round.[56] Just as the Tralee Gaelic football league was getting underway, calls for a seven-a-side inter-firm soccer league were being made in the same town.[57] This drew interest from some thirty-two teams in the first round – a huge number in a staunch Gaelic footballing community.[58] The final of the inter-firm Gaelic football league between Civil Services and either Liebherr or Builders was to be the curtain raiser at the annual Whit Sunday football tournament in Killarney in June of 1971.[59] That year saw a further expansion of the Tralee inter-firms soccer league and the increased activity necessitated the founding of a town board to ensure its proper running.[60] This was again followed by the seven-a-side tournament, restricted to thirty-two teams in total that year.[61] The increased popularity of playing soccer in this period was likely aided by the deletion of the ban on GAA athletes playing foreign games, which was stricken from the Association rules in 1971.

With the popularity of factory leagues growing, new leagues were also organised. The Pubs League, a Waterford innovation, comprising city-centre pubs, was first organised in 1966. As a site of social interaction, the pub was often central to the lives of working-class people over the course of the twentieth century in Ireland. Elizabeth Malcolm has written that 'one of the principal centres of popular culture in Ireland today is the public house. The pub, in both town and country, is the focus of working-class social life . . . a place to meet, to drink, to eat, to conduct business, to make friends . . . or simply to pass the time.'[62] Injury was an ever present worry to players in such leagues, as it might mean missing work. One of the first mentions of the Pub League in the *Munster Express* highlights these concerns. We are told of an injured player who 'has a young family, three children in all, and they are now feeling the pinch of his long unemployment . . . his affairs are at the lowest ebb'. The author of the piece urges 'If we let down one of our own in this instance, it's going to lower our nationwide reputation for sportsmanship and generosity.'[63]

Such dangers to personal health notwithstanding, the new pub league was immensely popular – just as popular in fact as the factory league, but was 'supposed to be a light-hearted competition and the rules must be designed to retain the light-heartedness as far as practicable.'[64] A meeting was held in the city's Municipal Library to determine the rules of eligibility, and according to the *Munster Express*'s soccer correspondent 'it will undoubtedly be stressed that pubs should select their teams from their own customers and not go recruiting outsiders, and especially non-drinkers, for the purpose of this kind of unfair "packing".'[65] The rules for the league were highly specific with a minimum requirement of four players over 35 years of age. Entrance to the league was set at £1 per team.[66] Although popular, it was nevertheless the focus of an attack at the 1967 AGM of the Waterford and District Football League despite both the Pubs League and Factory League being instrumental that year for maintaining the finances of the Waterford and District Football

League. Indeed, there had been thirty-eight entries into the Factory League that year.[67] The attack on both leagues is a fine example of the antagonisms that can exist in any voluntary organisation where the interests of different subsections clash; those in the more traditional roles of the general committee concerned about the running of the traditional winter-season fixture list than the more informal, if popular, summer-time factory and pubs leagues. The bulk of teams in the Pubs League were from the city centre, with some from the countryside and Wexford.[68] Their prize was the Phoenix Cup, donated by Phoenix Ale, brewed in Cherry's.[69] The Pubs League was much looked forward to again in 1968, with still more wrangling over eligibility (some teetotallers had slipped through the tight regulations), as was the factory league which had forty-five applicants. Such large numbers caused something of a headache for the organising committee since it contained nearly every single industrial and service employer in the city and surrounding area.[70] Making sure that fixtures were arranged and played in a timely fashion when such large numbers were involved was no mean feat. The pubs league was a smaller affair, with thirty-nine pubs taking part.[71]

That year's final was between the Munster Bar and Doyle's. The Munster won, and spurred on by their victory that summer, the following year we learn 'already, the present champions, The Munster, and former champions, Walsh's of Ballybricken are into their stride with trials and friendlies lined up to have them fully tuned when the competition gets under way.' As the correspondent for the paper put it 'this is now a deadly-earnest, keenly-contested and highly-prized championship and the rules that were intended to keep the spirit of fun should now be discarded and let the best horse jump the ditch – so to speak.'[72] There were 'rumblings that quite a few premises feel that the competition is getting altogether too professional and that it's nearly time to revert to its original form of a "bit of gas for the customers".'[73] The Munster Bar started their season as defending champions winning the Gallwey Cup, a charity game to start the new pubs league season. The final was contested by Keane's and Caulfield's, going to a replay which Keane's eventually won 2-0.[74]

By 1972, the pubs league had grown elsewhere in Munster with Cork and Limerick establishing leagues, and a new competition called the Smithwick Inter-Cities Pub Competition. Waterford pub Graces were drawn to play against The Bell Tavern of Limerick with the winners to play Cork Pubs League champions in Turner's Cross, Cork city. As ever, with pub league season approaching, the usual trouble was brewing over eligibility and transfer of players from one pub to another. The soccer correspondent of the *Munster Express* poked fun at the latter, writing 'there will be some major surprises in the line out of one local team in the forthcoming Pub League. Rumour has it that one over-35 is getting a transfer to De Lacey's from a neighbouring pub for a fee of 6 large bottles.'[75] In 1973, the largest number of pubs yet took part with forty teams entered into the competition in Waterford. That year in Carrick-on-Suir, a pubs league was established by the local soccer team, Carrick United. The competition's spread shows what a centre of social interaction the pub then was in Ireland.[76] It provides a window into working-class culture in Ireland in the twentieth century: the Pubs League was a sporting outlet for friends whose lives were organised around the traditional centres of their communities. Emmet O'Connor has written that in Waterford, 'live variety was popularized after 1962 by the phenomenally successful Tops of the Town. [It] illustrates the degree to which social being sprang from the communities created by the factories; the entries read like a litany for industrial life. Working class Waterford was indeed a "factory town".'[77] The same litany can be found in the teams of the factory leagues and the pubs leagues. The Tops, a variety show of comedy, musical and dance numbers, should be seen as an extension of the communities fostered in the sporting factory league. First organised in 1962 by the De La Salle Brothers fundraising for St Stephen's Street school, the prize was £100, and a trophy fabricated by the Waterford Glass. Entries were nearly identical to the factory soccer and hurling leagues.[78] This crossover between the two was in personnel as well as the workplaces, like 'Tommy Fitzgerald (of City soccer fame) a versatile compere even though his opening shot was the unusual one of "golfer".'[79] This crossover goes some way in showing how working-class

Waterford people spent their leisure time. The Tops continued, growing into a national phenomenon, sponsored by cigarette company Player & Wills. By 1973, the final was being held in the Gaiety Theatre and there was national prize money of £500 for winners and £400 for runners-up. Local heats were put on in towns across the country.[80] Not losing sight of its original aims, the proceeds went to locally-based charities.[81]

CONCLUSION

As Ireland entered a new era on joining the European Economic Community in 1973, the various leagues continued in one form or another for a further twenty-five years or so in working-class communities across the country. For many of these leagues however, their heyday was the 1950s, 1960s and 1970s. Changes in Irish life and culture had a huge impact especially on how and where working-class people spent their leisure time, summer evenings and summer holidays. These factory teams and leagues existed in both the good and the bad times. They grabbed hold of the imagination of working people from Dublin to Galway, Waterford to Tralee, in Cork and Killarney, Limerick and Roscrea, Carrick-on-Suir and Scariff. This chapter has shown that sport as a part of working-class life in Ireland was connected with the two chief institutions of adult life in Ireland at that time: work and the pub. Importantly, people's formation of teams was of their own accord and the use of their factory name was not an official dispensation from management but a reflection of their common bond as workmates. People really got behind these teams. That they could organise such competitions of their own accord and see that they continued to run successfully for many years is a great testament to the abilities of working-class people. E.P. Thompson wondered 'if the purposive notation of time-use becomes less compulsive, then people might have to re-learn some of the arts of living lost in the industrial revolution: how to fill … their day with enriched, more leisurely, personal and social relations; how to break down once more the barriers between work and life.'[82] This chapter has shown people blurring the boundary of work and life through these leagues that they played in and organised themselves; the result of the sociability of work rather than being the result of top-down benevolence so often associated with sport and the workplace. Whether on the pitch, in the pub or under stage-lights, in a working-week these were the brightest couple of hours.

Chapter Ten

'I Never Would Return Again to Plough the Rocks of Bawn': Irishmen in Post-War Britain[1]

Sara Goek

Come all you loyal heroes wherever that you be
Don't work for any master, 'til you know what your work will be,
For you must rise up early, from clear daylight 'til dawn
And I'm afraid you'll never be able to plough the rocks of Bawn.

Oh rise up lovely Sweeney and give your horse some hay
And give him a good feed of oats, before you go away
Don't feed him on soft turnip, put him out on your green lawn
Or I'm afraid he'll never be able to plough the rocks of Bawn.

And my curse attend you Sweeney, you have me nearly robbed
You're sitting by the fireside with a *duidín* in your gob
You're sitting by the fireside from clear daylight 'til dawn
And I'm afraid you'll never be able to plough the rocks of Bawn.

And my shoes they are well worn now, my stockings they are thin
My heart is always trembling, afraid I might give in

My heart is always trembling, from the clear daylight 'til the dawn
And I'm afraid I'll never be able to plough the rocks of Bawn.

And I wish the Queen of England would send for me in time
And place me in some regiment, all in my youth and prime
I would fight for Ireland's glory from the clear daylight 'til the dawn
And I never would return again to plough the rocks of Bawn.[2]

The traditional song 'The Rocks of Bawn', though likely originating in the mid-nineteenth century, enjoyed popularity in the post-Second World War era. Its message provides a metaphor for many of the ambiguities in Irishmen's experiences of migration to Britain: hard work, attitudes towards their homeland, reasons for leaving, sense of community, and views of return. The contexts in which it featured, including the version above sung by Connemara sean-nós singer Joe Heaney on the recording *Irish Music in London Pubs*, further reinforce this significance. It is a ballad, a 'come all ye' as indicated by the first line, but though Bawn may originally have referred to a specific place and Sweeney to a particular person, ultimately the power of the song resulted from the ability of many people to relate to it. It addresses the hardships faced by agricultural labourers in Ireland – the long hours, poverty, and insecurity of their position. The first, fourth, and fifth verses take the perspective of the song's hero, a *spailpín* or hired labourer, who carries out an unending, thankless job for little return. Verses two and three come from the perspective of his employer, who first entreats and then curses him. It contains a palpable sense of injustice because the horse gets hay, oats, and time to graze on the 'green lawn', while Sweeney has worn shoes and stockings and receives criticism for smoking his pipe. The repetition of the last line of each verse, 'never be able to plough the rocks of Bawn', accentuates the ultimate futility of the situation of workers like Sweeney because, of course, rocks cannot be ploughed.[3]

Irish people in general would have understood the song's message, but agricultural labourers and small farmers in particular would have commiserated with Sweeney's circumstances and, like him, considered leaving for England a viable alternative. This study draws on original oral histories with traditional musicians and singers who emigrated from Ireland, mostly from rural areas, to Britain between 1945 and 1970. These types of sources offer a unique perspective and can remedy the perception expressed by writer and navvy Dónall Mac Amhlaigh that 'historians have written books about the Irish in Britain without ever really knowing the Irish immigrant labouring class. They can quote you the number of people who came to Skipton Hiring Fair, but they can't tell you what those workers felt and what they thought.'[4] In recent years more historians have recognised the value of oral sources for rectifying that imbalance, including Ultan Cowley, Sharon Lambert, Sarah O'Brien, and Seán Sorohan, and this research follows in their footsteps while also drawing on a range of interdisciplinary perspectives.[5] The Irish in Britain never shared one homogenous identity, as this examination based on class and gender reveals, but individual life stories offer insights into their varied experiences, labouring men's projection of common values and culture, and the intertwining and dynamic roles of class and ethnicity in their lives.

The interviews begin with recollections of childhood, family, and the social and economic contexts of migration, which provide a key to understanding later life course decisions. Danny Meehan recalls that his father struggled to support a large family on twenty-five acres of mountainous land in Donegal, so he farmed, but 'he'd do work on the roads and he used to make creels and he'd sell turf and stuff just to supplement the financial problems my mom would have.'[6] This ability to mix forms of income played an important role in the family's survival, but offered few prospects for the future and eventually all but one of the eleven Meehan children emigrated. On a national scale 47 per cent of all employed men recorded on the 1951 census worked in agriculture, but this dropped to 31.7 per cent two decades later.[7] The mechanisation of agriculture combined with little industrial or other economic development left few options for most raised in rural areas, a fact acknowledged by the Commission on Emigration and Other Population Problems in its 1954 report.[8] Enda Delaney suggests another primary cause of mass migration was Ireland's inflexible class structure and constrained opportunities for social mobility before changes in education and industry in the mid-1960s.[9] Consequently, net migration between the 1946 and 1971 censuses amounted to an estimated loss of 665,766 people and the annual total peaked in 1957 at negative 58,000.[10]

The last verse of 'The Rocks of Bawn' contrasts these difficulties with the appeal of a steady job. At the very least an English regiment offered regular food and pay. Many nationalists saw joining the British Army or even emigration itself as traitorous acts and Lord Mayor of Cork Terence MacSwiney went so far as to say 'emigration is desertion!'[11] Though his view relates to an earlier generation, it persisted into the mid-twentieth century in the form of reluctance on the part of Irish politicians to confront the issue of emigration head-on in any serious, constructive way. 'The Rocks of Bawn' directly challenges the notion of desertion: the first line addresses the song to 'loyal heroes' and the singer says he would choose to enlist in a regiment 'to fight for Ireland's glory' rather than remain in his current situation. He expresses no shame in wanting better opportunities and fair employment. Oral histories confirm this feeling in the reasons given for emigration. When asked 'why did you decide to leave?' most answered initially with a simple statement about economic conditions: 'no work', 'there was no money', 'there was no employment much in Ireland', 'there was no work here at the time', 'it was a done thing nearly in our time'.[12] These phrases stress the primacy of employment and the normalcy of emigration. Some of the men had temporary or seasonal work, but not enough to sustain them permanently. The need to earn a living (and even the hope of riches) formed a central motivation for emigration, but other statements that followed these in the interviews suggested a far more complex process of reasoning. The desire to see more of the world, the influence of peers, and the presence of relatives abroad all played important roles in explaining the reasons for departure and choice of destination, while also rationalising the decision in personal and voluntary terms.

Of the many individuals unwilling to face a life of uncertain and poorly paid work in Ireland who opted to go abroad in the post-war era roughly 80 per cent went to Britain.[13] As Martin McMahon stated succinctly, 'you went to England with an empty pocket. You had a job within a week.'[14] The Commission on Emigration reported that of the men in receipt of travel permits, identity cards, and passports between 1947 and 1951, 42 per cent were unskilled workers and 31.3 per cent agricultural workers.[15] Once there, the construction crew often took the place of the army regiment mentioned in the last verse of 'The Rocks of Bawn' as the country rebuilt after the Second World War. Philip Donnellan's 1965 film *The Irishmen: An Impression of Exile* illustrates this connection as Joe Heaney sings that song on the soundtrack while images of heavy machinery and labourers fill the screen.[16] In 1971 74 per cent of Irishmen in Britain worked in the skilled manual, partly-skilled manual, and unskilled manual occupational categories, almost exactly the same figure as those whose last occupation reported by the Commission on Emigration was unskilled or agricultural labour twenty years previously.[17]

The 'unskilled' label given to the categories of employment, while practical for data collection, has the effect of denigrating the integrity and pride expressed by individuals. No one ever describes his own work with that term. In Steve Pyke and Timothy O'Grady's mixed-media novel, *I Could Read the Sky*, the protagonist, an Irish migrant in Britain, remembers and imagines all the skills he possessed: 'What I could do. I could mend nets. Thatch a roof. Build stairs. Make a basket from reeds. Splint the leg of a cow. Cut turf. Build a wall. Go three rounds with Joe in the ring Da put up in the barn. I could dance sets. Read the sky.'[18] These have a full existence in his memory and dreams while he sits alone in a flat in Kentish Town, dwelling on his past. Though a fictional representation, O'Grady based the work on oral histories with Irishmen in London and despite the element of sadness in the situations and memories of some says, 'I heard many hard stories, but I never heard a complaint'.[19] Numerous studies and media representations have focused on negative aspects of Irish experiences in Britain or the problematic nature of the group including discrimination, crime, mental illness, and social marginalisation. While these are valid concerns, commentators concomitantly neglect the positive personal and collective values migrants used to negotiate and rationalise the circumstances in which they found themselves and that they continually draw on to make sense of their life courses.

Many interviewees referred to a shared sense of male working culture based on similar backgrounds in rural Ireland and privileging of independence and hard work. Jimmy Ó Ceannabháin from Ros Muc in Connemara went to England in 1966 at age 16 and travelled around the country following job opportunities 'on the buildings' and learning carpentry: 'you met them from every county in Ireland and we were all in the same boat. Looking for work we were, there was no talk of unemployment or anything like that … We had to help ourselves, we didn't get any handouts, we didn't look for it, we looked for a job … We didn't get nothing but what we earned and proud of it.'[20] His use of the second person and first person plural indicates the emphasis placed on this sense of commonality, epitomised by the phrase 'we were all in the same boat'. He suggests that the men he encountered, though from different parts of Ireland, shared certain characteristics; they came to England for jobs, worked hard, and took pride in it. Perhaps the most familiar and evocative expression of this mentality comes from another Galway man, Dónall Mac Amhlaigh in his book *Dialann Deoraí*, translated by Valentin Iremonger as *An Irish Navvy*, a record of his experiences in England between 1951 and 1957.[21] He went first to Northampton to a job as a hospital ward orderly but left that for manual labour, attracted by prospects of higher wages and camaraderie, particularly with Connemara Irish-speakers, whom he praised highly. The only historical work to date that explores aspects of this male working culture is Ultan Cowley's *The Men Who Built Britain: A History of the Irish Navvy*, though Delaney also discusses the group in general terms.[22] Claims that the Irish 'built Britain' may have been overstated, but nonetheless persisted in popular memory and oral histories show a definite association of Irish male labourers with the building trade.[23]

While stressing the importance of self-sufficiency, Jimmy Ó Ceannabháin's use of 'we' and the statement 'we had to help ourselves' also highlight the significant role social networks played in emigration and employment. Each man had to do his share of the work or risk mockery for laziness, but if he ever needed a job or place to live he knew friends, relatives or neighbours from back in Ireland would look out for him. Packie Browne from Ballyduff, County Kerry recalls that when he first went to England in 1964, 'I went over with friends and worked with friends there. You got work straight away. The place I went to work I suppose there would have been twenty or thirty from the locality working there between Ballyduff and Ballybunion, so I knew everybody there.'[24] This lessened the sense of dislocation, so though Packie had never ridden a train before he left rural Kerry, he made the journey with friends and joined others who had left previously. Once in Britain, social networks continued to play an important role in finding employment and accommodation. Very often these related to place of origin in Ireland, but Liam Farrell from Tyrone recalls that on one particular building site 'there was two Mayo men and they had work way down in Kent and I worked with them and they wouldn't give you a job unless you were a musician!'[25] This highlights not only the importance of his self-identification as a musician, but also the respect others had for that craft and its place in the Irish community, where it served to both remind people of 'home' and facilitate social interactions within the ethnic group.

Danny Meehan emigrated at age 16 in 1957, first to Selby, Yorkshire, but he worked across Britain in construction jobs before settling in London as an independently employed stonemason. He reflected on the values and lifestyle of the workingmen he encountered:

> I had a lot of kindred spirits over there. Men who were like me, you know. They loved the hard work and they loved the fun in the pubs and they loved the music. They weren't men for

getting married for no obvious reason but that they didn't want to get tied down and they couldn't always relate well to other people, you see ... It's hard to explain it but that's the way it was ... But those men were always well valued by contractors because they had a lot of energy. They could do the job well and a bit of hard work never phased them so the contractors all loved that certain breed of man who travelled from job to job and if he had a decent dry warm bed he didn't need any fancy decorations or anything, you needed to get your head down, you know.[26]

He calls these men 'kindred spirits', referring to them in the third person plural, but clearly placing himself within their ranks. They had come from similar rural backgrounds and prized their independence and ability to engage in difficult manual labour without needing 'fancy' living conditions, qualities employers also privileged. Danny's statement that 'they weren't men for getting married' may also reflect a personal justification for why he never married. Many of these men, in male-dominated occupations and from a society with relatively rigid gender roles, may have found it difficult to talk or relate to women even if given the opportunity in pubs or dance halls. However, while he articulates the positive aspects of these qualities of Irish labouring men, English commentators highlighted the same traits for negative reasons, associating frequent movement and willingness to endure poor conditions with unreliability and an inability to think beyond short-term monetary gains.[27] Along with their propensity for hard work, according to Danny these men maintained an ability to enjoy life and appreciation for Irish culture; 'they loved the fun in the pubs and they loved the music'. He uses the sense of values imbued in him from youth to explain the course of his own life, his independence and work and he recognised similar traits in others. Though framed in personal terms, the above excerpt demonstrates an internalisation of aspects of the common image of the Irish navvy that dates back at least to the nineteenth century, the heroism and pride as well as the hardships.

Danny Meehan refers to the 'certain breed of man who travelled from job to job', pointing to the prevalence of transience, a long-standing but underemphasised feature of the Irish population in Britain. Studies tend to focus on settlement and community, particularly in urban centres such as London or Birmingham, an assumption based on statistics and institutional records that represent one moment and place in time. However, as David Fitzpatrick argues, transiency deserves equal mention and individual life histories can draw attention to it.[28] The interviews in this study highlight both sides of the coin: while music is often discussed in relation to places with large, established Irish populations (particularly London), recollections of work experiences point to high levels of mobility.

> JOHN GILDEA: I travelled around quite a bit. I lived in Birmingham, Coventry, Sculthorpe, Leeds, a while in Scotland, but most of my time I spent in the London borough of Croydon, that was the longest time I was anywhere.[29]

> JIMMY Ó CEANNABHÁIN: I lived in London, I lived in Birmingham, I lived in Nottingham, I lived in a lot of places. But that's how it was. You might have a couple of weeks work here, then you move with the contract to some other place and back and forth.[30]

> DANNY MEEHAN: I went to Selby in '57 ... Progressed on from there then, went to various places. Ended up in Wales. You had a lot of freedom: if you didn't like the ganger man or if you didn't like your digs you just moved on. Wanderlust. The wanderlust was in me anyway always. The curse of the travelling man ... It's just it's in your blood, you know, the wanderlust.[31]

Movement between geographical locales, particularly in the months or years immediately following initial migration, is associated most often with men in the construction industry, whether they worked with one company that sent them around the country or switched between operations.[32] However, the tendency to move between jobs in search of better conditions, higher wages, or other companions seems to have been widespread among Irishmen generally.

> BILLY CLIFFORD: People'd just be hopping in and out of jobs. There was so many jobs available, I suppose … You'd have no bother getting a job. In the earlier times I would've been at the apprentice stage and I got kicked around a bit and horrible old bits of jobs where you knew you were never going to learn anything … so you'd only stick them for six months or maybe a year and then you'd go on to try and get something a bit better.[33]

> MARTIN TREACY: I used to work at the buildings game. Bricklayers, that type of thing. Everything. If that went slack I'd go at something else. I was never out of work; there was plenty of work there.[34]

Billy Clifford worked in electronics and says 'in the ten years in London I must've had at least fifteen jobs.'[35] John Gildea held jobs for a time in a factory and a brewery, but he chose to go back to construction work because 'I liked to be with the Irish', again suggesting their perceived prevalence and influence in that sector. He valued the companionship of friends and fellow Irishmen on the building sites over having a good, indoor job in isolation from that community. When asked about his movement John said he was 'travelling for work, yeah. Typical Irishman.'[36] These men articulate their movements in positive, or at least neutral, terms, associating it with the availability of work (a contrast to Ireland), the search for better conditions, and individual agency.

Despite displacement and frequent mobility, for many men Irish cultural traditions, particularly music, offered one aspect of continuity in their lives. However, in the mid-twentieth century traditional music still had a strong association with rural populations, those disproportionately impacted by emigration, which raises the issue of social differentiation or class in both Ireland and Britain. Ben Lennon recalls that even in his musical family in Leitrim in the 1930s and 1940s,

> We had two situations ... The kitchen was for traditional music and the parlour was for sheet music that you would buy in the shop and all the hit songs of the day. It was a little bit up market as opposed to the diddly-di in the kitchen. I would have been ashamed to be seen carrying a fiddle case at that time. It was looked down on; Irish music was looked down on at that time.[37]

Migrants carried these attitudes and associations with them, despite entering a different society where they celebrated greater opportunities for social and economic advancement. Martin McMahon says, 'you were a very, very low individual playing traditional music. To the Irish. Even when we went to England they were all laughing at us, "what are you playing that rubbish for?"'[38] He adds, 'traditional music was a peasant's music. Who mixed with peasants only another peasant. You kept to yourself. Doctors had their own type of people, solicitors and priests and all the educated people, they mixed in a different world altogether even though it was the same country.'[39] These distinctions originated in occupational status, levels of education, and the rural/urban split in Irish society. Dónall Mac Amhlaigh commented, 'there was a great cleavage – the towns and cities were dominated by British and American cultural ideas, but poor rural people had their own culture up to a point.'[40] Gradually, with the impact of high-profile figures such as composer Seán Ó Riada in Ireland and the beginnings of the folk revival in Britain and America, attitudes towards traditional music changed and access to education and economic development altered Irish society. However, into the 1960s traditional music still carried connotations of poor rural people, an image middle-class immigrants or those seeking upward mobility in Britain sought to escape.

Music and culture played an important role in the development of ethnic identity, an under-emphasised facet of the immigrant experience in Britain, but the format and selection of that culture was not uniform. Unlike the many sentimental ballads favoured by immigrant audiences across the Irish diaspora, 'The Rocks of Bawn' contains an unadulterated picture of hardship in Ireland and the willingness to give up that life for one with more employment opportunities, steady wages and security. The popular Irish singers in Britain such as Delia Murphy and Bridie Gallagher never recorded 'The Rocks of Bawn', instead choosing more nostalgic or nationalistic fare. However, anecdotal evidence suggests the ballad commonly featured in pubs and two different singers tell remarkably similar stories about it. Teresa McMahon recalls that she learned it from her father in Tipperary and in London 'there were certain places, I can still hear it, I'd be walking in and in a very big laugh you'd hear "here comes The Rocks of Bawn" and everybody would start laughing … Obviously that was my nickname behind my back, for a laugh.'[41] Joe Heaney told almost exactly the same story and said, 'That's the name I was known by in Camden Town!'[42] In Teresa McMahon's case the laughter contained a sense of derision and perhaps rejection of the bad memories of Ireland brought to mind by the song, but Heaney also said of the pub audiences, '"The Rocks of Bawn" was their favourite' and anytime someone sang a good song 'you'd get silence'.[43] Certainly both these recollections suggest the immigrant audiences recognised the ballad's message, whether they accepted or mocked it.

The presence or absence of 'The Rocks of Bawn' in different contexts reflects the extent to which socialisation patterns among the Irish in Britain mirrored class divisions existing in Ireland. The Galtymore, the largest of the London dance halls, had two ballrooms, the larger of which featured 'modern' dances and the smaller céilí dances. For the same price you could move between the two, but one commentator noted that a more 'west of Ireland' crowd tended to favour the latter side.[44] Certain venues also tended to attract different types of audiences. Tomás Ó Canainn comes originally from a family in rural Derry, but he grew up in the city, achieved a university education in Belfast and went to Liverpool for his PhD. He always maintained an interest in traditional music and the Irish language and recalled an incident from shortly after he arrived in England:

> I can remember when I went to Liverpool the first time I was trying to find out where there were Irish things available, particularly music, and I remember talking to our local priest in the church I was going to, Christ the King Church in Liverpool, and he was from Cork, a place that I knew nothing about at that time, but his name was Father O'Callaghan. I always remember his advice; he was very respectable. He said 'yes, they're down there in St Mary's, Highfield Street, but don't go near them, they're a very rough crowd,' sort of typical Irish lower classes. So that convinced me that that's where I wanted to go when he told me! That's when I went down and discovered the céilís there on a Sunday night and discovered the music. Even though he was warning me off it, he was the man that directed me to it.[45]

Priests represented a higher echelon of society from the 'peasants' who played traditional music, as Martin McMahon suggested. To Fr O'Callaghan, a young man studying for a PhD belonged with a higher social class and should avoid the 'very rough crowd' that attended the dance halls featuring Irish music. This anecdote illustrates the tension between the desire to share an Irish ethnic identity and persistent class distinctions in interpretations of that identity.

Mass emigration from rural areas in Ireland where cultural traditions flourished had the effect of creating excellent conditions for music to thrive in Britain. In practice, no interviewees seemed particularly focused on or bothered by its 'lower class' associations, choosing instead to highlight positive features of the communities centred on music. Vincent Campbell recalls that even when he worked on a hydroelectric scheme in a remote area of Scotland he lived with many others from Donegal:

We used to have fiddle players from Donegal [and] when the weekend would come, we'd go out to the canteen … have a few drinks, then come in with a big row of beds down one side and up the other side, like a big hall, and we used to sit on the beds then and take out the fiddles and the melodeons and we'd have home away from home. It kept us going 'til we got out of it. That's the way we passed the time.[46]

For first-generation migrants music provided a form of entertainment, much as it had in Ireland, as well as reminding them of 'home'. It features most prominently in discussions of the Irish in urban centres, particularly London. Jimmy Ó Ceannabháin explained the situation in his own terms:

The cream of Ireland was in London that time playing music. They had to do the same thing we all done, pack the suitcase and go. There was better music in London that time than there was in Ireland because there was work there, there was music there and they associated together good and you met people from the whole of the country. We'd all left the same conditions and there's no point in being shy telling you that.[47]

However, when he says 'we'd all left the same conditions' he refers to a particular type of people that he associated with – the men and women from rural Ireland who chose to go to dance halls and pubs where traditional music featured. Reg Hall notes that in post-war London 'almost exclusively, the immigrant musicians and singers were manual workers', predominantly male and from rural backgrounds.[48] Despite clear recognition of Irish social stratification and the low status of traditional music, most interviewees like Ó Ceannabháin never or only rarely used the term 'class'.

These venues and the crowds who attended them played an important role in migrants' adjustment processes. Teresa McMahon said the transition from rural Ireland to urban England 'was an awful culture shock. You went out of the middle of the country into this. The music really was the thing. That was fantastic. The dancing too.' Her husband Martin added a third element: 'I'll tell you what it was – it was music, drink, and dancing!'[49] Kevin Burke, born in London to parents from Sligo, says that when he went to pub sessions from a young age in the 1960s for the Irish immigrant clientele,

> The music was definitely a draw, but accompanying that was a chance to meet their friends and neighbours and hang out and it was definitely a community centre kind of atmosphere as well. Exchange views or news from home, gossip from back in Ireland, you know, but also a lot of these people would be working together for a while and then one guy would leave and go to another job and then at the weekend he'd meet his buddies and they'd be talking about the new job versus the old job, 'oh yeah this is a lot better, maybe you should come with me, I could get you a start there maybe', so there was a lot of that going on. Of course a lot of the younger people, a lot of the single people would be looking to meet girls and boys, for the young attraction angle. That was definitely part of the attraction of going to these places – meeting members of the opposite sex. But mainly it was just a hang, a place to hang, and great music alongside it.[50]

A combination of difficult working lives, inhospitable or crowded accommodation, the need to counter the sense of dislocation or loneliness arising from migration, and prospects of a space to mingle with members of the opposite sex all meant that pubs and dance halls played a central role in socialisation of the Irish in post-war Britain. Insularity characterised the communities that developed and pubs became 'a little enclave of Irish culture in this surrounding sea of Englishness'.[51] They served practical functions as well: publicans cashed wage cheques for their clients, received and sent mail, and sometimes served food. Once a predominantly male domain, by the mid-1950s pubs had expanded to include women, but they and the 'Irishness' developed in them feature more prominently in men's experiences. Irish women were more likely to have employment that provided live-in accommodation, such as in the hospitality and healthcare sectors, to integrate more easily within the workforce and host society, and to exhibit a desire for upward social mobility.[52] The role of pubs and dance halls has previously received little attention from historians because unlike formal institutions such as the Catholic Church or Gaelic Athletic Association, this type of informal culture can prove difficult to address using documentary sources.

The importance of pubs for socialisation combined with poor living and working conditions could produce negative side effects, including a relatively rough life style, competitive rivalries, and over-dependence on alcohol. These elements sometimes led to fights occurring. Kevin McDermott from Cavan worked in London as a fireman and recalls: 'At about eleven o'clock on a Saturday those fireman … they used to go out and stand on the balcony and watch the Irish beat themselves out of the pub and round the front of the fire station and sort it out on the forecourt of the station. That was their entertainment. It was, really it was awful.'[53] Mac Amhlaigh mentions several fights in *Dialann Deoraí*, most between Irishmen, and Bernard Canavan suggests that these stemmed from social or geographical distinctions brought over from Ireland.[54] These types of incidents contributed to negative representations of the Irish, while also reinforcing the class divisions that may have caused them. As illustrated in Tomás Ó Canainn's anecdote about the priest in Liverpool, those Irish perceived of as 'respectable' or 'middle class' distanced themselves from the working class and rejected the stubbornly persistent stereotypes based on fighting and drinking.[55]

In the last line of 'The Rocks of Bawn' the protagonist proclaims that if given a place in an English regiment 'I never would return again to plough the rocks of Bawn', but the reality often proved far more complex as migrants struggled to reconcile competing images of Ireland. They held, on the one hand, memories of difficult or impoverished living conditions and few opportunities; 'I thought I would never see Ireland again and I never wanted to. The memories are too bad and they're still with me.'[56] On the other hand, despite decades spent in Britain many kept 'rooms over there with the Irish flag and shamrocks' and a lifelong desire to return 'home', perhaps without fully comprehending the extent to which their mental image was idealised or how much Ireland had changed in the intervening years.[57] The decision to return made by some provoked a re-evaluation of their lives both in Britain and Ireland, the lens through which they now view their past and present circumstances. Martin and Teresa McMahon returned in 1998, perhaps hoping to find resolution, but Martin came to the conclusion that after living abroad for so long 'there's a part of your life gone missing somewhere and you look for that 'til your end'.[58] In Britain, holding onto their Irish identity through participation in traditional music and dance provided one way in which migrants sought that missing piece. However, for some that never constituted a full substitute and others rejected its association with rural lifestyles. As this chapter argues, the Irish were not a monolithic group and significant divisions from pre-migration society based on education, occupation, regionalism, and rural/urban geography persisted among immigrant communities in Britain. Recognition of these differences appears in oral histories, but largely without recourse to the terminology of class or articulation of any sense of working-class solidarity that extended beyond ethnic boundaries.[59] Nonetheless, interviewees clearly identified with others from similar backgrounds that shared their experiences and values, the 'kindred spirits' found among male labourers, and venues featuring traditional music and dancing formed an important focal point for those communities.

Chapter Eleven

'As If You Were Something Under Their Shoe': Class, Gender and Status among Cork Textile Workers, 1930–70

Liam Cullinane

The sociologists Richard Breen and Christopher T. Whelan write that:

> In Ireland class distinctions are thought of as a typically English phenomenon. The popular impression is that rigid social class demarcation was left behind with the ending of landlordism and the demise of the Anglo-Irish ascendancy. It is true that class boundaries in Ireland are less ritualised, or less marked by cultural difference, than in some other countries. This has encouraged the notion that we are a classless society.[1]

The idea of Ireland as a society without class distinctions is by no means an exclusively modern one. In 1955, the *Irish Times* described as 'well informed' a French writer's view of Ireland as being 'financially stable and practically classless'.[2] In 1964, the president of University College Dublin condemned the claim that Irish education was 'class-ridden' as an example of 'the intervention of pseudo-problems' and argued that Irish society was in fact 'extremely classless'.[3] One year before that a district court judge in Limerick had refused to accept counsel's argument that farmers and farm labourers belonged to different social classes.[4]

Such a point of view has also permeated Irish historical writing. Diarmaid Ferriter for example, complains that class is a 'neglected aspect of Irish history'.[5] This in spite of the fact that the Ireland that emerged in the decades after independence was characterised by deep class divisions, not just in terms of inequality but also in terms of pervasive discrimination by the institutions that dominated the republic. As Ferriter asserts, 'Class differences were in fact blatantly enunciated well after independence.'[6] As such, the supposed 'classlessness' of Irish society, both historical and contemporary, is 'something of a myth'.[7] Yet, the question remains, to what extent were these divisions recognised by the working class themselves? The deferential agricultural labourers of Southern England and the communist militants of the Fiat factory in Turin were all members of a global working class and yet varied significantly in their level of class consciousness and awareness. Where does Ireland fit into this picture? Moreover, how were the realities of class experienced in the lives of ordinary workers and their families?

Share et al. have argued that: 'An analysis of the minutiae of everyday activities and relationships may allow us to focus on the dynamic living out of social structures, in other words, to capture something of the "lived experience" of class', contending that 'an insight into people's everyday lives can contribute to an understanding of how class groupings are produced and reproduced and how class consciousness, ideologies and class-related attitudes are sustained.'[8] Oral history is particularly useful in this regard as it allows us to examine the subjective dimensions of class and to discover how class was experienced and perceived in everyday life. To date, only a handful of researchers have attempted this in Ireland. Maura Cronin has used her access to the extensive interview collection at the Oral History Centre in Mary Immaculate College, Limerick to produce a broad survey of attitudes to class and status over the course of the twentieth century,[9] while Mary Muldowney has investigated the complicated relationship between gender, status, the family and the state in mid-twentieth-century Ireland through detailed analysis of oral testimony.[10] The topic also forms part of the subject matter of the pioneering research of Máire Leane and Elizabeth Kiely.[11] This chapter will further this line of research by examining perceptions of class and status among a small sample of manufacturing workers, all of whom were employed by the Sunbeam-Wolsey textile firm in Cork city between 1930 and 1970. This chapter aims to determine the extent to which respondents were aware of class and status divisions in society and how, as 'blue-collar' manufacturing workers, they experienced and responded to these divisions.

It would be far beyond the scope of a brief chapter to capture the manifold dimensions of class as experienced by the narrators. Because of this, the chapter will focus on the experience of institutional discrimination by the Church and the education system, conducting close readings of a small number of narratives rather than a broad, far-reaching survey. Additionally, as Sunbeam-Wolsey's workforce was composed primarily of female workers, the chapter will also investigate the relationship between gender, class and status as it emerges in the oral testimony. Through the use of oral history then, this essay will investigate whether the Ireland inhabited by these narrators was the same classless idyll suggested by the president of University College Dublin and other commentators.

EDUCATION, RELIGION AND CLASS

Education and class were closely connected in twentieth-century Ireland. Both the Christian Brothers and the various orders of nuns which dominated the Irish education system were suspected by many narrators of being biased against working-class pupils. John O'Shea recalled his education at the North Monastery secondary school:

> And that was one of the terrible gripes I had. I was told that I'd be driving a donkey-butt all me life. Eh, like, we, I think that we in Gurranabraher [a working-class area in Cork city]

were treated a little bit differently than others. Now I could be completely wrong but they were looking for someone to bring turf to the school boilerhouse, they'd call me. Whether it was because I was very successful with donkeys or whether I was related to the donkey in some way but ... I noticed that and especially there was a period, a very interesting period in the North Mon where you were obliged to pay a fee ... I don't know was it or how long it lasted, the fee-paying. But as far as I know it was about two pounds odd per quarter or per half-year maybe. But we didn't have two pounds to rub together between us and God you know? And eh. But now, they didn't refuse to teach us. But Liam, they showed it to you like. You were shown that you were there, that you were and you were freeloading.[12]

Rena M. tellingly describes how class differences among her schoolmates have persisted right up until the present day:

I mean even now. Even now when we go to a school reunion, we had one now two years ago, a school reunion, and we could see money. There was about twenty of us on one table and then there was about ten behind us, you know, spread out like that, but we could see the thing that was over on this table with all the brain-boxes ... I mean they're very nice girls but they were brainy, no doubt about it, but then their people had businesses. They were all pushed to the front of the class and we were all pushed down the back.[13]

Rena goes on:

Oh yeah. No matter if we couldn't hear properly. You were down the back. What we call the grandies then, they were all up the front, and even up to this day that goes on. They all sit up at a round table up at the Country Club. The rest of us are over there and we'd be saying, 'I hope to God they don't come over!' We've no time for them now, cos they'd no time for us in school. The nuns were mad about them, cos they had businesses, and if you were the ordinary working person, if you had brains fine, you were good, but if you hadn't brains like.[14]

Two aspects of this quotation stand out. Firstly, it gives an indication of how deeply entrenched class divisions appear to have been in Ireland. The class lines drawn in the classroom in the 1940s and 1950s remain in place fifty years later, a fact Rena is keen to emphasise through the use of 'even now' as well as through repeating the visual metaphor of class, the 'grandies' up the top in the classroom with the working-class pupils forced to the back. This hierarchy is reproduced in the school reunion, again through the organisation of seating. What the whole narrative suggests is the consistency in class divisions from youth to old age. Rena's narrative would thus indicate that class divisions in Ireland, even if less formalised than Britain, were far from fluid and emphasises that discrimination in the classroom determined the opportunities and life-choices available to working-class women.

All the narrators in the sample, like the overwhelming majority of Irish schoolchildren, were educated in religious institutions. Religion was central to almost all aspects of life in Ireland's deeply confessional society. With regard to class, the Church promoted co-operation between workers and employers, and preached equality before God. Confraternities and other community-based religious activity could sometimes provide 'common ground for various social levels to meet as (temporary) equals',[15] but in practice religious activity frequently reflected rather than concealed the class structure of society. Diarmaid Ferriter explains that industrial schools, the classist segregation between 'choir sisters' and 'lay sisters' and a host of other practices represent 'an indication of a Church-endorsed class bias'.[16] He argues that: 'The truth was that those involved in the Church at all levels reflected the same political and class divisions which affected the rest of society'.[17]

Religious practice revealed class divisions in a variety of highly public forms. These included the order of seating in mass, the humiliating public payment of Christmas and Easter 'dues' and even the pecking order of the dead. In Cork, Mary Cronin recalled: 'When we were young the priest would come around for their dues ... And I can remember my mother ... She had nothing then. She'd even borrow maybe, and I'd say two and six, maybe five shillings to have when the priest would come. That all went on then ... If you gave more, they'd fall down at your feet.'[18] Similarly, Marilyn Silverman, in her anthropological research in Thomastown, County Kilkenny, quotes a local millworker who explained that: 'Father Doyle had three prices for graves. The most expensive was at the back, near to the cross, the medium-priced ones were behind the most expensive; and the ones that cost the least, for the poor, were near the entry gate and road. And the only difference was status.'[19]

For working-class people, a deep and genuine piety could easily co-exist alongside a critical attitude towards the clergy and other religious institutions. Their belief in Catholicism was 'essentialized, naturalised and timeless'[20] but they also 'saw the failings of a Church that not only differentiated and segregated people but that also discriminated against some of them.'[21] To take an example from John O'Shea, these contradictions emerge in his narrative when he describes how: 'We were completely and utterly cowed by our Church. We had no rights whatsoever' and, in the same breath, mentions that he is still 'a daily mass-goer ... a daily communicant' alongside the telling use of the phrases '*our* church' and '*our* clergy'.[22]

An illuminating example of this complicated relationship between working-class people and the Catholic faith is that offered by Kathleen F. In the course of an interview with Margaret Kearns of the Women's Oral History Project, she tells two stories. The first involves one of her colleagues on the factory floor:

> I'd like to tell you this. We'd two conveyors as I told you. There
> was this Eileen Keating. She was a lovely person. Now I told

you how many of us was on the floor. There was about over a hundred. And we got in in the morning and before the work started, she said prayers. And the whole floor stopped and said it with her and then, she said the angelus at twelve o'clock. Every day, twelve o'clock, she said the angelus. And, if we were working overtime, at six. That's honest now. The whole ... the men and all, stopped working and we all said the rosary and everything. She was that kind of ... she wasn't a gospel-thumper now if you know what I mean now. She was really genuinely holy you know? And everyone respected her and everyone, we all said the rosary and we said our prayers.[23]

Another story, indirectly related to the former, crops up later in the interview:

The church, normally at that time I think, thought you should keep to your station in life ... One particular instance I was going to a confraternity night ... This particular priest ... He came from Montenotte people. And he said [affecting a posh accent] He had been in the opera house the night before. And he's sitting in the grand circle and he saw two people from Gurra above ... in the grand circle and he thinks, he thought they should keep to their own. I saw this now. That they shouldn't have been in the grand circle, they should have been up in the Gods.[24]

The 'Gods' refers to the worst seating in the Opera House, high in the aisles and far from the stage, while the Grand Circle was the best and most expensive seating. Share et al. comment that: 'Everyday experiences of class awareness or of social inequality may also be defined by relationships to space. Class and inequality are often related to neighbourhood and "community".'[25] Kathleen here represents class in geographic terms; the social origins of the two women in the second story is demonstrated by the fact that they are from Gurra (Gurranabraher), a working-class area of Cork city, while the middle / upper class position of the priest is indicated by his being 'from Montenotte people', an affluent suburb. It is important to note that Kathleen did not perceive that this incident was merely the case of an individual snobbish priest. Rather, it is told in order to demonstrate her belief that the Church was actively engaged in the suppression of working-class people and was attempting to prevent social mobility. Elsewhere, she remarks: 'I think they [the Church] tried to keep 'em, the poor people down, y'know? They did. They didn't want them to get an education or anything … the Church kept the poor people poor and uneducated'.[26]

The relationship between these two narratives is important. Neither story is directly prompted by the interviewer. This would seem to indicate that the memory of clerical discrimination against the poor is particularly important to Kathleen, leading it to assume primacy in her recollections. A cursory interpretation of the first narrative would suggest that its function was to illustrate the piety and religious devotion of an older generation, in the context of an interview between an elderly woman and a much younger academic. This may be partly the case, but the first narrative assumes a greater significance when viewed in relation to the second. The difference highlighted implicitly is between the quiet, humble and understated piety of Eileen Keating, someone 'genuinely holy' and the hypocritical Church (another priest is described in the interview as a 'gospel-thumper'). The narrative locates real genuine spirituality in the person of Eileen while rejecting the skewed, corrupt version promulgated by the hierarchy. In particular, the first narrative emphasises the power and respect afforded to Eileen, who can halt the entire floor, 'men and all'. Her spiritual power and hard-earned respect contrasts sharply with the corporeal, material power of the Church demonstrated elsewhere in the interview.

Kathleen is by no means anti-clerical. In fact, she was a loyal member of the local confraternity. However, as we have seen, this religious devotion exists side-by-side with an acute sense that the poor were being repressed by the Church. This presents an apparent contradiction between doctrine and practice that was also noted by Silverman in her research in Thomastown. She writes that the perpetrators of class discrimination were seen to be 'the agents of the church – priests and nuns. However, the deficiencies of these agents were seen in relation to religious practice rather than belief. That priests mediated between human beings and God was not in question … the problem was that they did not do so impartially.'[27] In relating these stories, Kathleen reconciles the gulf between what she regards as true, genuine religious practice and the hypocrisy and repression of the Church. The effect of the two narratives is to implicate this repression as being rooted in the institutions and agents of the Church, rather than in the doctrines and beliefs of Catholicism itself, which is embodied in the 'genuine holiness' of Eileen Keating and the observant workers who join her in prayer.

The oral history interview provides not just a platform for narration but also for recall and reflection, and both these processes are intertwined. Kathleen, who is otherwise a self-confessed traditionalist with social and political views that would be regarded as quite conservative, thus communicates a story that not only reveals the power and classist nature of the Church, but also resists it. She was, at best, a reluctant trade unionist and her political affiliations were conservative. Even so, her testimony, like many of the other oral narratives, reflects acute class awareness as well as a perception that powerful institutions (in this case the Church) were operating against the interests of workers and to the benefit of the rich and powerful. Her testimony echoes the perceptions of most narrators, who were both devoutly Catholic and yet frequently recognised and resented the class bias of the Church.

GENDER AND STATUS

Among female workers, status was closely linked to the type of work one was engaged in, rather than other possible indicators such as pay or skill level. Rena M. describes the various tiers of this female status hierarchy: 'Oh yes, I mean there, what was called a good job then, a secretary in a solicitor's office, that was called a good job. Or, you work in one of the big shops in town – Woolworth's now or the Moderne, Brown Thomas when twas Cashs [*sic*] … They were all what you called good jobs.'[28]

Contemporary distinctions between clerical, service and manufacturing employment were of central importance and defined how working women perceived themselves and were perceived by others. Rena recalled the snobbery that she experienced when encountering former schoolmates who had 'gone on to office or shop work:

> Oh yeah, if you worked in a factory, you were looked down on … I mean, people that were in school with us like these brainboxes now that were at our reunion. They worked in shops now, you know. They'd say, 'God, you work in a factory, God'. That was the attitude, like. As if you were something under their shoe, like.[29]

Though Rena recalled that she and her friends would simply laugh off such remarks, she also remembered that other female workers were far more sensitive to this kind of snobbery: 'You see you'd even get people, you know, they may not be friends of mine, but you'd get people that time, "Oh I don't work in a factory". They'd actually deny it.'[30] Even among factory workers there was a status division based on the workplace:

> Like, the Sunbeam now was a very good factory, Dunlops was a very good factory, Fords was a good factory. ESB, all them. They were all good, what were considered good factories, but I mean the likes of Lee Boot or Hanover or, em, there was another one there in North Main Street, they were down-class. They were considered the down-class like.[31]

Attitudes towards manual and white-collar work were explicitly gendered. The most valued jobs for men, as identified by Rena and other narrators, were workplaces like the Electricity Supply Board (ESB), Ford's and Dunlop. The prestige afforded these (predominately male) workplaces was due primarily to their high levels of pay and skill. Similarly, tradesmen and craft-workers (almost exclusively men) were cited as being 'higher up' due to their good wages, job security and useful skills.[32] White-collar employment and the particular type of prestige accorded to it also varied depending on gender. The high standing associated with *male* clerical work differed radically from that attributed to their female counterparts. Aidan Kelly describes the typical male white-collar worker in the early decades of the twentieth century:

> Prestige was the dominant element in his social profile; unable to reach or match the social plane of his superiors he responded by establishing a clear gap between himself and the great mass of manual workers. He owned his own house, took annual holidays and provided at the least a good secondary education for his children. This social station was enhanced by the treatment meted out by employers; he received a salary, not wages, he was paid monthly not weekly, he received sickness benefit and a pension on retirement, he worked fewer hours than a manual worker, and above all was called 'staff', not a worker.[33]

The positive attributes associated with male white-collar employment are reflective of gender ideology, his high standing determined primarily by his skill, independence, financial security and ability to provide for his family. Female white-collar employees were likewise afforded a high level of prestige, but for very different reasons. Mary Muldowney comments that in her research into working women in the period prior to and during the Second World War she found that 'One of the most frequently voiced opinions about occupational status was that factory work was inferior to other occupations, especially for women'.[34] The perceived inferiority of manufacturing employment for women was not related to income but to respectability. Muldowney suggests that: 'A job might be well paid but if it was not in a socially desirable employment sector, the women were dismissive of its appeal and it was clear that there was a correlation between the perceived suitability of the job for women – whether it involved "dirty" or manual work – and their attitude to it.'[35]

This assertion is supported by the accounts of female respondents. In Sunbeam, the gap in wages between female office staff and workers on the factory floor was minimal, yet the difference in status was significant. Billy Foley recalled:

> The office girls and the workers in the Sunbeam, there was a massive difference that time between them. They wouldn't even speak to one another. They wouldn't sit at one another's table. The girls in the office thought they were way above the workers … There used to be war over that like.[36]

Nancy Byrne worked in Sunbeam in the 1930s and observed a considerable gap between the office staff and the workers on the factory floor, noting: 'The office worker's hours were 9 to 6, life being much easier for them. Firstly, the boss never frequently visited their place of employment like he did in the factory. Also, their lives being much more pleasant, a tennis court and other sports being provided for them.'[37] While Nancy's recollections would suggest that clerical staff received more benefits than workers on the floor, most narrators indicated that differences in status were not related to levels of pay, but rather to the image associated with different kinds of work. Rena M. observed of female office and shop workers: 'But I don't know did they come out with as much money as we did. I think it was … The image of the thing. That they weren't factory workers.'[38] This view is corroborated by Billy Foley, who recalled: 'My own daughter actually started off in the office here and she left the office and went back down to the floor because she was getting more money on the floor. She was like her father. She didn't want a title, she wanted money.'[39]

This concern with 'image' and 'respectability' was clearly related to gender ideology. All women, to one extent or another, 'shared an awareness of paid employment that was related to the domestic role assigned to women in legal and social terms'.[40] Manufacturing work was disdained because it was perceived to be dirty, masculine and based on hard physical labour. In addition, there was a widespread perception that women in manufacturing employment were 'uncouth' and less respectable than their counterparts in more 'feminine' employment. Clerical and shop work on the other hand were perceived to be more feminine because such employment was clean, not primarily physical, and closer to the domestic ideal of the Irish woman. In Ireland's highly conservative society, the distinction between 'respectable' female employment and manufacturing employment was particularly strong, but it was by no means unique to it. Joan Sangster, for example, in her study of female manufacturing workers in Ontario, Canada, quotes one woman who recalls: 'There was an idea of toughness about women [factory workers] … if you were a good Christian living person, they thought you shouldn't be there … that work was for the rough and ready types, the uneducated'.[41] As Sangster further notes: 'Good work habits of clerical workers – punctuality, preciseness, politeness, pleasant personality – were essentially equated with "female" attributes'.[42]

These variations in status and prestige are ultimately indicative of deeper social forces. In the case of Ireland in these years, the family unit was accorded a central role both by the social teaching of the Church and by State policy at national level. The dominant assumption was of a male breadwinner and a female carer presiding over a large family. This assumption was underpinned by, amongst other things, the commitment to a family wage expounded by the government and supported by the trade union movement. For women, work was a necessary evil to be endured until marriage, with the majority of women 'largely accepting of the prevailing social and cultural norms which deemed the home as the appropriate sphere within which they would fulfil the prescribed roles of wife and mother'.[43] Thus, in the case of clerical work, the high status accorded men was distinctly related to their role as a breadwinner and an independent man possessing useful skills, while that accorded to women was related to the supposed 'femininity' of such work. Women who worked in manual labour, particularly factory work, were implicitly 'transgressing gender boundaries'[44] although, as essential contributors to household incomes, female workers had little choice other than to engage in this type of labour.

Despite the low status accorded to their employment, the dominant theme that emerges from the recollections of female manufacturing workers was one of pride in their working lives and mutual respect for their colleagues. Nancy Byrne recalls that: 'During my twelve years in the firm, I never heard a nasty word. I was appalled when people spoke badly of the girls because they were working in the factory.'[45] Similarly, Patsy Corcoran, when asked what having been a Sunbeam worker meant to her, simply replied: 'I'm proud. I'm very proud to have been a Sunbeam worker.'[46]

COMMUNICATING CLASS

Maura Cronin notes that in the 800 or so interviews conducted by Mary Immaculate College, 'interviewees have very seldom used the word "class" unless pressed to do so by the interviewer.'[47] However, the vocabulary of class is a great deal more complex. Terms like working class and middle class are, to some extent, British importations and may not necessarily be a natural part of the Irish lexicon. Rather, as we have seen in the narratives quoted here, more insular terms like 'grandies', 'big people', 'cottage people', 'money people', etc. appear as indicators of social class. Similarly, geographical representations of class are often employed, as in the case of both Kathleen F. and John O'Shea. John recalled various incidents of snobbery that he observed over the years, but noted that it was related primarily to place of origin rather than occupation:

I remember I was entertaining one night in a very popular golf club in Cork and ... I was a part of the entertainment and I happened to mention to one, one of the people who invited us actually, about a happening with reference to where we were reared [Gurranabraher] you know? And ah, he sidled up to me, and requested that I wouldn't mention it anymore you know? In other words, he was ashamed of where he came from.[48]

Again, narrators were quick to respond to this snobbery, stressing their pride in their working-class origins. John emphasised: 'I'm very proud of my roots. Poor as they were … it was a beautiful past where we were never hungry, where we got the best of cheap food and lots of it. And why should anybody deny where he came from or disown where he came from?'[49] Patsy Corcoran described the working-class Northsiders she worked with in Sunbeam as 'the salt of the earth'.[50]

The intimate connection between class and space that emerges so frequently in the interviews can be explained by the fact that Cork is a small city. The names of neighbourhoods, communities and even individual terraces and estates carry all sorts of connotations that can be readily understood by those familiar with the area. 'Blackrock', 'Mahon', 'Ballyphehane' or 'Mayfield' are not simply geographical indicators but designations which are dense with social meaning. While terminology like 'working class', 'middle class' etc. are rarely used by the narrators, they still communicate these concepts by other means. Therefore, the oral historian should not expect that respondents will simply describe class in the terms they expect. Rather, close inspection of the narratives, as well as a detailed knowledge of their historical context, is required in order to ascertain what they tell us about class and how it was experienced by working people.

CONCLUSION

Labour historiography has traditionally viewed the workplace and trade unions as central in generating class consciousness. However, such an approach is problematic when applied to female workers in early to mid-twentieth-century Ireland. Máire Leane and Elizabeth Kiely, in their research into Irish women in paid employment between 1930 and 1960, concluded that 'work did not provide a primary narrative identity for the women we interviewed.'[51] Primarily, this is because women's working lives in the early part of the twentieth century were often quite brief, frequently an interlude between school and marriage, which usually meant leaving the labour force. For example, a pension report produced by Sunbeam Wolsey in 1956 showed that there were twenty-three men over 55 years old on the payroll as compared to just four women, despite the fact that females made up the majority of the overall workforce. The report noted that 'very few of the female staff will ever reach pensionable age.'[52] Similarly, female workers, until the 1960s, were rarely able to play anything more than a subordinate role in the trade union movement. As such, women were often more likely to encounter class discrimination and division outside the workplace and the trade union movement, as in the case of Kathleen F. through discrimination on the part of the Church, or in the case of Rena M., the field of education. Work was still central to social identity, as the snobbery encountered by women in manufacturing jobs demonstrates, but was experienced very differently by men and women. As such, the experience of class cannot be analysed properly without paying appropriate attention to the interaction between class and gender.

While commentators such as the president of University College Dublin who claimed that Ireland was a classless society, or the district court judge in Limerick who denied the existence of class differences between farmers and their employees, may have been sincere in their views, these opinions were a luxury of the elite. Class divisions, as indicated by the narrators for this study, were central to life in twentieth-century Ireland. Overall, they articulate the existence of a very clear class identity, considering themselves as part of a broader working-class community for which class discrimination and snobbery, both societal and institutional, were a deeply resented reality of everyday life.

A NOTE ON THE INTERVIEWS

This chapter is based on a total of fifteen interviews with former employees of Sunbeam. Five of these interviews were conducted by me, eight were provided by the Cork Northside Folklore Project (CNFP) and two were taken from the Women in Irish Society Oral History Project. The latter are available online at http://www.ucc.ie/wisp/ohp/. The CNFP website can be found at http://www.ucc.ie/research/nfp/. All of my own interviewees were given the option of having their testimony stored in the CNFP archive in Cork city. I would like to thank Máire Leane, Elizabeth Kiely, Mary O'Driscoll, my interviewees and the staff of the CNFP for their assistance in the composition of this chapter.

Chapter Twelve

From Yeatsian Nightmares to Tallafornian Dreams: Reflections on Classism and Culture in 'Classless' Ireland

Michael Pierse

Following interviews with respondents regarding the issue of class in modern Irish society, Eileen M. Trauth noted a 'discrepancy' in the way Irish people talked about class as a lived, everyday reality; there was a pattern of 'professing to live in a classless society while at the same time sending strong signals about class consciousness.'[1] For any observer of Irish social and cultural life, this paradox is surely one of the nation's great curiosities, one of the more ignored elephants in a drawing room heaving with all sorts of carefully avoided taboos. Though 'Irish society is often thought of as a classless society', class feeling is pervasive; snobbery, too, is rife, as is its counterpoint – the mocking distaste for the archetypal 'poshie' that is so strong in working-class areas.[2] Yet Trauth, witnessing an apparent 'ambivalence about the class system', was perplexed. Perhaps, she speculated, 'people's comments about a classless society expressed wishful thinking about what *ought* to be the case.'[3]

However, there is little real evidence that this common evasiveness about class can be put down to lofty aspirations for a more egalitarian Ireland

— what 'ought to be'. And yet class politics are everywhere, apparent in everything from trivial everyday conversations, to 'white-collar boxing', to crime reporting, to employment patterns and social mobility. But perhaps Trauth comes close to the truth when she suggests that Ireland's postcolonial history may have something to do with the almost pathological tendency to downplay class, a 'legacy of colonialism that produced a rigid "us–them" situation'.[4]

THE 'FIGHT FOR COLLARS AND TIES'

If the nationalist movement ostensibly sought to paper over the cracks of social stratification, however, it too was always riven with internal class divisions. This idea is touched upon by Tom Garvin in his analysis of one of the key organisations active in the formation of Irish nationalist identity, the Gaelic League. Garvin notes League founder and future president of Ireland Douglas Hyde's complaints regarding the 'leftist influence'; as Hyde's organisation grew, it began to accommodate all sorts of heretofore unreachable elements, such as Larkinites, that swelled its ranks, making Hyde feel a little uncomfortable with the fruits of his own success — so much so that Garvin notes how he felt 'compelled to wear old clothes so as not to raise the ire of the new democracy'.[5] Hyde's inveighing against the 'penny dreadfuls' and 'shilling shockers' of English (and consequently Irish) popular culture – along with his advocacy of 'use of Anglo-Irish literature instead of English books' – had, as Declan Kiberd also comments, a great deal 'in common with the future strictures of F.R. Leavis', a well-known cultural critic whose views on the low-brow tenor of the age of mass production and mass literacy, 'the vulgarization of popular taste', are often enlisted in criticisms of the elitism of literary studies.[6] Hyde's relationship with socialists was also fractious. When Patrick Pearse made a speech in praise of Larkin as someone who at least 'was doing something', Hyde, who shared the same platform, was tellingly unimpressed.[7] Hyde irked men like Seán O'Casey, for whom class was a significant barrier to organisational unity. O'Casey felt alienated within the League, on specifically class grounds; his working-class attire, he claimed, was criticised by other members; the 'nicely-suited, white-collared respectable members' of the 'refined Gaelic League branches of Dublin ... knew nothing and cared less' for the working class, he would later claim. These 'fretful popinjays lisping Irish wrongly' were more interested in the 'fight for collars and ties' than the 'fight for Irish'.[8] And so, even amidst the fervour of national feeling that no doubt accompanied the expansion of Gaelic revivalism, class was a significant, if at times ignored, concern.

THE NOBLE AND THE BEGGARMAN?

Other nationalist figures equally at home with the dream-world of Gaelic primitivism also felt perturbed by the reality of a 'new democracy'. The W.B. Yeats who penned 'The Fisherman' (1916) – his tribute to the archetypal 'wise and simple' peasant – was foisted on generations of Irish secondary school students, who were often told of the fêted poet's quaint desire for an alliance of 'noble and beggarman'.[9] But this vision of class harmony (albeit with the beggarman firmly in his place) is most emphatically undermined by Yeats's most poisoned of plays, *Purgatory* (1938), which never graced a Leaving Certificate curriculum. In the play, Old Man stands forlorn with his teenage son in front of the burnt-out shell of an old Big House. He relates how he was born in the house, to a woman of wealthy stock who died giving birth to him; she had married beneath her, to his father, a stable hand, who subsequently squandered the wealth of the house and then, in a drunken state, burnt it down. Old Man, we are told, later murdered his father because of this 'capital offence', but he then also repeated the supposed dilution of blue blood by fathering a bastard son with 'a tinker's daughter'.[10] In turn, his gruesome murder of his own son in the play is depicted as an act of social cleansing, excused because 'had he grown up / He would have struck a woman's fancy / Begot, and passed pollution on'.[11] This grotesque, visceral repugnance for the lower orders – reminiscent of the xenophobe's fear of miscegenation – is tellingly twinned with a distaste for the lustful body, a sentiment repeated, in poems such as 'Sailing to Byzantium' (1926), as disdain for all that is 'fish, flesh or fowl … Whatever is begotten, born and dies'.[12]

Yeats's contempt for the plebeian centres on a curious parallel between corporeal and class loathing, which James Plunkett explored in his novel (later a major television drama series) *Strumpet City* (1969). His elitist priest, Fr O'Connor, is enraged and repulsed in equal measure by a trade union rabble 'driving the respectable off the sidewalks'; for O'Connor the Lockout period is a complete shock to the social order. The priest sees the workers as an animalistic, immoral multitude, and senses the 'near presence of evil' in these 'agitators', a mere 'mob' of 'hooligans'. He is even 'violently and repeatedly sick', because of the attendant sense 'of infirmity, of uncleanliness, of corruption'.[13] In the novel, O'Connor is a proponent of the rarefied culture of the rich that Yeats had glorified. In this regard, working-class poet Paula Meehan excoriates the Yeats who 'spied motley / From high Georgian windows' with his 'literary crew' – from a world in which 'the poor become clowns / In your private review'. But how is it that students have so long been exposed to Yeats the great, pluralist statesman and nationalist poet, and so little to Yeats the sinister, snobbish bigot?[14] Why have cultural critics often chosen to ignore or evade the swaggering class warrior in his work?

CLASS DISMISSED

As Maura Adshead writes regarding the Gaelic League, 'the failure – by the protagonists recorded and the political scientists recording – to explicitly recognise the class dimensions to this narrative point[s] to another peculiarity of Irish politics, that is, the steadfast refusal to acknowledge class in popular political discourse'.[15] It is all the more revealing that her point is made in relation to Hyde, a man who supposedly tried to unite Irish people around a singular idea; Hyde, like Yeats, wanted to bond everyone to an idealised image of Ireland — *just not those people over there.* In the Free State 'the idea was promulgated that because British rule and the Protestant Establishment had been overthrown, Ireland was somehow a classless society. The fact that this is not true is less important than the fact that so many believed it to be true and as a consequence, in Ireland *social* class did not translate into class *politics.*'[16] The relative weakness of the Irish left in Europe that Adshead identifies here is beyond doubt one of the defining anomalies of Irish life. But cultural studies scholars should surely be attending to obvious class inflections across a range of cultural production in Irish life? Why has the significant international, institutionally widespread study of Irish literature and film been subjected to so little thoroughgoing class analysis?

In Britain, such work has long been associated with cultural materialism – a Gramscian strain of critical analysis originating in the work of socialist literary critic Raymond Williams – which has had a profound impact on scholarship across a range of disciplines. In Shakespeare studies, for instance, there are many examples of 'high culture' being challenged by academics determined to expose classism masquerading as tradition. Scholarly refutations of 'bardolatry' have become commonplace in British cultural studies; statements like 'believing in Shakespeare is not altogether different from believing in Santa Claus' make sense to the extent that Shakespeare has become 'the imaginary projection of an important tradition of social desire.'[17] As with Yeats, the 'common view of Shakespeare as a unique, transcendent genius is a kind of just-so story', an unquestioned, popularly held 'fact' that can be argued to sustain cultural ideas that ultimately support forms of social inequality. For many Shakespeare scholars, the image of 'the Bard' as the 'transcendent genius of a universal human nature' has faded over recent decades, replaced – in academia if not always in popular culture – by a more considered distancing from the 'Shakespeare myth'.[18] The very idea of Shakespeare as an immutable, transcendent icon of cultural 'genius' presupposes a static world in which certain forms of cultural production remain above criticism; more broadly, this idea of 'high culture' as an ageless and infallible constant also supports a whole host of conservative, traditionalist social practices, such as monarchy for instance. Shakespeare is thus harnessed to the conservative process of indoctrination in schools and the public sphere. As Michael D. Bristol argues, encountering Shakespeare at school or at a local theatre production imbues children with 'pre-theoretical intuitions' that encourage the assimilation of 'bardolatry' rather than any critical distance or intellectual probity.[19] But whereas scholarship by leading cultural academics of various hues – such as Graham Holderness, Terence Hawkes, Stephen Greenblatt, Francis Barker, Jonathan Dollimore and Alan Sinfield – has dragged Shakespeare down from his ethereal perch into the world of real men and women his work supposedly depicts, far less of this vintage has been produced in relation to Irish studies. While postcolonial interpretations of writers like Yeats and Joyce are commonplace, there is comparatively little on their attitudes toward the less well off, or, moreover, on how their legacies have been (mis)represented since to bolster certain kinds of cultural practices.

WHAT'S WITH O'LEARY IN THE GRAVE?

In relation to Yeats, it is ironic and absurd that many Irish people regard his work as that of a crusading pluralist and nationalist — largely based on a naïve reading of a small selection of his writings. In the centenary year of the 1913 Lockout, Yeats's 'September 1913' (1913) will no doubt again feature in documentaries and historical accounts as some sort of vindication of the rights of the working class, but as Yug Mohit Chaudhry has argued, such readings can be accused of 'facilitating thereby a sanitised and "international" reading of Yeats as "the last Romantic"'; Yeats thereby becomes Ireland's Shakespeare.[20] Take this typical contribution by Dan Mulhall in the *Irish Times* (20 August 2012): 'The Irish labour movement was beginning to come into its own in the second decade of the 20th century, and it was the Dublin Lockout that inspired Yeats to put pen to paper in September 1913.'[21] According to this standard narrative, Yeats saw the suffering of the workers, due to the belligerence and greed of the bosses, led by William Martin Murphy, as evidence of the passing of 'romantic Ireland', giving rise to the famous refrain of the poem.[22] Yeats had begun to develop 'his own brand of nationalism, founded on the values of the nobleman and the peasant, which he imagined to be mutually compatible'. This is typical also of the uncomplicated picture that many have of Yeats. While Mulhall rightly adduces that Yeats 'developed an aversion to the values of the rising Catholic middle class', for him this is because Yeats 'blamed [it] for putting paid to the Romantic Ireland he had treasured since the days of his youth'. This Yeats, who would later write 'Easter 1916' (1920), 'was energised by the aspirations that inspired the Rising'. Aspirations like republicanism, socialism, internationalism, the extension of the franchise?

Like the Shakespeare who becomes transcendent through tradition, Yeats, in this version of events, is a sort of romantic dreamer, almost unavailable to the kind of socio-cultural deconstruction that literary critics normally engage in. It is perhaps significant that Mulhall is the Irish ambassador to Germany and that his words were originally delivered as part of a lecture given at the University of Münster. His is the sanitised version of Yeats that Ireland presents to itself and to the world, part of a culture industry linked with tourism — simplified and marketable, like Kerrygold or Killarney. That is not to say Mulhall's intentions are to reproduce a travesty of Yeats; rather, we must question the cultural assumptions, or as Bristol put it, the 'pre-theoretical intuitions', that inform his analysis.

The original title of Yeats's poem, 'Romance in Ireland / (On reading much of the correspondence against the Art Gallery)', immediately hints that the focus of the poem was not, in fact, the suffering of workers or the nationalism of John O'Leary. Indeed, for Yeats the inspiration for the poem was the failure of the authorities in Dublin to reciprocate Hugh Lane's offer of paintings with a fitting gallery to house them; high culture, not workers' rights, is our starting point. Another key indicator is the poem's first place of publication: Ireland's most staunchly and explicitly unionist newspaper at the time, the *Irish Times*. As Chaudhry notes, the idea of this newspaper publishing a poem with even remotely nationalist leanings should at least arouse suspicion. But was O'Leary not a legendary Fenian? 'Contrary to popular understanding, O'Leary was not the respected, left-wing, anti-establishment Irish nationalist of the physical force tradition.'[23] In fact, O'Leary was himself a landlord, opposed to the activities of the Irish Parliamentary Party and the Land League and particularly critical of direct actions such as boycotting. If, in 1880, O'Leary was indeed a Fenian, by 1913 he was 'a constitutional monarchist opposed to republican democracy and adult franchise in Ireland' whose brother described him as 'quite an Englishman and ... a conservative in politics'. As Yeats went about asserting his ascendancy heritage in these years, O'Leary was a perfect focus for his idealisation; his attitudes 'would have wedded him to the poem's context and struck a sympathetic chord with *Irish Times* readers, many of whom were landlords with similar views'.[24] When Yeats castigates those who 'fumble in the greasy till', it is not a criticism of capitalism's venality *per se*, but rather an attack on the parvenu and philistine Catholic middle class in particular; his attack on those who 'add prayer to shimmering prayer' is not a criticism of religious hypocrisy *per se*, but rather an attack on Catholic wealth in particular.[25] After several antagonistic exchanges with William Martin Murphy in various periodicals, Yeats had become increasingly incensed at the power and swagger of this *arriviste* class, of which Murphy was a leading luminary. When Yeats invokes nationalist heroes Edward Fitzgerald, Robert Emmet and Wolfe Tone, it is primarily as an upbraiding reminder to Murphy of the contribution of the Protestant ascendancy to the nation — not as a rallying call to republicanism. When he denounces those who have added 'the halfpence to the pence / And prayer to shivering prayer', Yeats condemns the alliance of Catholicism and capitalism — primarily because it is such a threat to his own caste.[26] In American academia, as Chaudhry rightly argues, this primary focus of the poem has been obscured by naïve misreadings, which 'have politicised the poem on the wrong side'.[27] While many in Ireland also re-imagine the Yeats of 'September 1913' as a crusader for the workers, nothing could be further from the truth. The real Yeats harboured rather more ugly ideas:

The whole system of Irish Catholicism pulls down the able and well-born as it pulls up the peasant, as I think it does. A long continuity of culture like that at Coole [Lady Augusta Gregory's ancestral home, emblematic for Yeats of Protestant cultural ascendancy] could not have arisen, and never has arisen, in a single Catholic family in Ireland since the middle ages.[28]

Against Yeats's obsession with Hugh Lane's paintings, the failure of elitist aesthetic practices to reflect the lives of the poor is underscored by other writers. In Act 3 of Oliver St John Gogarty's *Blight* (1917), a meeting of Dublin Corporation's Hospital Board is used to contrast the aesthetic concerns of the affluent with the material realities of the poor. City councillors opt to avoid reading a letter from the Local Government Board, 'calling attention to the urgent necessity of adopting some scheme for preventing the spread of the hidden plague' in the tenements, because of 'considerations of good taste'.[29] Instead, they pointedly turn their attention to lofty talk about Dublin's architecture and the building of an elaborate, ornate mortuary chapel. Gogarty's message – that in Dublin's corridors of power the aesthetics of death are more important than the proletariat's misery in life – was surely a direct retort to Yeats and his ilk. Yeats's poem may inspire great feelings of maudlin nostalgia for socialists today, but only as a great historical distortion.

REMEMBERING TO FORGET

The kind of culturally widespread, collective amnesia that underpins all of this is, of course, no accident. Those who scrambled for power in the 1920s and 1930s ensured that elite power would be cemented in the ensuing cultural hegemony. The selective treatment of the works of Seán O'Casey is a case in point. While his *Trilogy* plays – *The Shadow of a Gunman* (1923), *Juno and the Paycock* (1924) and *The Plough and the Stars* (1926) – remain staples in the repertoire of Irish theatrical production (and they do rake in the cash), O'Casey's many later, socialist and stylistically experimental works have elicited relatively scant commentary and support. As with Yeats, schoolchildren are fed on the relatively cosy O'Casey of the *Trilogy*, whose anti-nationalism may raise a few heckles, but whose backhanded, comic-tragic tribute to the Revolutionary Period posed little real threat to the new hegemony – as compared to the biting anti-clerical and anti-capitalist mockery of the new state in his middle and later plays. If the names of O'Casey's *Trilogy* plays roll effortlessly off the tongue of the average Irish 18-year-old, later works, such as *Within the Gates* (1933), *The Star Turns Red* (1940), or *Cock-a-Doodle Dandy* (1949) are more likely to evoke raised eyebrows. O'Casey's dogged commitment to the working class was a bad business decision, and he indeed anticipated how cultural exclusivism would affect his own legacy and that of other writers. *The Bishop's Bonfire* (1955), for instance, centres on the civic welcome for a bishop in which all heretical literature is to be burned – levelling a serious accusation of literary fascism against the Irish Government. This was prescient stuff indeed, for much of Dublin's working-class writing in the coming decades was to fall under the jack boot of Ireland's own cultural commissars. O'Casey stresses the class prejudice that underpinned censorship in an opinion voiced by the Canon to Father Boheroe. Poor minds cannot contend with freedom of expression, he explains: 'Can't you understand that their dim eyes are able only for a little light? Damn, it, man, can't you see Clooncoohy can never be other than he is?'[30] This elitism is, of course, reminiscent of Yeats's eugenics. In the Ireland that produced the fascist Blueshirt movement, the anti-communist Irish Christian Front, and continual attacks on and denunciations of left-wing politics from Church, State, and even the trade union movement, it is unsurprising that a full appreciation of O'Casey's core aesthetic and political values failed to emerge in popular consciousness, but it is perhaps surprising how the effects of this censorship endure. As Bernice Schrank laments, the 'general reluctance to deal with O'Casey's socialism is unfortunate because it artificially isolates O'Casey's technical achievements from his political concerns.'[31]

O'Casey was a victim of hegemonic reconstructions and deliberate censorship of his work, and the State control of books he condemned was, of course, one of the cornerstones of its class war. Consider, for instance, the case of Paul Smith. Anthony Burgess was 'sorely tempted' to use the term 'genius' to describe him.[32] John Jordan compared his novel *The Countrywoman* (1961) with the work of Emile Zola.[33] Its social realist style and political overtones even met with official Soviet approval, securing it a Russian translation and an inclusion in Volume Three of the Soviet *Concise Literary Encyclopaedia* as a notable work of 'social protest'.[34] His writing is of great significance, but most Irish people are unlikely to have ever heard of Paul Smith. *The Countrywoman*, with its realism and its forceful denunciations of poverty in the Free State, was always destined for the censor's bin. Lee Dunne is another writer whose literary career suffered from such censorship. Dunne – also a working-class Dub – again focussed on the privations of working-class life, and his work had a considerable following. *Goodbye to the Hill* (1965), as a novel, was a bestseller in Britain and the USA, selling over one million copies worldwide. It spawned a Hollywood movie, *Paddy* (1970), which was immediately banned by the Irish censors (only to be granted a 12A certification when passed by national censor John Kelleher in 2006).[35] In its most successful theatrical production, at the Regency Airport Hotel, from September 1989 until December 1992, *Goodbye* became Ireland's longest running play.[36] But despite this feat, Dunne's work has failed to receive any significant recognition from Ireland's cultural elites (by this I mean academia and arts bodies). In revealing commentary on Ireland's elitist cultural practices, Dunne complained about the Irish government's banning of paperback editions of his books (which the poor might afford), while letting the more expensive hardback editions through. 'Economic morality' of this kind infuriated him: 'I mean, a book that's dirty at four shillings is clean at twenty five?'[37] The attitude of censors towards his work recalls the paternalistic view of O'Casey's bishop.[38]

But there are more subtle forms of repression than censorship: the education system, the Arts Council, the various forms of regulation, support and reproduction in culture that promote one artefact over another all play their part. It is particularly notable in Irish literary studies and education that one of the great works of proletarian life, Robert Noonan's (Tressell) *The Ragged Trousered Philanthropists* (1910), written by an Irishman, is barely acknowledged in Ireland. Things like this do not simply 'happen'. These writers' legacies (or lack thereof in Ireland) reveal how, through censorship, cunning, snobbery or avoidance, the State has often denied working-class Irish people access to their own histories and to the cultural production that mirrors their experiences.

CLASSISM IN MODERN IRELAND: WHAT IS LEFT UNSAID

The repercussions of this discursive repression of class in Ireland are very much with us to this day. As I have argued, class inequality is pervasive but rarely acknowledged. Why is it, for instance, that RTÉ felt comfortable – during its major *Ireland's Greatest* (2010) initiative – having presenter Joe Duffy, who earned a whopping €408,889 in the middle of a deep recession, present the case for James Connolly, a radical socialist who must surely have somersaulted in his grave?[39] This glaring, even comic juxtaposition of Swiftian proportions was emblematic of the hidden-in-plain-sight nature of class inequalities in Irish media production; so profound is our national broadcaster's blindness to class issues that it did not even consider that the millionaire Duffy's advocacy of Connolly might be inappropriate, or risible.

As Helena Sheehan notes of the period from 1962–87 in Ireland, RTÉ was largely oblivious to working-class, city life: 'RTÉ had failed to come to terms with the real texture of contemporary urban life and particularly with its cutting edge … It had been most remiss with respect to its representation of working class life and strikingly negligent in relation to the most socially conscious and culturally advanced elements of urban life.'[40] Often broadcasters pick on the bad or mad in working-class life instead of shining a light on what is good, but it is not that programmes like Stuart Carolan's RTÉ drama *Love/Hate*, for instance, which has been accused of 'glorifying' criminality, should not be made – although they might be made better. The real concern is that what is not made, what is not commissioned by the national broadcaster, reveals a great deal in terms of how Irish society is allowed to see itself.[41] Drug dealing and 'gangland' crime are significant scourges in Irish working-class life, but the kind of things that are less immediate, but equally – perhaps even more – damaging, like white-collar criminality and political corruption, feature far less in terms of dramatisation and reportage.

This correlates with Ciaran McCullagh's analysis of crime and class in Ireland, which suggests how the manner in which classes of crime are depicted has a direct impact on the way in which crime is dealt with by the courts. Corporate crime fails to 'mobilise the stigma of criminality', perhaps because corporate criminals do not, in the main, emerge from or operate in working-class areas. 'In those few cases that come to the attention of the courts,' McCullagh adds, 'offenders are "let off" with a fine'. This anomaly has more to do with the class of the criminal than the class of crime, he argues: '[It is] in some contrast to the way in which the criminality of the working class is dealt with. At the most basic level there is a somewhat greater willingness to use prison as the sanction for the offences they commit'. In his scrutiny of 'getting the criminals we want', McCullagh attests to how criminality is associated with the working class in general public perceptions.[42] As Leslie J. Moran also observes, 'middle-class men are not culturally associated with violence as there is an assumption that violence (as pathology) is a characteristic of the criminal "Other", the working and underclass'.[43]

In the same week that *Love/Hate* received some of its most stinging criticism for graphic depictions of gangland violence, another story emerged and quickly disappeared: 'a substantial drop in the number of people convicted of white collar crime'.[44] The figures show that the number of people convicted of white collar crime dropped from 579 – just under a quarter of the offences in 2003 – to 178 in 2010, less than 15 per cent of the offences committed in that year. Compounding this dramatic decrease was the revelation of an increase in the number of white-collar crime offences over the same period. The figures also revealed that there were no solicitors or barristers, and only two full-time accountants employed by the Garda

Bureau of Fraud Investigation in 2012.[45] In this context, television drama such as *Love/Hate*, whatever the merits in terms of screenwriting, production and acting, cannot but be seen to reinforce the inordinate focus on the crimes committed by criminals from working-class areas, while white-collar crime still manages to get off scot free. This type of representational tilting can have very negative social consequences: as Maggie Wykes asserts of 1980s Britain, 'significant swathes of what characterised working-class life were associated with disorder, deviance and crime, enabling control and change through a range of policy and popular pressure during Thatcherism'.[46]

Despite the many serious issues in working-class areas, there is more of a tendency to trivialise than to analyse, as the popularity of reality shows like TV3's *Tallafornia* suggests. Donald Clarke's review of this series in the *Irish Times* reveals (though not intentionally) how ostensibly harmless popcorn TV can be detrimental because of what it presents and omits. 'It's easy to deride the vulgarity of label addiction and genital decoration, but it's harder to regret the celebration of upward mobility in contemporary popular culture,' he enthuses.

> Of course, we don't know how 'real' the subjects are. They do slip suspiciously easily into character types. But the colonisation of the mainstream by ambitious, funny, gregarious folk from unfairly maligned outer boroughs deserves at least a tentative cheer.[47]

Tallafornia's jolly glossing over of working-class areas is supposedly to be commended, even if we don't know how 'real' it all is. But what Clarke terms the 'celebration of upward mobility' that the programme depicts is concerning. In the fantasy land of *Tallafornia*, the working-class is on-the-up, enjoying the fruits of a newly mobile society and all of the consumerism it has to offer. This, again, propagates a pernicious myth. In its working paper, *Intergenerational Social Mobility: A Family Affair?* published by the Organisation for Economic Co-operation and Development (OECD) in

2009, it emerged that Ireland offers less educational mobility than the average OECD country. The paper elaborates that

> there is a statistically significant probability premium of achieving tertiary education associated with coming from a higher-educated family, while there is a probability penalty associated with growing up in a lower-educated family ... the penalty of coming from a low-educated family is particularly high in Ireland and Greece.[48]

Again, this reality is less likely to be borne out by 'reality' TV. Poverty and Ireland's socially sclerotic exclusivism are conveniently elided in favour of 'tentative cheer'.

REPRESENTING CLASS

It should be evident from all of this that how class is represented in Irish cultural production is an area where class analysis might be engaged more fully. One of the current hazards in this area is the slippage into semantic dishonesty and euphemism that is characteristic of how class is dealt with in Irish media discourse, as instanced by the current craze for the 'coping classes' – because calling people 'working class' is, well, somehow insulting and old-fashioned. But terms such as 'coping classes', and the deluded elasticity of 'middle class', serve a more sinister purpose, presenting an illogical and experientially artificial categorisation that has no basis in reality, but that does allow rich people to tell the poor 'we're all in this together'. In Ireland, this is belied, of course, by the recent revelation that 'the country's highest earners are paying a smaller share of income tax now than they did at the height of the boom'.[49]

Ideas of class are of little use unless they have a solid relationship with the realities of social experience. As anthropologist Chris Eipper wrote in his study of class in Bantry, County Cork, in 1986, 'class has to be analytically grasped as both an ideological encounter and as a material condition'.[50] This was the position taken by iconic historian E.P. Thompson, who argued the case for class as 'a relationship, not a thing'.[51] As Fintan O'Toole states, notions of an expanded, all-consuming middle class in advanced economies across the world are part of the 'great con job of our times'. The wealthy across these states are prospering, and incrementally increasing their share of society's spoils, while convincing the less well-off that we are all part of a broad middle; at the same time, wages are falling and austerity is sharpening the already gaping inequality. The con job is first ideological, then economic: 'Being middle class means you can identify with, and aspire to join, the elite. You don't need the two things that created a fairer distribution of the fruits of growth: trade unions and the welfare state'.[52] As Robin D.G. Kelley argues in the recent documentary *Class Dismissed – How TV Frames the Working Class*, 'it's very hard for people who see themselves as middle class to reconceive themselves as working class, because somehow, in this culture, working class is a failure'.[53] His comments relate specifically to the USA, but might as easily be applied to Ireland and, to a lesser extent, Britain. Yet there is a case to be made that many people are still very aware of being working class – even at the height of Ireland's ballooning affluence in 2005, a survey found that 30 per cent of the Republic's population still designated themselves working class.[54] A further instance could be the European Fiscal Treaty vote of 2012, in which the result was very much split along class lines.[55] Is it more so the case that middle-class policymakers and pundits have imagined the working class away?

Academics and others engaged in the business of cultural criticism and promotion must acknowledge their own culpability in this process. University humanities departments offer very little in terms of concrete interactions with working-class cultural life. Belfast shipyard worker and writer Thomas Carnduff complained in 1941 that,

> so far as I can remember, the University and the worker have
> little in common. It is an educational institution reserved to

certain classes of the community … You don't bother to explain to the working-classes what benefit they derive from your institution, if any.[56]

His complaint is still valid today. As Ken Worpole put the case in Britain, 'the fragmentation of working class historical and cultural consciousness now fiercely debated … is not exactly surprising given the fragmentation and lack of concern for the material artefacts of that consciousness.'[57] There is something very important, indeed at times epiphanic, for working-class people, in encountering books like *The Ragged Trousered Philanthropists* (1910) or films like *Brassed Off* (1996) for the first time. As John Berger put it, 'the pride with which a class first sees itself recognisably depicted in a permanent art is full of pleasure even if the art is flawed and the truth harsh. The depiction gives a historic resonance to their lives. A pride which was, before, an obstinate refusal of shame, becomes an affirmation.'[58] How much space do the institutions of the state such as the Department of Education, the universities and the Arts Council actually afford this large section of the population and their narratives? How much do the 'ideological state apparatuses', as Louis Althusser termed them, even wish to engage with the concept of culture in working-class life?[59] In the centenary year of the Lockout, class as a concept and a lived reality – as a culture, a 'relationship with tradition, a discourse of roots' – is evidently still an important battleground.[60] Not an anachronism, not a shibboleth, not some variety of doctrinaire socialist's fantasy, but a lived reality, a palpable part of everyday life. The importance of returning to class is that class returns to us. And perhaps what is most important in all of this is that we learn to question more of the class dynamics of Irish culture, as the true proponents of the Lockout – such as James Connolly, Jim Larkin and Seán O'Casey – would surely have hoped we would.

Notes

Chapter 1

1. Quote taken from F. Devine, *Organising History: A Centenary of SIPTU* (Dublin: Gill & Macmillan, 2009), p.53.
2. Devine, *Organising History*, p.44.
3. Arnold Wright, *Disturbed Dublin: The Story of the Great Strike of 1913–14* (London: Longmans, Green and Co., 1914), p.15.
4. C.A. Cameron, *Report upon the State of Public Health in the City of Dublin for the Year 1913* (Dublin: Sealy, Bryers & Walker, 1914), p.43. I am indebted to Dr Rhona McCord for this reference.
5. Ibid., p.258.
6. Wright, *Disturbed Dublin*, p.30.
7. '...the returns gave the rate in Dublin as 22, while the average rate for the 76 great towns of England and Wales was 13.9 – Birmingham was 15, Liverpool 18, Manchester 16, Blackburn 18, Huddersfield 19, Newcastle 10, Glasgow 15, and Belfast 16. Unfortunately it is no new thing for Dublin to head the list, as a matter of fact it usually does so', 'Dublin Topics', *Irish Times*, 9 April 1910, p.5.
8. L. Carroll, *In the Fever King's Preserves: Sir Charles Cameron and the Dublin Slums* (Dublin: A. & A. Farmer, 2011), p.57.
9. Ibid., p.160.
10. E. O'Connor, *A Labour History of Ireland 1824–2000* (Dublin: University College Dublin Press, 2011), p.51.
11. T. Morrissey, *William Martin Murphy* (Dundalk: Dundalgan Press, 1997), p.45.
12. 'Dispute in Dublin Newspaper Office', *Weekly Irish Times*, 23 August 1913, p.4.
13. P. Yeates, *Lockout: Dublin 1913* (Dublin: Gill & Macmillan, 2001), p.9.
14. Ibid., p.10.
15. O'Connor, *Labour History of Ireland*, p.78.
16. Workers' Union of Ireland, *1913: Jim Larkin and the Dublin Lock-out* (Dublin: Workers' Union of Ireland, 1964), p.23.

17. 'Dublin Tram Strike', *Irish Times*, 27 August 1913, p.9.

18. Anon, *Dublin Strikes 1913: Facts Regarding the Labour Disputes Contained in Speech of Mr. T.M. Healy, K.C., M.P., at Court of Enquiry Held in Dublin Castle on Wednesday October 1st, 1913* (Dublin: Acme Press, n.d.), p.20.

19. Yeates, *Lockout*, p.16.

20. 'Meeting in Beresford Place', *Weekly Irish Times*, 30 August 1913, p.4.

21. 'Interview with Mr. W.M. Murphy', *Weekly Irish Times*, 30 August 1913, p.4.

22. 'Labour Agitation in Dublin', *Irish Times*, 29 August 1913, p.7. The *Irish Times* mistakenly spelled Lawlor as Lalor.

23. 'The Defendants Before the Magistrate', *Irish Times*, 29 August 1913, p.7.

24. Yeates, *Lockout*, p.69.

25. '500 Hurt, 1 Dead in Dublin Riots', *New York Times*, 1 September 1913, p.1.

26. Devine, *Organising History*, p.56.

27. C.D. Greaves, *The Life and Times of James Connolly* (London: Lawrence & Wishart, 1961; 1986), p.309; 'James Connolly Released', *Irish Times*, 15 September 1913, p.7.

28. 'No Meeting in Sackville Street', *Weekly Irish Times*, 6 September 1913, p.5.

29. Yeates, *Lockout*, p.112.

30. 'Dublin Labour Crisis', *Irish Times*, 4 September 1913, p.7.

31. Ibid.

32. Workers' Union of Ireland, *1913*, p.39.

33. E. O'Connor, *James Larkin* (Cork: Cork University Press, 2002), p.44.

34. 'Labour Crisis in Dublin', *Weekly Irish Times*, 27 September 1913, p.3.

35. 'Meeting at Liberty Hall', *Irish Times*, 14 November 1913, p.7.

36. O'Connor, *James Larkin*, p.46.

37. 'Larkin in Manchester', *Weekly Irish Times*, 22 November 1913, p.5.

38. 'The employers' essential demand is for freedom from the intolerable tyranny of the Irish Transport Workers' Union, as that union is at present constituted. The English labour leaders must have much sympathy with this demand, for they have discovered for themselves the truth about Mr. Larkin and his methods.' From editorial, 'A New Development', *Weekly Irish Times*, 6 December 1913, p.10.

39. 'Trade Union Congress and Dublin dispute', *Weekly Irish Times*, 13 December 1913, p.11.

40. 'Dublin Labour Crisis', *Weekly Irish Times*, 27 December 1913, p.5.

41. W. O'Brien, *Forth the Banners Go* (Dublin: Three Candles Press, 1969), p.241.

42. 'Transport Union Repudiated', *Freeman's Journal*, 2 February 1914, p.7.

43. 'The End of the Strike', *Irish Times*, 3 February 1914, p.4.

44. O'Brien, *Forth the Banners Go*, p.241.

Notes

Chapter 2

1. Children's street song from 1913, sung to the tune of 'Alexander's Ragtime Band', cited in Donal Nevin 'On Larkin: A Miscellany', in Donal Nevin (ed.), *Jim Larkin: Lion of the Fold* (Dublin: Gill and Macmillan, 1998), p.466.

2. See for instance, Niall Crowley, 'Debate needed on legacy of Dublin lockout 1913', *Irish Times*, 4 January 2013.

3. Bureau of Military History Witness Statement (BMH WS) 0733 James O'Shea, p.2. These statements, collected from 1947–57, form an incredible resource for the study of the Irish revolutionary period and are now freely available and searchable online at http://www.bureauofmilitaryhistory.ie/ (accessed 13 March 2013).

4. C. Desmond Greaves, *The Irish Transport and General Workers' Union: The Formative Years 1909–1923* (Dublin: Gill and Macmillan, 1982), p.91.

5. Sean O'Casey, *Autobiographies II: Drums Under the Windows and Inishfallen, Fare Thee Well* (London: Faber and Faber, 2011 [1st ed. 1949]), p.172.

6. BMH WS 0258 Mrs MacDowell (Maeve Cavanagh), p.4.

7. Jim Larkin in his presidential address to the annual meeting of the Irish Trades Union Congress, 1 June 1914, cited in James Plunkett, 'Big Jim: A Loaf on the Table, a Flower in the Vase', in Donal Nevin (ed.), *Lion of the Fold*, p.112.

8. Cited in R.M. Fox, *Jim Larkin: The Rise of the Underman* (London: Lawrence & Wishart, 1957), p.73.

9. Oft-cited figures of weekly sales of more than 20,000 are questioned by James Curry as lacking evidence. He details the original source of these mistaken figures in his book *Artist of the Revolution: The Cartoons of Ernest Kavanagh (1884–1916)* (Cork: Mercier Press, 2012), pp.14–15.

10. See James Curry, *Artist of the Revolution*.

11. On the IWWU, see Mary Jones, *These Obstreperous Lassies: A History of the Irish Women Workers' Union* (Dublin: Gill and Macmillan, 1988). On Delia Larkin and the IWWU, see Theresa Moriarty, 'Delia Larkin: Relative Obscurity', in Donal Nevin (ed.), *Lion of the Fold*, pp.428–38, and James Curry, 'Delia Larkin: "More harm to the Big Fellow than any of the employers"?', *Saothar: Journal of the Irish Labour History Society*, 36 (2011), pp.19–25.

12. BMH WS 0889 Seamus Ua Caomhanaigh, p.38.

13. Virginia E. Glandon, *Arthur Griffith and the Advanced-Nationalist Press Ireland, 1900–1922* (New York: Peter Lang, 1985), p.45.

14. Haywood had been in France when he received a telegram from the *Daily Herald* inviting him to London to speak on behalf of Larkin, who was then in prison. The CGT gave him a check for 1,000 francs for the Dublin workers. When Haywood arrived

in London, Larkin had been released, and Haywood spoke alongside him at a mass rally in Albert Hall. Despite his years of campaigning work, Haywood said that 'I have never spoken in any meeting with more satisfaction than in this auditorium.' See Bill Haywood, *Bill Haywood's Book: The Autobiography of William D. Haywood* (London: Martin Lawrence Limited, 1929), pp.272–4.

15.   Donal Nevin, 'The Askwith Inquiry', in Nevin (ed.), *Lion of the Fold*, p.190.

16.   Ibid., p.191.

17.   See John Newsinger, *Rebel City: Larkin, Connolly and the Dublin Labour Movement* (London: The Merlin Press, 2004), pp.88–106 for a discussion on the *Daily Herald* and the Dublin Lockout.

18.   Trades Union Congress Parliamentary Committee, *Report of the Deputation appointed by the Manchester Congress to deal with the Trade Union Crisis in Dublin* (London: 1913), p.1. This and many other reports on the dispute are available for consultation in the TUC Library, London Metropolitan University.

19.   Ibid., p.2.

20.   Ibid., p.3.

21.   Ibid., p.4. The Chief Divisional Magistrate, E.G. Swifte, who sentenced many during the Lockout, including Larkin and Connolly, was a substantial shareholder in Murphy's Dublin United Tramway Company. The allegation was made by Walter Carpenter at a Socialist Party of Ireland rally on 15 September 1913 and never denied by Swifte. See Dublin Metropolitan Police report, National Archives of Ireland, CSO, CR 17597, cited in Pádraig Yeates, *Lockout: Dublin 1913* (Dublin: Gill and Macmillan, 2000), p.34.

22.   Trades Union Congress Parliamentary Committee, *Dublin Food Fund, Statement of Accounts and Complete List of Grants, Donations, Collections, and Personal Contributions* (London: 1914), p.4.

23.   Ibid., p.7.

24.   Ibid., pp.7–43.

25.   Ibid., pp.43–4.

26.   BMH WS 1650 Patrick O'Reilly, p.5.

27.   TUC Parliamentary Committee, *Dublin Food Fund*, p.4. See also Pádraig Yeates, *Lockout*, pp.321–327.

28.   BMH WS 0889 Seamus Ua Caomhanaigh, pp.37–8.

29.   *Liverpool Daily Post and Mercury*, 18 November 1913, cited in Bob Holton, *British Syndicalism, 1900–1914: Myths and Realities* (London: Pluto Press, 1976), p.193.

30.   BMH WS 0800 Michael O'Flanagan, p.1.

31.   BMH WS 1065 James Coss, p.1.

32.   BMH WS 0733 James O'Shea, p.5.

Notes

33.   BMH WS 0328 Gearoid Ua h-Uallachain, p.20.

34.   Bodleian Library, University of Oxford, MS. Asquith 38, f. 210 [this may now be fol. 32], 26 September 1913 cited in Leon Ó Broin, *The Chief Secretary: Augustine Birrell in Ireland* (London: Chatto & Windus, 1969), p.75.

Chapter 3

1.   Robert G. Lowery, 'Sean O'Casey and the Irish Worker (with an index, 1911–14)', in Robert G. Lowery (ed.), *O'Casey Annual 3* (London: Macmillan Press, 1984), p.41.

2.   'Dublin Printers' Bankruptcy. James Larkin Examined', *Irish Times*, 27 August 1913.

3.   Steven Dedalus Burch, *Andrew P. Wilson and the Early Irish and Scottish National Theatres, 1911–50* (Lewiston, New York: Edwin Mellen Press, 2008), pp.53–4.

4.   Francis Devine, 'Larkin and the ITGWU, 1909–1912', in Donal Nevin (ed.), *James Larkin: Lion of the Fold* (Dublin: Gill & Macmillan, 1998), p.35; Lowery, 'Sean O'Casey and the Irish Worker', pp.42–3.

5.   Burch, *Andrew P. Wilson*, pp.64–5.

6.   Lowery, 'Sean O'Casey and the Irish Worker', pp.61–2, 84. As 'Euchan' Wilson also replied to several critical letters from readers of the *Irish Worker*.

7.   'City T.C.'s Action. Mr. J. Larkin Sued For Libel', *Sunday Independent*, 26 January 1913.

8.   'Arouse Ye, Then!', *Irish Worker*, 28 September 1912.

9.   'Bill! A Tragedy in Three Acts. With Prologue and Epilogue', *Irish Worker*, 25 January 1913.

10.   Burch, *Andrew P. Wilson*, p.13.

11.   John Newsinger, *Rebel City. Larkin, Connolly and the Dublin Labour Movement* (London: Merlin Press, 2004), p.26.

12.   Burch, *Andrew P. Wilson*, p.26.

13.   Lowery, 'Sean O'Casey and the Irish Worker', p.44.

14.   Burch, *Andrew P. Wilson*, p.24. See David Krause (ed.), *The Letters of Sean O'Casey 1910–41*, Volume 1 (London: Cassell & Company, 1975), pp.13–27.

15.   See *Forth the Banners Go. Reminiscences of William O'Brien, as told to Edward MacLysaght, D. Litt* (Dublin: Three Candles Limited, 1969), p.260; William O'Brien Papers, National Library of Ireland (NLI), Ms. LO P 113 (61); 'Libel Action. Against Mr. James Larkin. By A City Councillor', *Freeman's Journal*, 23 January 1913; 'City T. C.'s Action. Mr. J. Larkin Sued For Libel', *Sunday Independent*, 26 January 1913.

16.   Burch, *Andrew P. Wilson*, p.57.

17.   'The Sackmender. A Parable', *Irish Worker*, 25 May 1912.

18.   'Women Workers' Column. The Sackmender', ibid., 1 June 1912.

19.   'Irish Workers' Dramatic Club', ibid., 8 June 1912.

20. 'Our Xmas', ibid., 28 December 1912.

21. 'The Suffrage! A Great Meeting and a Great Cause', ibid., 1 February 1913.

22. 'Wisdom', ibid., 13 July 1912.

23. 'The Assinine Law', ibid., 14 September 1912.

24. 'The Hass and 'Orse Show', ibid., 31 August 1912.

25. 'Ali Martin Baba and His Forty Thieves; Or the Victory of Shemus. A Christmas Phantasy in Three Spasms', ibid., 21 December 1912.

26. 'The Grasping Hand. A Tale of Murphy's Early Years', ibid., 2 August 1913.

27. 'Profit!', ibid., 12 October, 19 October, 26 October 1912.

28. Burch, *Andrew P. Wilson*, p.28.

29. For a facsimile edition of the *Irish Worker*'s 1912 *Christmas Number*, which contains the full text of Wilson's *Victims* and *Ali Martin Baba and His Forty Thieves* plays, see James Curry & Francis Devine (eds), *'Merry May Your Xmas Be & 1913 Free From Care': The Irish Worker 1912 Christmas Number* (Dublin: Irish Labour History Society, 2012).

30. Ben Levitas, 'Plumbing the Depths: Irish Realism and the Working Class from Shaw to O'Casey', *Irish University Review*, Vol. 33, No. 1, Special Issue: New Perspectives on the Irish Literary Revival (Spring – Summer 2003), p.141.

31. Christopher Murray, *Sean O'Casey. Writer at Work* (Dublin: Gill & Macmillan, 2004), p.95. See also Burch, *Andrew P. Wilson*, p.30; Levitas, 'Plumbing the Depths', p.141; Ben Levitas, *The Theatre of Nation. Irish Drama and Cultural Nationalism, 1890–1916* (Oxford: Clarendon Press, 2002), p.202.

32. 'Liberty Hall. The Irish Workers' Dramatic Club', *Irish Worker*, 28 December 1912.

33. The flyer advertising the *Irish Worker*'s 1912 *Christmas Number* revealed that the publication would feature a play called 'The Victims' by 'Euchan'. Yet when the *Christmas Number* was actually published this had been altered to 'Victims' by 'A. Patrick Wilson'. See William O'Brien Papers, NLI, Ms. LO P 113 (61). A. Patrick Wilson was the theatrical name which Wilson went by during his time in Ireland, a situation which came about due to his pretending to be 'a full-blooded Irishman' when auditioning for membership with the Abbey Theatre's second company in 1911. In Scotland he was instead known as Andrew P. Wilson. See Burch, *Andrew P. Wilson*, p.54.

34. Burch, *Andrew P. Wilson*, p.203.

35. Levitas, 'Plumbing the Depths', pp.141–2.

36. 'Liberty Hall. The Irish Workers' Dramatic Club', *Irish Worker*, 28 December 1912. Wilson directed all four plays, three of which he acted in alongside Delia Larkin.

37. Burch, *Andrew P. Wilson*, p.35.

38. 'Euchan in a New Role', *Irish Worker*, 17 May 1913.

39. *Victims and Poached* (Dublin: Liberty Hall Plays, no. 1, n.d.)

40. 'Some Casual Comments On Rolling Stones and Other Things', *Irish Worker*, 29 March 1913.

41. Lowery, 'Sean O'Casey and the Irish Worker', p.46.

42. 'Dublin Fanaticism', *Irish Worker*, 1 November 1913; 'Come off that Fence', *Irish Worker*, 13 December 1913.

43. 'Wisdom', ibid., 13 July 1912.

Chapter 4

1. Special thanks to Sara Goek who proofread and suggested improvements to this chapter. Thanks also to Prof David Brundage who made further suggestions.

2. Letter by Superintendent Howe, Dublin Metropolitan Police Detective Department, Dublin. 26 October 1914. Dublin Castle Special Branch Files. CO 904/206/233B. National Archives, Kew [hereafter listed as SBF]. From the Colonial Office Record Series Vol. 1: Sinn Féin and Republican Suspects 1899-1921 (Dublin: Eleclann, 2006). His luggage was reported as two 'portmanteux' and a black trunk.

3. Seán Mac Giollarnáth (Gerald O'Connor) and Diarmuid Ó Cearbhaill, 'James Connolly: A Study of his Work and Worth', *Journal of the Galway Archaeological and Historical Society*, 58 (2006), p.153; James Larkin, *In the Footsteps of Big Jim: A Family Biography* (Dublin: Blackwater Press, 1995), p.79; D. R. O'Connor Lysaght, 'The Irish Citizen Army, 1913–16: White, Larkin and Connolly', *History Ireland*, 14, 2, (March/April, 2006), p. 19; *Irish Worker*, 28 November 1914. Mollies, short for Molly Maguire, was an insult directed at the Ancient Order of Hibernians which had grown in the early decades of the twentieth century into a major sectarian, nationalist and anti-union force within the Irish Parliamentary Party. Larkin himself claimed 'the men who were responsible for that strike [Lockout] and the prolongation of it were J.D. Nugent [AOH national secretary] and the "scabs". He would teach them, as the United Irishmen did in past times, that they would have no sectarianism in this country.' Fergal McCluskey 'MAKE WAY FOR THE MOLLY MAGUIRES!' The Ancient Order of Hibernians and the Irish Parliamentary Party, 1902–14', *History Ireland*, 20, 1 (January/February 2012), p.36.

4. William O'Brien and Thomas Kennedy Papers, 23718/H (223), National Library of Ireland.

5. Mac Giollarnáth and Ó Cearbhaill, 'Connolly', pp.145–6.

6. R.M. Fox, *The History of the Irish Citizen Army* (Dublin: Cahill and Co. Ltd., 1944); Sean O'Casey, *The Story of the Irish Citizen Army* (London: Journeyman Press, 1980).

7. *The Gaelic American*, 21 November 1914. One letter writer in the same paper expressed his anti-English sentiments that 'if England had declared war on hell I would be pro-devil'.

8. *The Evening Herald*, 9 December 1914; *New York Tribune*, 16 November 1914.

9. Personal and Confidential, Directorate of Intelligence (Home Office), Monthly Review of Revolutionary Movements in British Dominions Overseas and Foreign Countries, No. 21, July 1920. CAB/24/111. National Archives, Kew.

10. Eugene V. Debs, 'The Catholic Blight', *Socialist Spirit*, 1 (December, 1901), p.14.

11. Eugene V. Debs to Fred D. Warren, 13 December 1912, *Letters*, Vol. 1, p.560 quoted in Jacob H. Dorn '"In Spiritual Communion": Eugene V. Debs and the Socialist Christians', *The Journal of the Gilded Age and the Progressive Era*, 2, 3, (July 2003), p.310.

12. John A. Ryan 'Introduction', in John A. Ryan and Joseph Husslein (eds), *The Church and Labor* (New York: Macmillan Company, 1920), p.x.

13. On regional variations within the American Catholic Church, see David Noel Doyle, *Irish-Americans, Native Rights, and National Empires: The Structure, Division, and Attitudes of the Catholic Minority in the Decade of Expansion, 1890–1901* (New York: Arno Press, 1976). On the battle between liberal and conservative forces within the American Catholic Church, see Robert D. Cross, *The Emergence of Liberal Catholicism in America, 1878–1902* (Cambridge: Harvard University Press, 1958); Marvin O'Connell, *John Ireland and the American Catholic Church* (St Paul: Minnesota Historical Society Press, 1988).

14. Allen Will, *Life of Cardinal Gibbons Archbishop of Baltimore* (New York: E.P. Dutton, 1922), pp.676–7; *America*, Vol. 2, No. 13, 8 January 1910 quoted in Marc Karson, 'The Catholic Church and the Political Development of American Trade Unionism (1900-1918)', *Industrial and Labor Relations Review*, 4 (July 1951), p.529.

15. Cardinal O'Connell, 'Pastoral Letter on Laborer's Rights', in Ryan & Husslein (eds), *The Church and Labor*, p.183.

16. Robert E. Doherty, 'Thomas J. Hagerty, the Church, and Socialism', *Labor History*, Vol. 3, No. 1 (Winter 1962), pp.39–56.

17. Benjamin Gitlow, *The Whole of Their Lives: Communism in America, a Personal History and Intimate Portrayal of Its Leaders* (New York: Charles Scribner's Sons, 1948), pp.38–9.

18. Emmet O'Connor, *James Larkin* (Cork: Cork University Press, 2002), p.46.

19. *New York Call*, 15 January 1915.

20. David M. Emmons, *Beyond the American Pale: The Irish in the West, 1845–1910* (Norman: University of Oklahoma Press, 2010), pp.328–9.

21. *New York Call*, 18 January 1915.

22. Ibid.

23. Ibid.

24. James Weinstein, *The Decline of Socialism in America 1912–1925* (New York: Rutgers University Press, 1984), pp.116–18.

Notes

25. Charles Leinenweber, 'Class and Ethnic Bases of New York City Socialism, 1904–1915', *Labor History*, Vol. 22, No. 1 (Winter, 1981), pp.47–9.

26. These historians include; Marc Karson, 'The Catholic Church and the Political Development of American Trade Unionism (1900–1918)', *Industrial and Labor Relations Review*, Vol. 4, No. 4 (July, 1951), pp.527–542; and Selig Perlman, *A Theory of the Labor Movement* (New York: Macmillan, 1928), p.169.

27. *Gaelic American*, 20 February 1915.

28. Ibid.

29. Pope Leo XIII, 'Rerum Novarum: Encyclical on the Condition of Labor (15 May 1891)', in Ryan & Husslein (eds), *The Church and Labor*, p.84.

30. Emmons, *Beyond the American Pale*, p.326.

31. Karson, 'The Catholic Church', p.528.

32. Ibid., pp.533–8. The Militia of Christ may have been given too much credit for their efforts to expunge socialist influence in the organisation since the leadership realised their conciliatory tone towards a pro-war orientated Wilson administration would alienate remaining socialist members of the AFL.

33. *Harpers Weekly*, 10 March 1915 from Samuel Gompers, *Labor and the Common Welfare* (New York, 1919), p.214.

34. For Socialist Party efforts to resist American entry to the war, see Alexander Trachtenberg, *The American Socialist and the War* (New York: The Rand School of Social Science, 1917).

35. David Montgomery, *The Fall of the House of Labor, The Workplace, the State, and American Labor Activism, 1865–1925* (New York: Press Syndicate of the University of Cambridge, 1987), pp.371, 375.

36. Ibid., p.370.

37. David M. Emmons, *The Butte Irish: Class and Ethnicity in an American Mining Town, 1875–1925* (Urbana: University of Illinois Press, 1990), p.13.

38. Ibid.

39. Fr Brosnan to his father, 18 February 1917. Brosnan Family Letters, in possession of Professor Kerby A. Miller, University of Missouri, Colombia.

40. Emmons, *Butte Irish*, p.278

41. Ibid., p.348.

42. Oscar A. Dingman, 1948. Montana Folklore Survey Project, 1979 AFS 1981/005, Box 2 Folder 41. Library of Congress, Archive of Folk Culture.

43. Unaccredited. Montana Folklore Survey Project, 1979 AFS 1981/005, Box 2 Folder 41. Library of Congress, Archive of Folk Culture. The Cornish referred to the Irish as 'savage' when the Parrott mine in Butte was purchased by Daly's Anaconda Company.

'Goodbye, birdie, savage got thee, no more place for we'. Wayland D. Hand, 'The Folklore, Customs, and Traditions of the Butte Miner', *California Folklore Quarterly*, 5, 1 (January 1946), p.178.

44. Seán Ó Dubhda, *An Duanaire Duibhneach* (Baile Atha Cliath: Oifig Diolta Foilseachain Rialtais, 1933), pp. 132–3. Translation by Dr Bruce D. Boling, Brown University, from Kerby A. Miller, *Emigrants and Exiles: Ireland and the Irish Exodus to North America* (New York: Oxford U.P., 1985), p.xiii.

45. Ó Dubhda, *An Duanaire Duibhneach,* pp.130–131. Translation by Dr Bruce D. Boling, transcript in possession of Professor Kerby A. Miller, University of Missouri, Colombia.

46. Emmons, *Beyond the American Pale*, p.306.

47. Larkin first visited Butte in September 1915 and when the acting mayor Michael Daniel O'Connell withdrew permission for Larkin to speak at the city auditorium at the last minute and the Finnish Workers' Club offered to host him he said 'I love my native land and I love my race, but when I see some of the Irish politicians and place hunters you have in Butte, my face crimsons with shame, and I am glad they did not remain in Ireland.' *Montana Socialist*, 9 October 1915. See Emmons, *Butte Irish*, pp.352–4.

48. *Montana Socialist*, 22 July 1916.

49. Ibid.

50. Ibid., Emmons, *Butte Irish*, p.358. Emmons offers an educated guess at the people Larkin was referring to; Judge Jeremiah J. Lynch, lawyer Walter Breen, editor James B. Mulcahy, and priest Rev. Michael Hannan.

51. *Montana Socialist*, 27 January 1917.

52. Emmons, *Butte Irish*, p.359.

53. Ibid., p.376.

54. Ibid., p.268.

55. Ibid., p.269. The event also allowed the Anaconda Company to establish a rustling card system that could be used by the company to blacklist workers.

56. Ibid., p.373.

57. Ibid., p.362.

58. Ibid., p.360

59. Ibid., pp.364–5. The Pearse–Connolly Club, the MMWU, the IWW and the Finnish Workers Club all shared the same address, 318 North Wyoming, Finlander Hall.

60. Ibid., p.365.

61. Ibid.

62. Ibid., p.398.

63. Ibid., pp.400–1.

64. Emmet Larkin, *James Larkin: Irish Labour Leader, 1876–1947* (Cambridge, MA: MIT Press, 1965), pp.217–18.

65. Ibid.

66. Larkin, *James Larkin*, p.211.

67. One telegram instructed, 'Government have directed that he must be watched and shadowed and his speeches taken down while in the States. If he traffics with the Enemy he can be arrested on his return.' Telegram from Dublin Metropolitan Police Detective Department. 28 October 1914. SBF.

68. Deputy Inspector General, R.I.C., Dublin Castle to Head Constable, Liverpool, 23 December 1914. SBF.

69. Directorate of Intelligence (Home Office), Report on Revolutionary Organisations in the United Kingdom. 7 August 1919. CAB/24/86. National Archives. Kew.

70. British Embassy, Washington D.C. 8 August 1917, SBF; E. O'Farrell, Undersecretary of State, Home Office, London, 10 September 1917, SBF; Chief Secretary's Office, Dublin Castle, 8 November 1917, SBF.

71. Cecil Rice to A. J. Balfour, 26 September 1916, SBF; Inspector General, R.I.C. Memo 64, undated. SBF.

72. Larkin, *James Larkin*, pp.237–43.

73. O'Connor, *James Larkin*, p.63.

74. *New York Times*, 20 April 1923; O'Connor, *James Larkin*, pp.68–9.

75. O'Connor, *James Larkin*, p.69.

76. Bertram Wolfe, *Strange Communists I Have Known* (New York: Stein and Day, 1965), p.64.

77. O'Connor, *James Larkin*, p.62.

78. James Larkin, LO P 113, William O'Brien Papers, National Library of Ireland. Undated.

79. Ibid.

80. Jack Carney to Jim Larkin, 10 September 1946, Ms 37989, Sean O'Casey papers. National Library of Ireland.

81. Larry Peterson, 'The One Big Union in International Perspective: Revolutionary Industrial Unionism 1900–1925', *Labour / Le Travail*, Vol. 7 (Spring, 1981), p.42.

82. This degree of marginalisation has gradually begun to loosen and it is hoped this trend will continue. See Enda Delaney, 'Directions in Historiography: Our Island Story? Towards a Transnational History of Late Modern Ireland', *Irish Historical Studies*, 37, 148 (Nov. 2011), pp.83–105.

Chapter 5

1. *Nationalist and Leinster Times*, 27 April 1918.

2. Emmet O'Connor, 'War and Syndicalism 1914–1923', in Donal Nevin (ed.), *Trade Union Century* (Cork: Mercier Press, 1994), p.54.

3.   Theresa Moriarty, 'Work, warfare and wages', in Adrian Gregory and Senia Pašeta (eds), *Ireland and the Great War: 'A war to unite us all'?* (Manchester: Manchester University Press, 2002), pp.74–5.

4.   Peter Murray, 'The First World War and a Dublin Distillery Workforce: Recruiting and Redundancy at John Power & Son, 1915–1917', *Saothar*, Vol. 15, (1990), pp.54–5.

5.   Edward Patrick Lahiff, 'Industry and Labour in Cork 1890–1921' (MA thesis, University College Cork, 1988), p.186.

6.   Moriarty, 'Work, warfare and wages', in Gregory and Pašeta (eds), *Ireland and the Great War*, pp.77, 79.

7.   John Newsinger, *Rebel City – Larkin, Connolly and the Dublin Labour Movement* (London: The Merlin Press, 2004), p.156.

8.   National Archives UK (NAUK), CO 904/157/166, Military Intelligence Reports, Southern District, March 1917.

9.   C. Desmond Greaves, *The Irish Transport and General Workers' Union – The Formative Years* (Dublin: Gill & Macmillan, 1982), pp.185–6, 191.

10. NAUK, CO 903/19/4/5, 10-11, 13, Judicial Division (JD) intelligence reports, 1918, Ulster, Antrim, Cavan, Donegal, Down, pp.1, 6–7, 9.

11. Newsinger, *Rebel City*, p.156.

12. Greaves, *The Irish Transport and General Workers' Union*, p.181.

13. Nevin (ed.), *Trade Union Century*, pp.433, 437, 441.

14. Conor Kostick, *Revolution in Ireland: Popular Militancy, 1917–23* (London: Pluto Press, 1996), p.32.

15. NAUK, CO 903/19/4/19, 25-6, 32-3, 37, 39-40, 42-3, 46-7, JD intelligence reports, 1918, pp.15, 21–2, 28–9, 33, 35–6, 38–9, 41–3.

16. Greaves, *The Irish Transport and General Workers' Union*, p.134.

17. Rosemary Cullen Owens, *Louie Bennett* (Cork: Cork University Press, 2001), p.69.

18. Greaves, *The Irish Transport and General Workers' Union*, p.191.

19. James Connolly, 'Conscription', in Prionsias Mac Aonghusa and Liam Ó Réagáin (eds), *The Best of Connolly* (Cork: The Mercier Press, 1967), p.184.

20. Jim Larkin, 'The Irish Rebellion', in National Archives of Ireland (NAI), Bureau of Military History (BMH), Witness Statement (WS) 1766, William O'Brien, pp.141–2.

21. James Connolly, 'The Friend of Small Nationalities', *Irish Worker*, 12 September 1914, cited in Desmond Ryan (ed.), *Socialism and Nationalism – A selection from the writings of James Connolly* (Dublin: The Three Candles, 1948), p.148.

22. Greaves, *The Irish Transport and General Workers' Union*, pp.160–1.

23. *The Workers' Republic*, 12 June 1915.

24. Ibid.

Notes

25. Ibid., 3 July 1915.

26. Ibid., 27 November 1915.

27. National Library of Ireland (NLI), Ms 17115 (v), Thomas Johnson papers, 'Some notes on the persuasive aspect of voluntary recruiting,' n.d.

28. Murray, 'The First World War and a Dublin Distillery Workforce', pp.48, 51; Thomas Neilan Crean, 'Labour and Politics in Kerry During the First World War', *Saothar*, Vol. 19, (1994) p.29.

29. J. Anthony Gaughan, *Thomas Johnson, 1872–1963* (Dublin: Kingdom Books, 1980), p.86.

30. *The Workers' Republic*, 5 June 1915.

31. Ibid., 19 June 1915.

32. Ibid., 13 November 1915.

33. Ibid., 4 December 1915.

34. Ibid., 13 November 1915.

35. Ibid.

36. Ibid., 27 November 1915.

37. Ibid., 18 December 1915.

38. NLI, POS 914, A/0215, Michael Collins papers, General Perishing's memoirs.

39. Parliamentary Archives (PA), London, LG/F/14/4/18, Lloyd George papers, Report from Derby (War Office) to Lloyd George, 25 January 1917.

40. NAUK, HO267/690/87, *Irish Opinion – Voice of Irish Labour*, 20 April 1918.

41. NAUK, HO267/690/71, *Irishman*, 20 April 1918.

42. *Cork Examiner*, 18 April 1918.

43. *Fermanagh Times*, 18 April 1918.

44. *Cork Examiner*, 15 April 1918.

45. *Cork Constitution*, 15 April 1918.

46. *Cork Examiner*, 15 April 1918.

47. Kostick, *Revolution in Ireland*, p.34.

48. NLI, MS 17,155 (ii), Johnson papers, handbills.

49. *Evening Telegraph*, 22 April 1918.

50. NAI, BMH, WS No. 1,755, Thomas Johnson, pp.18–21.

51. *Cork Weekly News*, 27 April 1918.

52. *Cork Examiner*, 22 April 1918.

53. Gaughan, *Thomas Johnson*, p.94.

54. *Cork Examiner*, 22 April 1918.

55. *Cork Weekly News*, 27 April 1918.

56. NLI, Ms 17, 115 (ii), Johnson papers, Letter from Shán Ó Cuiv to Thomas Johnson, n.d.

57. *Cork Weekly News*, 27 April 1918.

58. *Irish Opinion*, 27 April 1918.

59. Peter Hadden, *Troubled Times – Chapter 4*, http://www.socialistworld.net/pubs/tt/ch04. html (accessed 13 March 2013); Arthur Mitchell, *Labour in Irish politics, 1890–1930* (Dublin: Irish University Press, 1974), p.88; and John Brennan, 'Frongoch University and after, 1916–1919', in The Kerryman (ed.), *Dublin's fighting story – told by the men who made it, 1913–1921* (Tralee: The Kerryman Limited, n.d.), p.121.

60. Brennan, 'Frongoch University and after, 1916–1919', in The Kerryman (ed.), *Dublin's fighting story*, p.121.

61. Deirdre Lindsay, 'Labour against Conscription', in David Fitzpatrick, (ed.), *Ireland and the First World War* (Dublin: Trinity History Workshop, 1986), p.84.

62. Military Archives (MA), CD258/7/18, Johnson collection, *Freeman's Journal,* 23 and 24 April 1918.

63. *Evening Telegraph*, 23 and 24 April 1918.

64. NLI, MS 15,670, O'Brien papers, B. Leahy, 'The one-day strike in Ireland', *Freedom*, June 1918; and Frank Gallagher, *The Four Glorious Years 1918–1921* (2nd edn. Dublin: Blackwater Press, 2005), p.27.

65. MA, CD258/7/18, Johnson collection, *Freeman's Journal*, 23 and 24 April 1918.

66. Ibid.

67. *Irish News and the Belfast Morning News*, 23 April 1918.

68. MA, CD258/7/18, Johnson collection, *Freeman's Journal*, 23 and 24 April 1918.

69. *Belfast Telegraph*, 23 April 1918.

70. MA, CD258/7/18, Johnson collection, *Daily Mail*, 24 April 1918.

71. MA, CD258/7/18, Johnson collection, *Freeman's Journal*, 23 and 24 April 1918.

72. Rosemary Cullen Owens (ed.), *Did your granny have a hammer??? A history of the Irish Suffrage movement 1876–1922* (Dublin: Attic Press, 1985), p.19; Rosemary Owens, 'Votes for Ladies, Votes for Women- Organised Labour and the Suffrage Movement, 1876–1922', *Saothar*, Vol. 9, (1983), p.42.

73. MA, CD258/7/18, Johnson collection, *Freeman's Journal*, 23 and 24 April 1918.

74. *Cork Examiner*, 24 April 1918.

75. *Cork Examiner*, 24 April 1918 and *Cork Weekly Examiner*, 27 April 1918.

76. *Cork Weekly Examiner*, 27 April 1918.

77. *Irish Opinion*, 27 April 1918.

78. *Bottom Dog*, 27 April 1918.

79. *Irish Times*, 23 and 24 April 1918.

80. David Fitzpatrick, 'Strikes in Ireland, 1914-21', *Saothar*, Vol. 6 (1980), pp.30, 36; Peter Hadden, *Troubled Times*.

Notes

81. NAUK, CO 904/167/89, Press censor report, August 1918.

82. Greaves, *The Irish Transport and General Workers' Union*, pp.206–8.

83. *Irish Opinion*, 27 April 1918.

84. MA, CD258/7/18, Johnson Collection, *Daily Mail*, 24 April 1918.

85. Greaves, *The Irish Transport and General Workers' Union*, p.202; Kostick, *Revolution in Ireland*, p.36.

86. *Belfast Telegraph*, 23 April 1918.

87. David Fitzpatrick, *Politics and Irish life 1913–1921 – Provincial experience of war and revolution* (Cork: Cork University Press, 1998), p.211; Gaughan, *Thomas Johnson*, p.117; and Emmet O'Connor, 'War and Syndicalism 1914-1923', in Nevin (ed.), *Trade Union Century*, p.56.

88. NLI, MS 15,653 (2), O'Brien papers, Letter probably to O'Brien, cannot read sender signature, n.d.

89. NAUK, CO 903/19/4/25, JD intelligence reports, Kerry, Munster, 1918, p.21.

90. *Irish Independent*, 2 April 1918 and *Irish News and the Belfast Morning News*, 2 April 1918.

91. John Horne, 'James Connolly and the Great Divide: Ireland, Europe and the First World War', *Saothar*, Vol. 31, 2006, pp.75–6.

92. Gaughan, *Thomas Johnson*, p.120.

93. *Irish Opinion*, 2 November 1918.

94. D.R. O'Connor Lysaght, Speech commenting on Brendan Halligan's paper, *The Irish Labour History Society Annual General Meeting*, 9 May 2009, www.socialistdemocracy.org/History/HistoryOnTheDemocraticProgrammeOfTheFirstDail.html (accessed 13 March 2013).

95. Fitzpatrick, *Politics and Irish life 1913–1921*, p.211.

96. Greaves, *The Irish Transport and General Workers' Union*, p.221.

97. Newsinger, *Rebel City*, p.157.

98. Lil Conlon, *Cumann na mBan and the Women of Ireland 1913–25* (Kilkenny: The Kilkenny People, 1969), pp.59–61.

99. *Irish Opinion*, 1 June 1918.

100. Ibid., 8 June 1918.

101. Rosemary Cullen Owens, *Smashing Times: A History of the Irish Women's Suffrage Movement, 1889–1922* (Dublin: Attic Press, 1984), p.121.

102. *The Workers' Republic*, 18 December 1915.

103. Charlotte Fallon, *Soul of Fire: A Biography of Mary MacSwiney* (Cork and Dublin: Mercier Press, 1986), p.42.

104. *Irish Citizen*, May and June 1918.

105. *The Irish Citizen*, 19 April 1918, in Cullen Owens (ed.), *Did your granny have a hammer???*.

106. Ibid.

107. Maria Luddy, *Women in Ireland, 1800–1918, A Documentary History* (Cork: Cork University Press, 1995), p.286.

108. This granted the vote to British and Irish women over the age of 30.

109. Cullen Owens, *Louie Bennett*, p.41.

Chapter 6

1. Letter to An Cigire, Special Branch from Thomas Keelan, D/O (24 September 1934). Contained within 'Activities of the Animal Gang in Dublin Metropolitan Division' (JUS 2008/117/291), National Archives of Ireland (Hereafter NAI).

2. Brian Hanley, *The IRA 1926–1936* (Dublin: Four Courts Press, 2002), p.83.

3. George William Panter, 'Eighteenth Century Dublin Street Cries' in *The Journal of the Royal Society of Antiquaries of Ireland*,15,1 (30 June 1924), pp.68–86, p.74.

4. Alan J. Lee, *The Origins of the Popular Press in England, 1855–1914* (London: Taylor and Francis, 1976), p.65.

5. 'The Newsboys' in *Irish Times*, 11 October 1882.

6. 'The Tired Newsboys!' in *Irish Times*, 20 December 1884.

7. Pádraig Yeates, *Lockout: Dublin 1913* (Dublin: Gill & Macmillan, 2000), p.9.

8. 'Newsboys Strike' in *Irish Times*, 21 August 1911, p.10.

9. Ernie O'Malley, *Army Without Banners: Adventures of an Irish Volunteer* (Boston: Houghton Mifflin, 1937), p.17.

10. Emmet O'Connor, *James Larkin* (Cork: Cork University Press, 2002), p.97.

11. 'Belvedere Newsboys' Club: New Premises Open' in *Irish Times*, 27 November 1929.

12. 'Fine Work of Newsboys' Club' in *Irish Press,* 9 December 1931.

13. Ibid.

14. 'How We Carried On' in *An Phoblacht*, 22 October 1933.

15. 'Mrs. Skeffington's Release' in *Irish Times*, 22 February 1933.

16. 'Mr. Mulcahy and the Newsboys' in *Irish Press*, 10 April 1934.

17. 'Dublin Strike' in *The Times* (London), 27 July 1934.

18. 'Press Still Silent in Dublin Strike' in *New York Times*, 17 September 1934.

19. Hanley, *The IRA 1926–1936*, p.8.

20. Front page of *An Phoblacht*, 6 October 1934.

21. The comments on the number of Dublin newsboys trading on the streets were made in the Dáil by Independent TD John Good on 17 May 1934. Dáil Éireann Debates Vol.5, No.9 (17 May 1934) available at: http://www.oireachtas-debates.gov.ie/ (accessed 13 March 2013).

Notes

22. 'Remember the Newsboys' in *Irish Independent*, 7 December 1934.
23. Ibid.
24. 'Disturbances created by Newsboys at Frederick Lane' (JUS 8/67), NAI.
25. Letter to An Cigire, Special Branch from Thomas Keelan, D/O (24 September 1934). Contained within 'Activities of the Animal Gang in Dublin Metropolitan Division' (JUS 2008/117/291), NAI.
26. Pat Feeley notes that the gangs were 'drawn from the men who tended the cattle on cross-channel boats' in his article 'The Siege of 64 Great Strand Street', in *Old Limerick Journal*, 9 (Winter 1981), pp.22–4.
27. Front page of *An Phoblacht*, 15 September 1934.
28. Ibid.
29. Ibid.
30. Front page of *An Phoblacht*, 29 September 1934.
31. Report entitled 'Armed Raids in "C" District' (24 September 1934) in 'Activities of the Animal Gang in Dublin Metropolitan Division' (JUS 2008/117/291), NAI.
32. 'House in the Navy' in *Irish Times*, 28 September 1932, p.2.
33. Report entitled 'Alleged Armed Hold-Up at the Ardee Hall, 38 Talbot Street, Dublin on 25 September, 1934' (26 September 1934) within 'Activities of the Animal Gang in Dublin Metropolitan Division' (JUS 2008/117/291), NAI.
34. Ibid.
35. Ibid.
36. 'Men questioned by armed men at Corporation Street', report (27 September 1934) submitted by M.O'Callaghan, Cigire. Report within 'Activities of the Animal Gang in Dublin Metropolitan Division' (JUS 2008/117/291), NAI.
37. Ibid.
38. Front page of *An Phoblacht*, 29 September 1934.
39. Ibid.
40. 'Dublin Strike Ends' in *The Times* (London), 1 October 1934.
41. Letter to An Cigire, Special Branch from Thomas Keelan, D/O (24 September 1934). Contained within 'Activities of the Animal Gang in Dublin Metropolitan Division' (JUS 2008/117/291), NAI.
42. This *An Phoblacht* cut-out is contained within 'Activities of the Animal Gang in Dublin Metropolitan Division' (JUS 2008/117/291), NAI.
43. Ibid.
44. Murray Fraser, *John Bull's Other Homes: State Housing and British Policy in Ireland, 1883–1922* (Liverpool: Liverpool University Press, 1996), p.84. The failures of the Corporation Buildings project is well documented in Ruth McManus's *Dublin 1910–1940: Shaping the City and Suburbs* (Dublin: Four Courts Press, 2002).

45. Lorcan Collins, *James Connolly* (Dublin: O'Brien Press, 2012), p.208.
46. Crime Reporter 'Crime in Dublin' in *The Bell*, December 1942 (Vol.5 No.3) pp.174–179, p.178.
47. 'The Animal Gang: City Assault Cases' in *Irish Times*, 9 October 1934.
48. 'The 'Animal Gang: Father and Son Sentenced for Attack of Police' in *Irish Times*, 13 November 1934.
49. 'Corporation Dwellings Criticised' in *Irish Times*, 24 October 1935.
50. 'Iron Bars and Lead Piping: Dublin Gang War' in *Irish Times*, 11 February 1936.
51. 'Assault on a Dublin Guard' in *Irish Times*, 21 September 1935.
52. 'Animal Gang Again: Ten Young Men Remanded' in *Irish Times*, 11 April 1935.
53. 'Bricks and Communism' in *Irish Times*, 21 October 1931.
54. R.M. Douglas, *Architects of the Resurrection: Ailtirí na hAiséirghe and the fascist 'new order' in Ireland* (Manchester: Manchester University Press, 2009), p.22.
55. Bob Doyle, *Brigadista: An Irishman's Fight Against Fascism* (Dublin: Currach Press, 2006), p.32.
56. 'Anti-Communist Frenzy' in *Irish Times*, 29 March 1982.
57. 'Veteran who stayed true to the ideals of the Spanish War' in *Irish Times*, 9 August 2003.
58. Report entitled 'Connolly House, Great Strand Street, attacked and damaged by Riotous Crowd' (20 March 1933) within 'Anti-Communist Demonstrations' (JUS 8/711), NAI.
59. See, for example, Manus O'Riordan, 'Communism in Dublin in the 1930s: The Struggle against Fascism', in H.Gustav Klaus (ed.), *Strong Words, Brave Words: The Poetry, Life and Times of Thomas O'Brien* (Dublin: O'Brien Press, 1994), pp.215–239, p.220. Also, Pat Feeley, 'The Siege of 64 Great Strand Street', in *Old Limerick Journal*, 9 (Winter 1981) pp.22–4.
60. Doyle, *Brigadista*, p.38.
61. Ibid.
62. Ibid.
63. Peadar O'Donnell, *Salud! An Irishman in Spain* (London: Methuen, 1937), p.7.
64. Ibid.
65. Ibid., p.8.
66. H. Gustav Klaus quotes Fitzpatrick's poem in his introduction to H.Gustav Klaus (ed.), *Strong Words, Brave Words: The Poetry, Life and Times of Thomas O'Brien* (Dublin: O'Brien Press, 1994), p.18.
67. Rosamond Jacob sent a copy of this threatening letter she received from someone using the name of the 'Animal Gang' to the *Irish Press* newspaper, which published it on 13 May 1936. The paper didn't appear to take the threat too seriously, noting how the writer had incorrectly referred to Rosamond as 'Mr. Jacob'.

68. Donal Ó Drisceoil, *Peadar O'Donnell* (Cork: Cork University Press, 2001), p.93.

69. Jack White detailed the experience of being attacked by those he called 'pious hooligans' in the pages of the CNT-AIT bulletin in 1936. The CNT were an anarchist union and revolutionary movement in Spain which White was sympathetic towards. These memories were reprinted in 2005 as an appendix to White's memoir *Misfit: A Revolutionary Life* (Dublin: Livewire, 2005).

70. Fearghal McGarry, *Irish Politics and the Spanish Civil War* (Cork: Cork University Press, 1999) p.91.

71. Ibid.

72. The 'Letter to the Editor' from Frank Ryan and George Gilmore in the wake of the anti-communist violence was published in several Irish newspapers, for example *Irish Times*, 1 May 1936.

73. The St Patrick's Anti-Communist League was founded in March 1933, just prior to the outbreak of severe anti-communist violence in the city. Its members pledged to 'uphold the Faith, Hope and Charity St. Patrick brought to Ireland'. Information on the grouping is contained within 'Anti-Communist Demonstrations' (JUS 8/711, NAI).

74. Kevin Kearns, *Dublin Tenement Life* (Dublin: Gill & Macmillan, 2006), p.56.

Chapter 7

1. Edward Fahy, 'Reformatory Schools in Ireland', *Hermathena*, LX (Nov 1942), p.61.

2. *States of Fear*, narr., Áine Lawlor, writ., prod., dir., Mary Rafferty, RTÉ, Ireland, 27 April 1999.

3. The report of the commission was published on the 20 May 2009. The commission was set up in 2000. For a copy of the report see www.childabusecommission.ie (accessed 13 March 2013).

4. The industrial school system in Britain was based on a Continental model, and by the 1850s, Germany, Switzerland and the Scandinavian countries had over a hundred institutions catering for criminal and destitute children.

5. There had developed a growing critique of institutionalisation in the United States and other western societies from the late-nineteenth century. In 1886, W.P. Letchworth in the United States referred to children becoming 'institutionalized', yet in Ireland this option would be repeatedly chosen. Robert H. Bremner et al., *Children and Youth in America: A Documentary History, Vol. 2: 1866–1932* (Cambridge, MA: Harvard University Press, 1971), p.296.

6. Before research began, agreements for confidentiality and the protection of subjects of the case records were negotiated with the Irish Society for the Prevention of Cruelty to Children (ISPCC) and throughout, not only are all names fictional, the numbers of

case records represent a system developed specifically for this research and not actual agency case numbers. I have chosen to use John Byrne's name in this piece as I believe his family were attempting to secure justice during 1935, and chose to place his name in the public domain. To have used a pseudonym would have been to ignore this public appeal.

7. Annual Report (AR) Dublin Branch NSPCC 1948–49 (ISPCC, Limerick), pp.5–6. This essay draws on research and findings from my PhD thesis. See S. Buckley, 'Protecting "the family cell"? Child Welfare, the NSPCC and the State in Ireland, 1880–1944' (PhD thesis, University College Cork, 2010). See also S. Buckley, 'Child neglect, poverty and class: the NSPCC in Ireland, 1889–1938 – a case study', *Saothar: Journal of Irish Labour History,* 33, (2008), pp.57–72; M. Luddy, 'The early years of the NSPCC in Ireland', *Éire-Ireland,* 44, no.1 & 2 (2009); *Women and Philanthropy in Nineteenth-Century Ireland* (Cambridge: Cambridge University Press, 1995), pp.68–96. For a discussion of the NSPCC in Britain, see G. Behlmer, *Child Abuse and Moral Reform in England, 1870–1908* (Stanford, CA: Stanford University Press, 1982); Tom Cockburn, 'Child abuse and protection: The Manchester Boys' and Girls' Refuges and the NSPCC, 1884–1894', *Manchester Sociology Occasional Papers* (1995), pp.1-44; Susan Creighton, *Trends in Child Abuse 1977–82: The Fourth Report on the Children Placed on NSPCC Special Unit Registers* (London: NSPCC, 1984); Gary Clapton, '"Yesterday's men": The inspectors of the Royal Scottish Society for the Prevention of Cruelty to Children (RSSPCC), 1888–1968', *British Journal of Social Work,* 39(6), (2009), pp.1043–1062; Harry Hendrick, *Child Welfare: Historical Dimensions, Contemporary Debates* (Bristol: Policy Press, 2003); Sue Wise, *Child Abuse: The NSPCC Version* (Manchester: Feminist Praxis, 1991); NSPCC, *NSPCC: The First Hundred Years* (London: NSPCC, 1984).
8. AR Dublin Branch NSPCC, 1900–1901, p.15.
9. Louise A. Jackson, *Child Sexual Abuse in Victorian England* (London: Routledge, 2000), p.133.
10. Linda Mahood, *Feminism and Voluntary Action: Eglantyne Jebb and Save the Children, 1876–1928* (London: Palgrave MacMillan, 2009).
11. Kevin Kearns, *Dublin's Lost Heroines: Mammies and Grannies in a Vanished Dublin* (Dublin: Gill & Macmillan, 2004), p.126.
12. Article 42, Section 1, *Bunreacht na hÉireann.*
13. Article 41, Section 1, *Bunreacht na hÉireann.*
14. There were 133 cases of neglect investigated by the inspector in 1937, with 14 cases resulting in committal to industrial schools. AR Wexford District Branch, 1937 (ISPCC, Limerick).

15. AR Waterford and District Branch, 1939 and AR Waterford and District Branch, 1940 (ISPCC, Limerick).

16. CF #99. Case-files of the NSPCC (ISPCC Limerick).

17. CF#221.

18. CF#65.

19. CF#02.

20. Ibid.

21. CF #13.

22. CF #77.

23. CF #60.

24. CF #104.

25. CF #117.

26. 'Schoolboy's Death: Evidence at the Inquest', *Irish Times*, 27 April 1935; 'Death of Artane Schoolboy: Allegations of a Scuffle with Teacher', *Irish Press*, 27 April 1935; 'Boy's Mysterious Death: No Mark of Violence', *Irish Independent*, 27 April 1935.

27. Letter signed by Lawrence Wright, Secretary of the Irish Labour Defence League, 16 May 1935, *Sheehy Skeffington Papers*, National Library of Ireland. Thank you to Donal O'Drisceoil for providing me with this reference.

28. Ibid.

29. 'Schoolboy's Death', *Irish Times*.

30. *Irish Independent*, 27 April 1935.

31. 'Number and Causes of Deaths Amongst Pupils in Industrial Schools', *Department of Education Annual Report, 1934–35*, p.222.

32. Case-files of the NSPCC (ISPCC Limerick).

Chapter 8

1. The author would like to thank the School of History and Anthropology, Queen's University Belfast for the award of a J.C. Beckett Bursary in 2008 which facilitated the research on which this article is based. Thanks also to Dr Daniel Brown, Dr Glenda Mock and Dr Seán Byers for reading prior drafts. Any mistakes are the author's.

2. *Northern Whig*, 13 October 1942.

3. Ibid., 14 October 1942.

4. Ian S. Wood, *Britain, Ireland and the Second World War* (Edinburgh: Edinburgh University Press, 2010), p.178.

5. Ibid., p.182.

6. Jonathan Bardon, *A History of Ulster* (Belfast: Blackstaff Press, 1992), p.562.

7. I.S. Wood, *Britain*, p.173.

8. Brian Barton, *Brookeborough: The Making of A Prime Minister* (Belfast: Institute of Irish Studies, Queen's University Belfast, 1988), p.172.

9. Ibid., p.173.

10. Graham Walker, *A History of the Ulster Unionist Party: Protest, Pragmatism and Pessimism* (Manchester: Manchester University Press, 2004), p.88.

11. Brian Barton, 'Northern Ireland: The Impact of War, 1939–45', in Brian Girvin and Geoffrey Roberts (eds), *Ireland and the Second World War* (Dublin and Portland, OR: Four Courts Press, 2000), p.69; Graham Walker, *The Politics of Frustration: Harry Midgley and the Failure of Labour in Northern Ireland* (Manchester: Manchester University Press, 1985), pp.127–8.

12. Graham Walker, *The Politics of Frustration*, p.91.

13. Ibid., pp.112–13.

14. Boyd Black, 'A Triumph of Voluntarism? Industrial Relations and Strikes in Northern Ireland in World War Two', *Labour History Review*, 70 (2005), p.20 (cited hereafter as 'Voluntarism?').

15. David Edgerton, *Britain's War Machine: Weapons, Resources and Experts in the Second World War* (London: Penguin, 2011), p.123.

16. Boyd Black, 'Voluntarism?', p.9.

17. Mark Donnelly, *Britain in the Second World War* (London and New York: Routledge, 1999), p.55.

18. J.W. Blake, *Northern Ireland in the Second World War* (1956; repr. Belfast: Blackstaff Press, 2000), p.24.

19. Philip Ollerenshaw, 'War, Industrial Mobilisation and Society in Northern Ireland, 1939–1945', *Contemporary European History*, 16 (2007), p.186.

20. Mark Donnelly, *Britain in the Second World War*, p.55.

21. Ibid., p.56.

22. Notes of meeting between the Minister of Commerce and trade union leaders, 10 July 1941 (COM/61/589, Public Records Office of Northern Ireland (PRONI), Ministry of Commerce papers).

23. E.H. Cooper to H.R. Chapman, 14 May 1942 (COM/61/655, PRONI, Ministry of Commerce papers).

24. Meeting with trade union officials, 24 April 1941 (COM/28/7, PRONI, Ministry of Commerce papers).

25. All quotes from Scottish labour inspectors contained in Report on the visitation of technical representatives from the Ministry of Labour and National Service (Scottish region) to Northern Ireland, 13 to 24 January 1942 (CAB/9/CD/208/1, PRONI, Cabinet papers).

Notes

26. Factors affecting production, 1 September 1941 (COM/61/589, PRONI, Ministry of Commerce papers).

27. W.P. Kemp to J.M. Andrews, 23 September 1941 (CAB/9/C/22/1, PRONI, Cabinet papers).

28. Shop Stewards committee (Belfast) to Herbert Morrison, 28 August 1942 (CAB/9/22/1, PRONI, Cabinet papers).

29. J.F. Gordon to J.M. Andrews, 5 Nov. 1942 (CAB/9/22/1, PRONI, Cabinet papers).

30. J.M. Andrews' statement to the press on the disputes at Mackies and Short and Harland, *Belfast Newsletter*, 15 October 1942.

31. A 'closed shop' is one in which only trade union members may be employed. Employment is, therefore, 'closed' to non-trade unionists.

32. E.H. Cooper to Major McConnell, 25 September 1942 (COM/61/589, PRONI, Ministry of Commerce papers).

33. I. S. Wood, *Britain*, p.183.

34. Boyd Black, 'Voluntarism?', p.12.

35. Jonathan Bardon, *Ulster*, p.578.

36. David Richardson, 'The Career of John Miller Andrews, 1871–1956', PhD dissertation (Queen's University Belfast, 1998), p.253.

37. Diary of Sir Basil Brooke, 1st Viscount Brookeborough, 6 October 1942 (D/3004/D/33, PRONI, Brookeborough papers).

38. E.H. Cooper to H.R. Chapman, 8 October 1942 (COM/61/655, PRONI, Ministry of Commerce papers).

39. Diary of Sir Basil Brooke, 1st Viscount Brookeborough, 8 October 1942 (D/3004/D/33, PRONI, Brookeborough papers).

40. Telegram from Beattie to J.M. Andrews, 12 October 1942 (CAB/9/22/1, PRONI, Cabinet papers).

41. Quotes from the debate at Stormont can be found in *Hansard N.I. (Commons)* vol. 25, cols. 2719–31 (13 October 1942).

42. *Belfast Newsletter*, 30 October 1942.

43. *Northern Whig*, 16 October 1942.

44. Ibid.

45. *Belfast Telegraph*, 16 October 1942.

46. Ibid.

47. Ibid.

48. Ibid.

49. *Northern Whig*, 16 October 1942.

50. Text of resolution passed at Belfast shipyard meeting, 16 October 1942 (CAB/9/22/1, PRONI, Cabinet papers).

51. *Belfast Newsletter*, 17 October 1942; *Northern Whig*, 17 October 1942.

52. *Northern Whig*, 17 October 1942.

53. Diary of Sir Basil Brooke, 1st Viscount Brookeborough, 18 October 1942 (D/3004/D/33, PRONI, Brookeborough papers).

54. All quotes from the Court of Inquiry can be found in J.C. Davidson, *Report of the court of inquiry into the causes and circumstances of the trade dispute at the Balmoral dispersal unit of Messrs. Short and Harland Limited on 4 October 1942* (Belfast: H.M. Stationery Office, 1942) (cited hereafter as *Court of Inquiry*).

55. *Northern Whig*, 23 October 1942.

56. Ibid.

57. *Belfast Telegraph*, 23 October 1942.

58. *Irish News*, 28 October 1942.

59. Boyd Black, 'Voluntarism?', p.14.

60. *Belfast Newsletter*, 2 November 1942.

61. Ibid., 30 October 1942; *Belfast Telegraph*, 30 October 1942.

62. Boyd Black, 'Voluntarism?', pp.10, 12.

63. Ibid., p.88.

64. David Edgerton, *Britain's War Machine*, p.4.

65. By 1943 60 per cent of Northern Irish employees in engineering establishments were covered by a JPC. Boyd Black, 'Voluntarism?', p.19.

66. E.H. Cooper to H.R. Chapman, 14 October 1942 (COM/61/655, PRONI, Ministry of Commerce papers).

67. *Hansard N.I. (Commons)*, vol. 25, col. 2964 (29 October 1942).

68. *Court of Inquiry*, Day 2, p.180.

69. Diary of Sir Basil Brooke, 1st Viscount Brookeborough, 8 October 1942 (D/3004/D/33, PRONI, Brookeborough papers).

70. Harry Midgley resigned from the NILP in December 1942 and founded the pro-British Commonwealth Labour Party. See Graham Walker, *The Politics of Frustration*, pp.135–6.

71. Philip Ollerenshaw, 'Northern Ireland, 1939–45', p.188.

72. *Irish News*, 31 October 1942; *Northern Whig*, 31 October 1942.

73. Boyd Black, 'Voluntarism?', p.6.

74. *Hansard N.I. (Commons)* vol. 25, cols. 2726-7 (13 October 1942).

75. *Belfast Newsletter*, 15 October 1942.

76. Ibid., 24 March 1942.

77. Diary of Sir Basil Brooke, 1st Viscount Brookeborough, 22 June 1942 (D/3004/D/33, PRONI, Brookeborough papers).

78. *Court of Inquiry*, Day 1, p.7.

Notes

79. Geoffrey Field, 'Social Patriotism and the British Working Class: Appearance and Disappearance of a Tradition', in *International Labor and Working-Class History*, 42 (1992), p.24.
80. For Peggy Bell's testimony see *Court of Inquiry*, Day 2, pp. 11–14.
81. Jonathan Bardon, *Ulster*, p. 580.
82. Figures calculated from *Ulster Year book, 1938* (Belfast: H. M. Stationary Office, 1938), p. 163; *Ulster Year book, 1947* (Belfast: H. M. Stationary Office, 1947), p. 171.
83. H.A. Clegg, *A History of British Trade Unions since 1889: Vol. 2, 1911–33* (Oxford: Clarendon Press, 1985), p.215.
84. *Court of Inquiry*, Day 2, p.128.
85. Resolution adopted at Communist Party public meeting, Belfast, 16 August 1942 (CAB/9/CD/208/1, PRONI, Cabinet papers).
86. Ronnie Munck and Bill Rolston, *Belfast in the Thirties: An Oral History* (Belfast: Blackstaff Press, 1987), p.139.
87. J.C. MacDermott to J.M. Andrews, 2 November 1942 (CAB/9/C/22/1, PRONI, Cabinet papers).
88. For description of the 1944 dispute in Belfast, see Boyd Black, 'Voluntarism?', pp.13–14; Michael Farrell, *Northern Ireland: The Orange State* (2nd ed., London: Verso, 1980), pp.174–6; J.F. Harbinson, 'A History of the Northern Ireland Labour Party, 1891–1949'(PhD thesis, Queen's University Belfast, 1966), pp.165–9; I.S. Wood, *Britain*, pp.179–80. However, the only detailed research conducted on the 1944 dispute thus far is C.J. V. Loughlin, 'Anti-Fascist and Anti-Management: the Belfast Munitions Strike of 1944' (B.A. thesis, Queen's University Belfast, 2008).

Chapter 9

1. This chapter developed from a working paper given at the University College Cork School of History Research Seminar Series in winter 2011. I am grateful to several people who read and critiqued earlier drafts in particular Niall Murphy, Peter Hession and Dr Daryl Leeworthy.
2. The Gaelic Athletic Association (GAA) was founded in 1884 to promote hurling, Gaelic football and athletics in Ireland.
3. Dáil Éireann – Volume 35 – 05 June 1930, Finance Bill, 1930 – Committee Stage. Available online at www.oireachtas-debates.gov.ie (accessed 13 March 2013).
4. To gain a comprehensive understanding of football in England before the Second World War, see T. Mason's *Association Football and English Society, 1863–1915* (Brighton: Harvester Press 1980); quote is from E. Hobsbawm, *Uncommon People: Resistance, Rebellion and Jazz* (London: Abacus, 1998), p.89.

5.   Basketball, for instance, was especially popular in Cork and Kerry. In Tralee, it was sufficiently popular as a sport to have its own inter-firms league established in 1964.

6.   C. Mac Gearailt, *A Decade of Galway Inter-Firm GAA* (Dublin: Tara Publishing, 1978), p.1.

7.   In Cork in the 1920s teams such as Tramways and Steampacket were part of the Munster Senior League. In others, like the Leinster Senior League, work-oriented football was represented by clubs like the Butcher's Social Union Football Club and Railway Union, along with the Civil Service teams. For details of these, see *Cork Examiner* and *Football Sports Weekly*.

8.   C.S. Andrews, *Dublin Made Me* (Dublin: Mercier Press 1979), p.12.

9.   *Evening Echo* [Cork], 18 March 1926.

10. *Munster Express*, 15 May 1931. Notice reads: 'There were 24 delegates representing 12 Waterford City firms, who intend competing in the new Employers' Football League present at the meeting of the Waterford and District Football League held on Monday night.'

11. *Football Sports Weekly*, 7 May 1927.

12. The Waterford and District Football League was founded in the Catholic Young Men's Society Hall in 1924. Although the Employers' League did not take off under that name an approximation, called the Mid-Summer League, made up of teams from the various centres of employment in the city was active in 1931, *Munster Express*, 31 July 1931.

13. *Munster Express*, 24 September 1937.

14. *Southern Star*, 29 August 1936.

15. *Kerryman*, 9 April 1938; 16 April 1938. At the end of the season of the newly expanded Waterford and North Munster Football League, we learn that ten teams made up the factory section of the league, *Munster Express*, 12 August 1938.

16. In Section A were Liptons, Boyles, Cannocks, Todds and Great Southern Railway (Bus Dept.); Section B comprised of the ESB, Limerick Shoe and Slipper Works 'B' Team, Ranks, Shannon Foundry, James McMahons and Geary and Cleeves; Section C was made up of the following teams: Limerick Shoe and Slipper Works 'A' team, Great Southern Railways, Spaights, Employment Exchange, Limerick Leader newspaper, Shannon Shoes, CBS and Lanigan Bros. *Kerryman*, 17 December 1938.

17. *Limerick Leader*, 1 April 1939; 17 June 1939; 1 July 1939.

18. Ibid., 5 August 1939.

19. *Munster Express*, 2 August 1940.

20. *Limerick Leader*, 21 October 1942.

21. Ibid., 17 June 1944.

22. One of the few works to reconsider the 1950s as a decade is T. Garvin, *News from a New Republic* (Dublin: Gill and Macmillan, 2010).

Notes

23. C. Mac Gearailt, *A Decade of Galway Inter-Firm GAA* (Dublin: Tara Publishing, 1978).

24. *Meath Chronicle*, 7 July 1951; *Westmeath Examiner*, 21 December 1957; *Anglo-Celt*, 14 March 1959.

25. J. Cassidy, *Buses, Trains and Gaelic Games: A History of CIÉ GAA Clubs* (Dublin: Original Writing, 2009), p.26.

26. Ibid., p.176.

27. *Munster Express*, 19 December 1947.

28. The following teams competed in the league: CIÉ, Transport United, H&A Hamilton, J&LF Goodbody, Civil Service, Graves', McDonnell's, Allied Ironfounders, Waterford Flour Mills, Printers, Clover Meats, Builders' United, Piltown, the Waterford Glass Co., Grocers, Bakers, and Bottlers. See *Munster Express*, 5 March 1948; 12 March 1948; 26 March 1948; 23 April 1948; 30 April 1948.

29. *Munster Express*, 14 January 1949.

30. Ibid., 14 July 1950.

31. Ibid., 4 April 1952.

32. In the first division there were the following teams: Public Authority, Bottlers United, CIÉ, Clover Meats, Rockingham United, Denny's A, Tycor A, Waterford Glass Co., and Allied Ironfounders. Division two comprised of Port & Docks, Graves' & Co., J. Hearne & Co. (Builders), Gas Co., Accountants, Hearne & Co. (Drapers), Tycor B, Combined Garages, ACEC, Printers, Denny's B, and Snowcream United. Ibid., 6 June 1952.

33. Ibid., 18 July 1952.

34. Ibid., 1 August 1952.

35. Ibid., 11 July 1952.

36. Ibid., 25 July 1952.

37. Ibid., 26 September 1952. Another, much less likely sport, took to establishing a factory element to its own league. The Waterford and District Table Tennis League, which was made up of three men's divisions and a mixed division, also had two factory league divisions. The teams competing in these divisions were Accountants, Drapers, Bottlers, Hearne's (two teams), Public Authorities (two teams), Denny's, Graves' (two teams), Crokers, Glass Factory, and Tycor. This league would continue on throughout the winter in Waterford.

38. Ibid., 20 March 1953.

39. Ibid., 17 April 1953; 1 May 1953; 22 May 1953.

40. Ibid., 5 June 1953; 10 July 1953. Years later, in east Cork, when Calor Gas Midleton won the inter-firm hurling league, they were celebrated at the company's social club annual dinner, *Kerryman*, 5 December 1970.

41. *Munster Express*, 7 August 1953; 28 August 1953; 25 September 1953.

42. Ibid., 30 October 1953.

43. Ibid., 12 February 1954.

44. Ibid., 28 May 1954.

45. Ibid., 6 August 1954; 20 August 1954.

46. See *Munster Express*, 17 August 1956, 11 April 1958 and 25 April 1958. On the cup tournaments, see 1 July 1955, 20 July 1955 and 7 December 1956.

47. Ibid., 16 May 1958.

48. Ibid., 23 May 1958.

49. Waterford was unusually stable in that period too, a happy confluence of local initiative and government policy, according to J.M. Hearne, 'Industry in Waterford City, 1932–1962', in William Nolan, Thomas Power, and Des Cowman (eds), *Waterford: History and Society* (Dublin: Geography Publications, 1992), pp.685–706. Those playing at the top level of Irish football were often working full-time and were caught up in Factory League fever. Of the sixteen players for Waterford FC who lined out against Manchester United in the first round of the European Cup in September 1968 there was a cabinet maker, a glass cutter, a fitter, a machinist, a glass blower and a printer. See 'Pen Portraits', *Waterford v Manchester United Official Programme*, 18 September 1968.

50. *Kerryman*, 22 September 1962.

51. *Nenagh Guardian*, 23 April 1966; 10 February 1968; 16 March 1968; 28 March 1968; 27 April 1968; 29 March 1969.

52. *Kerryman*, 21 June 1969.

53. Ibid., 28 June 1969.

54. Ibid., 20 December 1969.

55. Ibid., 6 June 1970.

56. *Nenagh Guardian*, 13 June 1970.

57. *Kerryman*, 4 July 1970.

58. Ibid., 19 September 1970.

59. Ibid., 29 May 1971.

60. Ibid.

61. Ibid., 28 August 1971.

62. Elizabeth Malcolm, 'The Rise of the Pub: A Study in the Disciplining of Popular Culture', in James S. Donnelly and Kirby A. Miller, *Irish Popular Culture 1650–1850* (Dublin: Irish Academic Press, 1998), p.50.

63. *Munster Express*, 24 February 1967.

64. Ibid., 12 May 1967.

65. Ibid., 2 June 1967.

66. Ibid., 16 June 1967.

67. Ibid., 19 May 1967.

68. Ibid., 23 June 1967.

69. Cherry's brewery had its own factory league side at the time.

70. *Munster Express*, 31 May 1968.

71. Ibid., 5 July 1968.

72. Ibid., 16 May 1969.

73. Ibid., 4 July 1969.

74. Ibid., 15 August 1969.

75. Ibid., 8 June 1973.

76. Compare this to 'the astonishingly fabricated notion of the Irish pub, created from Singapore ... to San Francisco, drawing from a literal storehouse of bric-a-brac that would never be seen in an Irish pub in Ireland', as R.F. Foster saw it in *Luck and the Irish* (Oxford: Oxford University Press, 2008), p.156.

77. E. O'Connor, *A Labour History of Waterford* (Waterford: Waterford Council of Trade Unions, 1989), p.309.

78. Goodbody's 'A'; Hearne's Drapers; Ironfounders; Denny's; Goodbody's 'B'; Sack and Bag; Mental Hospital; ACEC; Waterford Glass; Hearne and Sons; Gold Crust; Paper Mills; Snowcream; Clover Meats; L&N Tea Co., *Munster Express*, 12 January 1962.

79. *Munster Express*, 16 February 1962.

80. These were Waterford, Cork, Dublin, Drogheda, Galway, Killarney, Wexford, Sligo and Limerick. Incidentally almost all of them are major soccer playing centres in Ireland. For Drogheda, the expansion coincides with the same ten-year period they entered the League of Ireland. The Tops, later the John Player Tops and aired on RTÉ, would run until 1996.

81. *Irish Independent*, 12 October 1973.

82. E.P. Thompson, 'Time, Work-Discipline and Industrial Capitalism', *Past & Present*, 38 (1), pp.56–97 (1967).

Chapter 10

1. I would like to thank Andy Bielenberg and Alan Noonan for their comments on an earlier draft of this work.

2. 'The Rocks of Bawn' (traditional), as sung by Joe Heaney on *Irish Music in London Pubs*, Smithsonian Folkways Records, FG3575 (1965).

3. Heaney can be heard singing this song and giving his own interpretation by way of introduction online at the Joe Heaney Archive / *Cartlann Seosamh Ó hÉanaí*, www. joeheaney.org (accessed 13 March 2013). He places it in the context of both Ireland's history under English rule and his own native area of Connemara, known for its rough and rock-strewn landscape. Sean Williams and Lillis Ó Laoire give their analysis of its

content and   Heaney's version in their book, *Bright Star of the West: Joe Heaney, Irish Song Man* (New York: Oxford University Press, 2011), pp.128–32.

4.   Skipton in Yorkshire had a hiring fair frequented by Irish seasonal agricultural labourers. Dónall Mac Amhlaigh in N. Gray (ed.), *Writers Talking* (London: Caliban Books, 1989), p.184.

5.   U. Cowley, *The Men Who Built Britain: A History of the Irish Navvy* (Dublin: Wolfhound Press, 2001); S. Lambert, *Irish Women in Lancashire, 1922–1960: Their Story* (Lancashire, UK: Centre for North-West Regional Studies, University of Lancashire, 2001); S. O'Brien, 'Irish Associational Culture and Identity in Post-War Birmingham' (PhD thesis, Limerick: Mary Immaculate College, 2009); S. Sorohan, *Irish London During the Troubles* (Dublin and Portland, OR: Irish Academic Press, 2012).

6.   Danny Meehan, interview with the author, 11 June 2012.

7.   The total size of the group went from 444,792 to 263,593. This figure for employment in agriculture includes farmers and families assisting, agricultural labourers, foresters, and turf workers. When women are included the total population occupied in agriculture went from 512,510 to 288,909. Data compiled from Table 4, Volume 3, Part 1, *Census of Population of Ireland, 1951* (Dublin: Central Statistics Office/The Stationary Office, 1954) and Table 5, Volume 4, *Census of Population of Ireland, 1971* (Dublin: Central Statistics Office/The Stationary Office, 1975).

8.   Commission on Emigration and Other Population Problems, *Reports* (Dublin: Stationery Office, 1954); T. Connolly, 'The Commission on Emigration, 1945–1954', in D. Keogh, F. O'Shea & C. Quinlan (eds), *The Lost Decade: Ireland in the 1950s* (Douglas, Cork: Mercier Press, 2004), p.89; A. Bielenberg & R. Ryan, *An Economic History of Ireland Since Independence* (Oxon, UK: Routledge, 2013), pp.57–9.

9.   E. Delaney, *The Irish in Post-War Britain* (Oxford: Oxford University Press, 2007), pp.32–3.

10.   Table 1, Volume 4, *Census of Population of Ireland, 2006* (Dublin:Central Statistics Office/ The StationaryOffice, 2007); National Economic and Social Council, *The Economic and Social Implications of Emigration* (Dublin: NESC, 1991), p.55.

11.   B. Canavan, 'Story-tellers and writers: Irish Identity in Emigrant Labourers' Autobiographies, 1870–1970', in P. O'Sullivan (ed.), *The Irish World Wide: History, Heritage, Identity*, Vol.3, *The Creative Migrant* (London: Leicester University Press, 1994), p.168.

12.   John Gildea, interview with the author, 9 February 2011; Danny Meehan, interview with the author, 11 June 2012; Jimmy Marshall, interview with the author, 10 October 2009; Packie Browne, interview with the author, 6 November 2010; Vincent Campbell, interview with the author, 12 June 2012.

Notes

13. E. Delaney, *Irish Emigration Since 1921* (Dublin: Economic and Social History Society of Ireland, 2002), p.10.
14. Martin McMahon, interview with the author, 6 December 2010.
15. The 'unskilled labourers' category includes builders' labourers. Table 31 in Commission on Emigration, *Reports*, p.322; E. Delaney, *Demography, State & Society: Irish Migration to Britain, 1921–1971* (Liverpool: Liverpool University Press, 2000), p.181.
16. P. Donnellan, *The Irishmen: An Impression of Exile* [film] (BBC, 1965); Williams & Ó Laoire, *Bright Star of the West*, p.131.
17. J.A. Jackson, 'The Irish in Britain', in P.J. Drudy (ed.), *Ireland and Britain since 1922*, Irish Studies 5 (Cambridge: Cambridge University Press, 1986), p.130.
18. T. O'Grady & S. Pyke, *I Could Read the Sky* (London: Harvill Press, 1997), p.37.
19. T. O'Grady, 'Memory, Photography, Ireland', *Irish Studies Review*, 14, 2 (2006), p.261.
20. Jimmy Ó Ceannbháin, interview with the author, 8 January 2011. Martin McMahon also used the phrase 'we were all in the same boat' to describe this feeling (interview with the author, 6 December 2010).
21. D. Mac Amhlaigh, *Dialann Deoraí* (Dublin: An Clóchomhar, 1960).
22. Cowley, *The Men Who Built Britain*; Delaney, *The Irish in Post-War Britain*.
23. Though the Irish made up only 5.5 per cent of the construction labour force in England and Wales in 1951, they accounted for 25 per cent in Scotland. These figures do not include those of Irish descent and may underestimate or over-generalise for Great Britain as a whole because they do not account for regional differences or hiring preferences of certain contractors, small and large. For example, it is estimated that at least half the 19,000-strong workforce on construction of the M1, Britain's first motorway in the late 1950s, was Irish. As Cowley asserts, the issue requires examination in qualitative as well as quantitative terms. Cowley, *The Men Who Built Britain*, p.122, p.151; U. Cowley, 'The Irish in British Construction Industry' (2002), http://ics-www. leeds.ac.uk/papers/vp01.cfm?outfit=ids&requesttimeout=500&folder=15& paper=108 (accessed 13 March 2013); E. MacColl, C. Parker & P. Seeger, *Song of a Road* (BBC, 1959; Topic Records, 2008).
24. Packie Browne, interview with the author, 6 November 2010.
25. The working 'gang' in this instance included several highly respected London-based Irish musicians: Liam Farrell (Tyrone, banjo), Bobby Casey (Clare, fiddle), Máirtín Byrnes (Galway, fiddle), Raymond Roland (Galway / Meath, accordion), and Johnny Collins (flute). Liam Farrell, interview with the author, 1 July 2012.
26. Danny Meehan, interview with the author, 11 June 2012.
27. Delaney, *The Irish in Post-War Britain*, p.200; S. Fielding, *Class and Ethnicity: Irish Catholics in England, 1880–1939* (Buckingham: Open University Press, 1993), pp.25–6.

28. David Fitzpatrick, 'The Irish in Britain: Settlers or Transients?' in P. Buckland & J. Belchem (eds), *The Irish in British Labour History: Conference Proceedings in Irish Studies, No.1* (Liverpool: Institute of Irish Studies, University of Liverpool & Society for the Study of Labour History, March 1992), p.1.

29. John Gildea, interview with the author, 9 February 2011.

30. Jimmy Ó Ceannabháin, interview with the author, 8 January 2011.

31. Danny Meehan, interview with the author, 11 June 2012.

32. Delaney, *The Irish in Post-War Britain*, pp.112–16.

33. Billy was born in England to parents from Kerry, grew up mostly in Ireland, but moved back to London with them for ten years, 1959–1969. Billy Clifford, interview with the author, 8 April 2011.

34. Martin Treacy, interview with the author, 8 January 2011.

35. Billy Clifford, interview with the author, 8 April 2011.

36. John Gildea, interview with the author, 9 February 2011.

37. Ben Lennon, interview with the author, 3 April 2011.

38. Martin McMahon, interview with the author, 6 December 2010.

39. Ibid.

40. Dónall Mac Amhlaigh in Gray (ed.), *Writers Talking*, p.172. For a discussion of class and other themes in Mac Amhlaigh's writings see Máirín Nic Eoin, 'An Scríbhneoir agus Imirce Éigeantach: Scrúdú ar Shaothar Cruthaitheach Dhónaill Mhic Amhlaigh', *Oghma*, 2 (1990), pp.92–104.

41. Teresa McMahon, interview with the author, 6 December 2010.

42. Joe Heaney, interview with Mick Moloney, 1981, quoted in L. Mac Con Iomaire, *Seosamh Ó hÉanaí: Nár Fágha Mé Bás Choíche* (Indreabhán, Conamara: Cló Iar-Chonnachta, 2007), pp.193–4.

43. Ibid, pp.184–5.

44. Reg Hall, interview with the author, 3 July 2012.

45. Tomás Ó Canainn, interview with the author, 9 December 2010.

46. Vincent Campbell, interview with the author, 12 June 2012.

47. Jimmy Ó Ceannabháin, interview with the author, 8 January 2011.

48. There were female musicians, but in smaller numbers and many played piano rather than melody instruments. R. Hall, 'Irish Music and Dance in London, 1890–1970: A Socio-Cultural History' (PhD thesis, University of Sussex, 1994), p.308.

49. Martin & Teresa McMahon, interview with the author, 6 December 2010.

50. Kevin Burke, interview with the author, 12 May 2012.

51. Ibid; R. Hall, 'Irish Music and Dance in London', p.305.

52. O'Brien, 'Irish Associational Culture and Identity in Post-War Birmingham', pp.152–3.

Notes

53. Kevin McDermott, interview with the author, 10 December 2011.

54. Canavan, 'Story-tellers and Writers', p.165.

55. Delaney, *The Irish in Post-War Britain*, p.198; S. O'Brien, 'Narrative Encounters with the Irish in Birmingham', in N. Cronin, S. Crosson & J. Eastlake (eds), *Anáil an Bhéil Bheo: Orality and Modern Irish Culture* (Newcastle upon Tyne: Cambridge Scholars Publishing, 2009), p.162.

56. Martin McMahon, interview with the author, 6 December 2010.

57. Teresa McMahon, interview with the author, 6 December 2010.

58. Martin McMahon, interview with the author, 6 December 2010.

59. Dónall Mac Amhlaigh said of the English working classes, 'I didn't seem to have a lot in common with them. I couldn't relax with them or enjoy their company very much … It seemed to me that we were on a different wavelength completely. I stayed among Irish friends almost exclusively … You could live a completely expatriate life among your own people.' In N. Gray (ed.), *Writers Talking*, p.175. On relationships between class and ethnicity see Fielding, *Class and Ethnicity*, pp.14–18; and S. O'Brien, 'Irish Associational Culture and Identity in Post-War Birmingham', pp.165–6.

Chapter 11

1. R. Breen and C. Whelan, *Social Mobility and Social Class in Ireland* (Dublin: Gill and Macmillan, 1996), p.1.

2. *Irish Times*, 16 July 1955.

3. *Irish Independent*, 29 June 1964.

4. D. Ferriter, *The Transformation of Ireland: 1900–2000* (London: Profile, 2005), p.7.

5. Ibid.

6. Ibid.

7. P. Share, H. Tovey and M. Corcoran, *A Sociology of Ireland* (Dublin: Gill and Macmillan, 2007), p.175.

8. Ibid, pp.181–189.

9. M. Cronin, 'Class and Status in Twentieth Century Ireland: The Evidence of Oral History', *Saothar*, 32 (2007), pp.33–43.

10. M. Muldowney, 'We were conscious of the sort of people we mixed with', *The History of the Family*, No.13, Vol.4 (2008), pp.402–415.

11. M. Leane and E. Kiely, *Irish Women at Work, 1930–1960: An Oral History* (Kildare: Irish Academic Press, 2012).

12. Interview with John Richard O'Shea, Parklands, 12 October 2012.

13. Interview with Rena M., conducted by Clodagh O'Driscoll, Women's Oral History Project, 20 September 2011. Transcript kindly provided by Máire Leane and Elizabeth Kiely.

14. Ibid.

15. Cronin, 'Class and Status', p.39.

16. Ferriter, *Transformation*, p.333.

17. Ibid.

18. Interview with Mary Cronin, Farranree, 22 October 2012.

19. M. Silverman, *An Irish Working Class: Explorations in Political Economy and Hegemony, 1800–1950* (Toronto: University of Toronto Press, 2001), p.361.

20. Ibid, p.362.

21. Ibid, p.363.

22. John Richard O'Shea.

23. Interview with Kathleen F. conducted by Margaret Kearns, 21 August 2001, Women's Oral History Project. http://www.ucc.ie/acad/appsoc/OralHistoryProject/Audio/interviews/FitzgibbonK1.wma (accessed 13 March 2013).

24. Ibid.

25. Share et al, *A Sociology of Ireland*, p.189.

26. Kathleen F.

27. Silverman, *An Irish Working Class*, p.363.

28. Rena M.

29. Ibid.

30. Ibid.

31. Ibid.

32. Mary Cronin.

33. A. Kelly, 'White-Collar Trade Unionism' in D. Nevin (ed.), *Trade Unions and Change in Irish Society* (Cork: Mercier, 1980), p.67.

34. Muldowney, 'We were conscious', p.409.

35. Ibid., p.411.

36. Cork Northside Folklore Project (CNFP): SR300, Billy Foley, 'Guided Tour of Sunbeam', Date of recording unavailable.

37. CNFP: SR Number Unavailable, Nancy Byrne, 6 June 2002.

38. Rena M.

39. Billy Foley.

40. Muldowney, 'We were conscious', p.411.

41. J. Sangster, *Earning Respect: The Lives of Working Women in Small Town Ontario: 1920–1960* (Toronto: University of Toronto Press, 1995), p.110.

42. Ibid., p.161.

43. M. Leane and E. Kiely, *Irish Women at Work*, p.109.

44. Muldowney, 'We were conscious', p.410.

Notes

45. Nancy Byrne.

46. Interview with Patsy Corcoran, Wilton, 2 October 2012.

47. Cronin, 'Class and Status', p.34.

48. John Richard O'Shea.

49. Ibid.

50. Patsy Corcoran.

51. E. Kiely and M. Leane, *Irish Women at Work*, p.188.

52. T.J. Sexton (Auditor), 'Proposed Pension Scheme Preliminary Report – 5th October, 1956', Cork City and County Archives, Sunbeam Business Files B505/BND31/1 Temp 72.

Chapter 12

1. Eileen M. Trauth, *The Culture of an Information Economy – Influences and Impacts in the Republic of Ireland* (Dordrecht, The Netherlands: Kluwer, 2000), p.96.

2. Perry Share, Hilary Tovey and Mary P. Corcoran, *A Sociology of Ireland* (Dublin: Gill & Macmillan, 2007), p.170.

3. Trauth, *The Culture of an Information Economy*, p.96. (Emphasis in original.)

4. Ibid., p.96.

5. Tom Garvin, 'The politics of language and literature in pre-independence Ireland', *Irish Political Studies*, 2:1, p.59.

6. Douglas Hyde, 'Necessity for De-Anglicising Ireland', in Charles Gavan Duffy, George Sigerson and Douglas Hyde (eds), *The Revival of Irish Literature* (London, 1894); Declan Kiberd, *Inventing Ireland* (London: Vintage, 1996), pp.144–5.

7. William Delany, *The Green and the Red: Revolutionary Republicanism and Socialism in Irish History* (London: Writer's Showcase, 2001), p.361.

8. Seán O'Casey, *Drums under the Windows* (New York: Macmillan, 1950), pp.27, 92.

9. W.B. Yeats, 'The Fisherman', in *W.B. Yeats, A Critical Edition of the Major Works* (Oxford: Oxford University Press, 1997), pp.68–9.

10. W.B. Yeats and Richard J. Finneran (ed.), *The Yeats Reader* (New York: Palgrave, 2002), pp.261–2.

11. Ibid., p.266.

12. Ibid., p.84.

13. James Plunkett, *Strumpet City* (London: Hutchinson, 1969), pp.293, 212, 213.

14. Paula Meehan, 'The Apprentice', in *Return and No Blame* (Dublin: Beaver Row, 1984), p.27.

15. Maura Adshead, 'Commentary by Maura Adshead', in Conor McGrath and Eoin O'Malley (eds), *Irish Political Studies Reader: Key Contributions* (New York: Routledge, 2008), p.191.

16. Ibid., pp.191–2.

17. Michael D. Bristol, 'Shakespeare the Myth', in David Scott Kastan (ed.), *A Companion to Shakespeare* (Oxford: Blackwell, 1999), p.490.

18. Ibid., p.490–91.

19. Ibid., pp.497, 501.

20. Yug Mohit Chaudhry, *Yeats, the Irish Literary Revival and the Politics of Print* (Cork: Cork University Press, 2001), p.3.

21. Dan Mulhall, 'The Strange Death of Romantic Ireland', *Irish Times*, 30 August 2012. This essay is an edited version of a lecture Mulhall gave at the University of Münster.

22. 'Romantic Ireland's dead and gone / It's with O'Leary in the grave'.

23. Chaudhry, *Yeats, the Irish Literary Revival and the Politics of Print*, p.5.

24. Ibid., pp.12–13.

25. W.B. Yeats, 'September 1913', *The Yeats Reader*, p.44.

26. Ibid.

27. Chaudhry, *Yeats, the Irish Literary Revival and the Politics of Print*, p.13.

28. W.B. Yeats and Denis Donoghue (ed.), *Memoirs* (London: Macmillan, 1972), p.271.

29. Oliver St John Gogarty, *The Plays of Oliver St. John Gogarty* (Delaware: Proscenium, 1973), p.47.

30. Sean O'Casey, *The Bishop's Bonfire: A Sad Play Within the Tune of a Polka* (London: Macmillan, 1955), p.79.

31. Bernice Schrank, *Sean O'Casey: A Research and Production Sourcebook* (London: Greenwood, 1996), p.11.

32. Anthony Burgess, 'In the twilight zone', *Observer*, 18 November 1962, p.25.

33. John Jordan, 'Slumlands Tragedy', *Irish Times*, 3 March 1962, p.9.

34. See Alla Sarukhanyan, 'Irish Literature in Russia', *Irish Times*, 4 July 1968, p.13; see also Seamus Ó Coigligh, 'Irish writing a la Russe', *Irish Times*, 21 July 1966, p.8.

35. Larissa Nolan, 'Film banned for 35 years coming to a screen soon', *Irish Independent*, 13 August 2006.

36. Mary Russell, '"Goodbye to the Hill" and hello to a "Mousetrap"', *Irish Times*, 9 July 1992.

37. Interview conducted with the present author, 27 November 2007.

38. 'Can't you understand that their dim eyes are able only for a little light? Damn, it, man, can't you see Clooncoohy can never be other than he is?'; Sean O'Casey, *The Bishop's Bonfire*, p.79.

39. Alison Healy, 'Pat Kenny again RTÉ's best-paid presenter', *Irish Times*, 10 October 2009.

40. Helena Sheehan, *Irish Television Drama: A Society and its Stories* (Dublin: RTÉ, 1987; re-published in a revised edition on CD-ROM, 2004), p.131.

Notes

41. Barry Duggan, 'Gun victim's father says new RTÉ drama glorifies criminals', *Irish Independent*, 14 October 2010.

42. Ciaran McCullagh, 'Getting The Criminals We Want: The social production of the criminal population', in Patrick Clancy et al. (eds), *Irish Society: Sociological Perspectives* (Dublin: Institute of Public Administration, 1999), p.424.

43. Leslie J. Moran, 'Homophobic Violence: The Hidden Injuries of Class', in Sally R. Munt (ed.), *Cultural Studies and the Working Class* (London: Cassell, 2000), p.209.

44. Helen Moorhouse, 'Great, but did we really have to see a graphic rape?', *Irish Independent*, 14 November 2012.

45. Anon., 'Substantial drop in number of white collar crime convictions', http://www.rte.ie/news/2012/1118/white-collar-crime-figures.html (accessed 13 March 2013).

46. Maggie Wykes, *News, Crime and Culture* (London: Pluto, 2001), p.82.

47. Donald Clarke, 'Behind "Tallafornia" vulgarity lurks message of social mobility', 24 March 2012.

48. Orsetta Causa, Sophie Dantan and Åsa Johansson, *Intergenerational Social Mobility in European OECD Countries* (Paris: Organisation de Coopération et de Développement Économiques, 2009), p.18.

49. Paul Melia, 'Wealthiest paying less tax now than at height of boom', *Irish Independent*, 21 December 2012.

50. Chris Eipper, *The Ruling Trinity: A Community Study of Church, State and Business in Ireland* (Aldershot: Gower, 1986), p.12.

51. E.P. Thompson, *The Making of the English Working Class* (London: Penguin 1980), pp.9–10.

52. Fintan O'Toole, 'Getting stuck in the middle with you', *Irish Times*, 14 February 2012.

53. *Class Dismissed – How TV frames the Working Class*. Dir. Loretta Alper. The Media Education Foundation. 2005.

54. In the Amárach survey, 50 per cent saw themselves as middle class; cited in David McWilliams, *The Pope's Children: The Irish Economic Triumph and the Rise of Ireland's New Elite* (NJ: Wiley, 2008), p.26.

55. Anon., 'Working class areas reject treaty', http://www.irishexaminer.com/breakingnews/ireland/working-class-areas-reject-treaty-553870.html (accessed 13 March 2013); Carl O'Brien, 'Far stronger No vote in poorer areas suggests shift to class politics for some', *Irish Times*, 2 June 2012.

56. Thomas Carnduff, 'Letter to the Editor', *The New Northman*, 9(1) Spring, 1941.

57. Ken Worpole, *Dockers and Detectives – Popular Reading: Popular Writing* (London: Verso, 1983), p.10.

58. John Berger, *About Looking* (London: Bloomsbury, 2009; orig. 1980), p.82.

59.   Louis Althusser, 'Ideology and the Ideological State Apparatuses', in John Storey (ed.), *Cultural Theory and Popular Culture: A Reader* (London: Harvester Wheatsheaf, 1994), pp.336–46.

60.   Andy Medhurst, 'If Anywhere: Class Identifications and Cultural Studies Academics', in Sally R. Munt (ed.), *Cultural Studies and the Working Class, Subject to Change* (London: Cassell, 2000), p.20.

Index

Index

Index

Index

Index